Playing on an Uneven Field

ALSO BY YUYA KIUCHI

Fifty Shades and Popular Culture (2017)
Edited by Yuya Kiuchi and Francisco A. Villarruel

The Young Are Making Their World:
Essays on the Power of Youth Culture (2016)
Edited by Yuya Kiuchi

Soccer Culture in America:
Essays on the World's Sport in Red, White and Blue (2014)
Edited by Yuya Kiuchi

BY MATHEW J. BARTKOWIAK
AND YUYA KIUCHI

The Music of Counterculture Cinema:
A Critical Study of 1960s and 1970s Soundtracks (2015)

Packaging Baseball: How Marketing Embellishes
the Cultural Experience (2012)

ALL FROM MCFARLAND

Playing on an Uneven Field

Essays on Exclusion and Inclusion in Sports

Edited by YUYA KIUCHI

McFarland & Company, Inc., Publishers
Jefferson, North Carolina

ISBN (print) 978-1-4766-7714-9
ISBN (ebook) 978-1-4766-3548-4

Library of Congress and British Library
Cataloguing data are available

Front cover: Australian Christie Dawes in the lead
of the 5,000-meter T54 at the 2012 Summer Paralympic Games
in London (Australia Paralympic Committee)

Printed in the United States of America

*McFarland & Company, Inc., Publishers
Box 611, Jefferson, North Carolina 28640
www.mcfarlandpub.com*

Acknowledgments

Nobody writes a book alone. This is especially true when the book is a collection of essays authored by multiple experts. My name appears on the cover of the book, but this is a book that was only made possible thanks to a countless number of people. First, I would like to thank all the authors who made this book project possible. Some of them are my old friends. Some others are my colleagues. The book also includes some I had the privilege of working with for the first time. All of them generously shared their expert knowledge and personal experiences with me in their manuscripts. Thank you for your contribution and putting up with my constant email inquiries.

This is my sixth book with McFarland. As always, many people from McFarland assisted me in the process. Thank you for your continuous support for my projects.

I would like to thank my wife, Nichole. As is the case with any of my writing projects, she read everything I wrote for this project and gave me feedback. Thank you, Nicki.

Contents

Introduction

YUYA KIUCHI

The world of sport is unfair. Despite its promise to be fair and equal, sport is filled with unfairness, inequality, discrimination, prejudice, and exclusion. This is because sport does not exist in a vacuum. Instead, it is enmeshed in an intricate international and domestic structure that perpetuates and sometimes takes advantage of injustices that exist in the world. Even in just the last several years, fans have thrown bananas at black soccer players, female athletes continue to be paid less even when they outperform their male counterparts, gender minorities face invasive interrogations, and the rising cost of youth sports has made it extremely difficult for non-wealthy families to support their children's athletic endeavors. From TV coverage to sponsorship revenue, the gap between the Olympics and the Paralympics is immense. The list continues.

Anecdotally, as someone who has officiated both top-level amateur and professional soccer games as a referee on three different continents, I understand and have experienced the exclusion, prejudice, and discrimination that takes place on soccer fields. In a local youth match, I sent a player off for foul and abusive language, namely race-based taunting, toward me. A 16-year-old recreational player did not believe that I, despite my background in officiating professional matches, was qualified to referee his game because my Asian eyes were not open enough to see fouls. I have heard many similar stories from not only officials but also from other participants in many other sports.

Simultaneously, some organizational bodies and leagues have taken steps toward equality. The "No to Racism" campaign has become a staple in international soccer. An increasing number of athletes have come out about their sexuality and sexual preferences. There are efforts to be inclusive of athletes who wear a hijab or other religious outfits. Although they are most likely politically motivated, efforts to unite North and South Korean athletes at the

Olympics is a progressive move. In this context, this book aims to explore the question, What does the intersection between sports and equality look like today?

The reality, of course, is mixed. Take soccer, one of the most popular sports in the world. In March 2016, five top players from the U.S. Women's National Team (USWNT) filed a wage-discrimination complaint, claiming that U.S. Soccer, the national organizing body, paid USWNT players about a quarter of what it paid their male counterparts (Das, "Pay Disparity"). The complaint came just several months after the USWNT had its game at Aloha Stadium in Hawai'i canceled due to its artificial playing surface, which was considered unplayable and dangerous (Das, "U.S. Soccer Sues"). Fans and players wondered if the men's team would ever have been scheduled to play in such an environment.

The pay-gap debate raises an interesting question: What are the athletes paid for? Are soccer players on a national team paid for their result (i.e., winning a match, a tournament, or a championship)? Are they paid for the revenue they generate for the governing body? Or are they paid for the number of days they spend away from home to be involved in their national team activities? In reality, the USWNT generated more revenue than the U.S. Men's National Team (USMNT) in 2016, after the USWNT won the World Cup. The USWNT brought in a profit of more than six million dollars whereas the USMNT brought in less than a third. Although USMNT teams play more games to qualify for the World Cup, USWNT teams plays more games as a whole. For example, between 2012 and 2016, the USMNT played 76 games while the USWNT played 110 (Das, "Pay Disparity"). Most significantly, the USWNT has won the World Cup three times, whereas the best result for the USMNT is the bronze medal from the inaugural tournament in 1930. The best result in recent history is making the quarterfinals in 2002. For the 2018 World Cup, the USMNT did not even quality.

Carli Lloyd wrote eloquently in the *New York Times* on this issue. "If I were a male soccer player who won a World Cup for the United States, my bonus would be $390,000. Because I am a female soccer player, the bonus I got for our World Cup victory last summer was $75,000. The men get almost $69,000 for making a World Cup roster. As women, we get $15,000 for making the World Cup team." She recognizes that "men's World Cup generates vastly more money globally than the women's event," but as noted above, the USWNT generates more profit than the USMNT for U.S. Soccer, the employer of these players. Lloyd continues,

> I was on the road for about 260 days last year. When I am traveling internationally, I get $60 a day for expenses. Michael Bradley gets $75. Maybe they figure that women are smaller and thus eat less.
>
> When Hope Solo or Alex Morgan, say, makes a sponsor appearance for U.S. Soc-

cer, she gets $3,000. When Geoff Cameron or Jermaine Jones makes the same sort of appearance, he gets $3,750.

The gap between male and female experiences is evident.

But such a gender gap in soccer is not only in the United States. When the women's World Cup took place in Canada in 2015, all the games were played on artificial turf fields. Despite recent developments in the artificial turf technology and FIFA's study that claimed "there was very little difference in the incidence, nature and causes of injuries observed during games played on artificial turf compared with those played on grass" after the 2005 FIFA U-17 Championship in Peru (*FIFA U-17* 9), players have agreed that turf irritates and burns when they slide. Dr. Bojan Žorić, the USWNT physician, commented, "[The research] can show that there are more injuries and that there are not more injuries. You don't have a great answer. That's with regard to acute injuries…. The body is by far more fatigued, there's a longer recovery rate, there's certainly more of a feeling of being worn down after practicing and playing on turf" (Bird). Soccer fans remember a picture Sydney Leroux Dwyer shared of her bruised and bleeding legs after a match played on a turf field in 2013.

Across the Atlantic, professional female soccer players in the French league, D1 Féminine, collectively make the equivalent of $13.6 million. The figure is $12.2 million in Frauen Bundesliga (Germany), $5.5 million in FA Women's Super League (England), and $3.4 million in Damallsvenskan (Sweden). Adding these numbers from these four highest-paying European leagues together and combining it with the $5.4 million that National Women's Soccer League players make in the United States, $1.7 million in New Zealand, and $837,656 in Mexico, these female players are jointly underpaid by more than a million dollars than Neymar, a male Brazilian player who makes more than $43 million a year at Paris Saint-Germain (PSG) (McCarthy).

Soccer is not unique. The same types of gaps exist in other sports. Consider how often NBA games are on TV compared to WNBA games. How much more attention fans pay to the men's March Madness games in college basketball than the women's tournament. How many times we have heard of a coach, after winning a championship or a tournament, getting "promoted" from the women's team to the men's team.

Even female athletes' achievements are not celebrated like male counterparts' achievements. In 2017, the New England Patriots (Super Bowl champions), the Houston Astros (World Series winners), and the Pittsburgh Penguins (NHL champions) were all invited to the White House to celebrate their victories. The Golden State Warriors were also invited, until President Trump withdrew the invitation after Stephen Curry announced that the team would not visit the White House. But the 2017 WNBA champions the Minnesota Lynx never received an invitation, even though they had been invited in 2011, 2013, and 2015 after their championship victories (Wallace).

Women are often pushed aside to the accessory role. Cheerleaders appear on sports broadcasts on TV but they are not the main event. How often do we see cheerleaders participate in a cheerleading competition? North Korea's cheerleading squad caught media attention during the Winter Olympics in 2018. The so-called "army of beauties" has a history of being forced to partake in "erotic games" and "parties devoted entirely to sex" ("There's a Sinister Side"). They are rarely taken seriously as athletes. They are shown and treated as accessories.

In the United States, the horrible working conditions and treatment of professional team cheerleaders have long been known. John M. Crewdson reported back in 1978 about the experience of the Dallas Cowboys cheerleaders. He wrote,

> The cheerleaders get paid next to nothing—$15 a game…. Because of the strong Christian ethic that infuses the Cowboys program (Tom Landry, the coach, and Roger Staubach, the quarterback, are devoutly religious), the cheerleaders cannot appear where alcohol is served, cannot attend parties of any sort, cannot even wear jewelry with their brief costumes.
>   They do make some money from modeling, promotional and television appearances, though not enough to live on.

A recent lawsuit filed by an attorney representing two NFL cheerleaders reveals that things have not changed much over 40 years. Furthermore, Washington Redskins cheerleaders stated that they had to participate in a topless photo shoot with an audience overseeing the shoot (Macur).

In motor racing, grid girls play a similar role to cheerleaders. Frequently dressed in tight-fitting and exposing clothes or swimsuits, they stand beside a car and hold a board that displays the name of the driver who drives the car. In 2018, Formula 1 decided to stop having grid girls. Sean Bratches, managing director of commercial operations for Formula 1, stated, "While the practice of employing grid girls has been a staple of Formula 1 grand prix for decades, we feel this custom does not resonate with our brand values and clearly is at odds with modern day societal norms." However, 60 percent of those surveyed by the BBC responded that grid girls should remain in Formula 1 ("Formula 1").

What appears to be a positive move by Formula 1 was undermined by both Michel Boeri, president of the Automobile Club de Monaco, and Lewis Hamilton, the defending champion of Formula 1. In early April, only a few months after Formula 1's announcement to stop employing grid girls, Boeri declared that Monaco GP would have grid girls. He argued, "They're pretty, and the cameras will be on them once again" ("They're Pretty"). In response to this announcement, Hamilton shared a screenshot of five grid girls wearing skintight jumpsuits with exposed cleavage with the comment "Thank you Jesus" on his Instagram (Hamilton).

In general, athletic organizations, sponsors, and other parties have begun to reconsider their use of women as accessories to their events. The Professional Darts Corporation also in 2018 decided not to use walk-on girls. The Women's Sports Trust stated, "We strongly encourage sports such as cycling, boxing and UDC to follow darts and Formula 1 and reconsider the use of podium girls, ring girls and octagon girls. This is not a matter of feminist versus models, which seems to be the way many people want to portray this story. These changes are taking place because global businesses are making a considered choice about how women should be valued and portrayed in their sports in 2018. They deserve significant credit for doing so" ("Formula 1"). Sports, often dominated by male figures in organizers' board rooms, media board rooms, and audiences, still have long ways to go to truly respond to the call by the Women's Sports Trust.

Of course, it is not just women who face exclusion, discrimination, and prejudice in sports. There are, for example, entry barriers for many economically disadvantaged families and youth. Youth sports today is a $15.3 billion industry (Barone). Consider the story of Ian, a 14-year-old boy from Orlando, Florida. In the summer of 2017, he visited Scotland with his parents not for a relaxing summer vacation but to participate in the U.S. Kids Gold European Championship at the Royal Musselburgh Golf Club. The family spent close to $5,000 during this 10-day trip. Dwight Davis, Ian's father, explains that the family has spent "well in the six figures" on Ian's golf since he started playing. The family also spends $60,000 on the annual tuition at Bishop Gate Golf Academy (Shell).

Writing for *USA Today*, Shell reports that almost 20 percent of American families spend $1,000 or more per month on youth sports per child. Just as a reference point, Shell notes that the average mortgage payment for Americans is $1,030 per month. Just over 60 percent of American families spend between $100 to $499 per month per child on youth sports. Eight percent spend more than $2,000 per month. The consequence of this expense is not small. One in three parents admit that they do not contribute to their retirement account on a regular basis due to sports-related expenses.

Some parents may argue that the investment will pay off when their children are admitted to a top division university with a full-ride scholarship. But according to the NCAA, about 1 percent of high school basketball players actually play in Division 1 basketball. The numbers are 2.6 percent for football, 2 percent for golf, and 4.6 percent for ice hockey. About 1.1 percent of college players end up professionally in basketball, 1.5 percent in football, and 5.6 percent in hockey (Shell). The high cost of youth sports limits the ability to participate. Jacob Bogage reports "athletic participation for kids ages 6 through 12 is down almost 8 percent over the last decade.... Children from low-income households are half as likely to play one day's worth of team sports than children from households earning at least $100,000." There is a very strong correlation between a family's income and children's likelihood of participating in a team sport.

It is not just playing a sport that can be costly. Eli Hoff wrote that Minnesota may be experiencing a soccer referee shortage because of the costs associated with buying equipment and annual recertification. Even though many teenagers officiate soccer games and make anywhere between $10 to $50 per game (or more if they officiate higher-level games), and may work multiple games per day to end up with a few hundred dollars in a weekend (often they are paid in cash), the initial investment of equipment, referee jerseys, and so on could easily be a few hundred dollars before they start officiating. Or, even at a higher level, if one wants to pursue his dream to officiate at the professional level, it is expected he travel multiple times a year to various tournaments to be evaluated by a limited number of referee mentors. Although state associations may cover the travel cost and referees may receive per diems, prospective officials have to take time away from school or work for which they are not compensated. Not everyone has a job that allows him to be gone for a week at a time, several times a year. Not everyone can take time off from work and afford not to be paid.

Think about immigrant communities that are also known for not participating in organized sport leagues. For example, in many communities in the United States, there is a booming Latino soccer league. Both at the youth and adult levels, it is rarely affiliated with U.S. Soccer or other national organizations. An administrative officer has admitted that it is often the I.D. requirement that prevents such leagues from being part of a larger organization. This is not to say that the players lack identification. It is a sense of distrust Latino and other minority communities have about submitting an I.D. and how their information may be used that makes them uncomfortable.

Of course, there are many other ways in which sports can be exclusive. People with different abilities and disabilities face challenges. If you are in charge of school sports, what do you do with transgender or intersex athletes? How do you provide accommodations? How do you ensure that all of your student athletes are treated fairly? As the designer of a new sport complex, are you aware that you will have to have a locker room for both home and away teams but also the officials who may consist of both males and females?

What does fairness and inclusion mean for someone like Kayla Montgomery? She was a high school track and field runner who was featured by Lindsay Crouse in the *New York Times*. Kayla, who was diagnosed with multiple sclerosis a few years prior, turned out to be one of the fastest runners in the United States. Crouse wrote, "Because M.S. blocks nerve signals from Montgomery's legs to her brain, particularly as her body temperature increases, she can move at steady speeds that cause other runners pain she cannot sense, creating the peculiar circumstance in which the symptoms of a disease might confer an athletic advantage." At the same time, any disruption to the activity, i.e., finishing the race, leads Kayla to lose control over her own body. This is why, just after the finish line, her coach waited for her to arrive so that she would not fall to the ground. When what gives Kayla an athletic advantage is a serious illness, most would hesitate to characterize it an unfair advantage. But if one plays the role of the devil's advocate, could one argue that she does have an unfair advantage? What would her peer athletes say as they might try to gain a full-ride athletic scholarship at a Division I university?

What about Mack Beggs, a high school wrestler who identified himself as a male and took a low dose of testosterone but was forced to wrestle in the girls' division? When Mack entered the Texas girls' Class 6A 110-pound division in February 2018, he had a 32–0 record. The year before, his record was 56–0. He had asked to wrestle in the boys' division, but he was required to play according to the gender on his birth certificate, according to Texas public schools (Schilken). What is fair for Mack? What is fair for other athletes?

With all of these nuances and intricacies in mind, this book discusses sports and exclusion and inclusion. Most of the essays focus on certain groups of athletes, major athletic events, legal structures, and so on. Two case studies conclude the book. They demonstrate how inclusion and exclusion takes place, what people experience, and how experiences are discussed.

Andrew Guest characterizes soccer as the most commonly employed vehicle for using sport to address global social problems. Sports for Development and Peace (SDP) programs try to take advantage of the near universality of the game and its raw emotional appeal to address inequality, promote health, facilitate youth development, empower girls and women, and confront other social justice issues. While these efforts are well intentioned, the raw emotional appeal of soccer can also incline its proponents toward oversimplifying culture, development, and global inequality. Guest uses examples of four different SDP programs employing soccer toward specific international development goals to analyze both the promise and peril of these endeavors. The argument is that if soccer is to make any contributions to global development its supporters must think less about how much we love the game and more about the complexities of international development work.

Glen Duerr investigates a core advantage in international politics: state sovereignty. Obviously, state sovereignty is also a major disadvantage to an out-group, people who are not represented by a recognized independent country. In tandem with this puzzle, this essay focuses on the CONIFA World Cup, a biennial soccer tournament, contested by a smattering of unrecognized states throughout the world. The maximalist goal for many participating associations is to gain de jure international recognition in the world. Thus, playing in the CONIFA World Cup plausibly helps to agitate for such a goal. This essay investigates the various geopolitical situations of the member associations, and why they participate in CONIFA tournaments. Duerr also discusses prominent subnational movements that have avoided CONIFA competitions.

The idea of sports as an environment where anyone is welcome as long as they "can play the game" has been tested by the extent to which homophobia has been present in that environment. Cedrick Heraux looks to assess the progress that has been made in sports at the professional level regarding this phenomenon. While certain high-profile athletes were able to come out some decades ago, the emphasis remained on their overall ability and success in their sport as a major contributing factor to that decision. Over time, the attitudes of fellow athletes, fans, and sports organizing bodies have seemingly changed to be more positive towards gay athletes, yet there remain relatively few who are openly gay in the United States' major sporting leagues, and most of those are women. Arguably, this is because, while society and the law have become more progressive, the institution of sports (that is, managers, coaches, and governing bodies) has failed to follow suit.

Meghan E. Fox and Francisco A. Villarruel argue that femininity prescriptions in the United States have long contributed to the pervasive social thought about women and their afforded roles in society. These ideological prejudices have historically sought to discourage women's participation in sports as it was deemed "too competitive, too strenuous, and too unfeminine" (Pieper 50). Post–World War I gender norms further perpetuated these societal views of sports as a masculine activity and deemed a woman who opted to play sports as an "amazon" or "muscle moll" (Pieper 50; McDonagh and Pappano 187). It was not until 1972 with the passage of Title IX and the Equal Rights Amendment (ERA) that the U.S. Congress offered some regulatory relief towards gender inequality by providing women greater access to educational resources, including sports. While there are critics that argue Title IX has had unintended outcomes of condoning sex segregation in contact sports reinforcing the notion women should not play with men, there are others that have touted the successes (McDonagh and Pappano 28). Today, it is estimated that nearly 150,000 women participate in collegiate sports compared to 30,000 before the legislation was passed. These opportunities are considered a pathway for lifelong success as women can play sports and then contribute in a meaningful way to society because of educational scholarships.

It has been reported as many as 80 percent of women executives identify their sports experiences as an influential factor in their career success (Schachter). In this essay, these long standing societal stereotypes about women in sports, under-recognition of women's athletic talent, systemic causes of related inequalities, and the dire need for better outcomes in gender equality and equity in athletics will be discussed. The complex role of Title IX as a solution as well as a transition from a commercial to a participation model of athletics will be evaluated for their merit to alleviate gender inequality.

Linda K. Fuller argues that despite having the "double whammy" discriminations of gender and disability, sportswomen in wheelchairs nevertheless have an increasingly impressive sports record that continues to grow. Their multisport events vary only in that they are performed by athletes with various physical and/or sensory abilities. This essay reviews the literature on wheelchair sportswomen, introduces a theoretical background based on Gendered Critical Discourse Analysis (GCDA), and a description of the following wheelchair sports in which the women athletes participate: archery, athletics, badminton, basketball, biathlon, curling, cycling, equestrianism, fencing, para-triathlon, powerlifting, rowing, rugby, shooting, skiing, softball, and tennis. Female para-athletes' biggest problem, it turns out, is winning over perceptions of them not as "supercrips" but instead as "regular" people who just happen to participate in, and excel at, various sports—in their wheelchairs.

Joshua R. Pate and Robin Hardin characterize disability as often overlooked and invisible within sport, and especially within the university sport management classroom. They explore how disability has been invisible within sport and how sport management educators can combat this oversight by infusing disability within curriculum. Using DePauw's framework in which disability is viewed in sport in three stages—namely, Invisibility of Disability, Visibility of Disability, and (In)Visibility of Disability, Pate and Hardin argue that sport lives primarily in DePauw's first two stages where disability is either excluded altogether or highlighted as inspirational. Yet, athletes with disabilities do not want to be inspiring; they want to be perceived as athletes. Disability sport is often minimized or overlooked within sport management higher education curriculum. The sport management classroom is the initial setting where this awareness can be enhanced if faculty include disability sport within their course content. The authors claim that excluding sport for people with disabilities from the sport management classroom may be simple oversight, but can be countered with proactive educators who aim to infuse disability in a similar manner they do for demographic areas within the industry. Excluding disability sport from the sport management classroom suggests it is not worthy of emerging professionals pursuing careers in this industry, is not valued, or simply does not exist. It is the educator's responsibility to promote inclusivity and better prepare a well-rounded sport professional.

LaToya T. Brackett shares an analysis of racial policing in American sports, particularly in regard to the NFL and the NBA. It first looks at the history of the integration of sports throughout American society, followed by a contextualization of how, despite integrating, a type of policing was created and has continued in relation to black athletes. Utilizing the concept of what is defined as the "white gaze," Brackett considers how the management of American sports must please and conform to the need of a white audience. This lens perpetuates the privileging of whites and the disadvantaging of people of color in the sports industry. It creates an industry that is inequitable. There may be lawful ways in which the industry is equally accessible by all people, on all levels, but most essential to understanding a continual policing of black players is the ways in which their behavior and presence is managed in a way that is not at the same requirements of white players. Brackett discusses three major ways in which the white gaze promotes and perpetuates racism in the sports industry. A black player receives racist responses particularly when they are being analyzed related to their (1) association with violence, (2) personal dress and (3) the way in which they stylize their way of play. Specific incidents with black players are compared to specific and similar incidents with white players. The rules and regulations of both the NBA and NFL are analyzed in regard to the way they focus on policing style and culture of black players. The essay closes with contemporary commentary on black player protests and the white gaze that has policed and defined such protest as wrong. The essay recognizes that despite the majority of both NFL and NBA players being black, the sports are indeed managed by and defined for whites only.

Benjamin James Dettmar focuses on the Olympics. When the first summer Olympic Games of the modern era took place in Athens, Greece, in 1896, 241 athletes competed and all were male. The most recent summer Olympics in Rio de Janeiro, Brazil, had 11,238 athletes with approximately 42 percent being female. How do we go from 0 percent to 42 percent over the course of 120 years and 31 Olympics? Was this a smooth process? What controversies did we see? Do we now have equality? And what exactly does equality mean? Dettmar charts the continuing quest for gender equality within the summer Olympics. The essay also examines equality within the sports that are currently offered as well as those that have been offered historically: how male and female athletes are treated differently by the governing International Olympic Committee (IOC); how female athletes have been "sex-tested"; how they are treated by media, commentators, and sponsors, how male political figures continue to dominate at both the National Olympic Committee

(NOC) level and the IOC level. Individual stories of athletes such as Lina Radke, Babe Didrikson, and Fanny Blankers-Koen surface in Dettmar's study. The essay concludes by assessing where the Olympics are in terms of equality as we head into Tokyo, Japan, 2020.

Corey Shouse focuses on the mid–1980s, glorious years for Colombian cyclists in the Tour de France. Luis Herrera, Fabio Parra and others claimed numerous stage victories and podiums in the world's most important cycling event. Unfortunately, the European press, peloton and fans often openly ridiculed the Colombian racers as "Indians" and "narcotraffickers," while the Colombian press simultaneously celebrated their compatriots as idealized representatives of a noble people stigmatized by the darkest years of the cocaine trade and insurgency violence. Through close analysis of national press archives and interviews with racers and fans, Shouse forwards a double-edged analysis of the barrier braking experiences of Colombians in the European peloton and their role in confronting and reconfiguring ideas of race, class and national identity at home and abroad.

Danielle Sarver Coombs and Jack Kucek examine the Aston Villa Football Club, a founding member of England's football association, located in central Birmingham, England. The club's specific location, Aston, is an ethnically diverse area, consisting largely of Southeast Asian immigrants. The area faces significant challenges in a number of areas, ranging from economics and employment to education and health care. As one of the largest and most prominent residents of Aston, the club and its owners have a unique position from which to potentially affect change. The authors explore some of the ways Aston Villa has attempted to have a positive impact on its environs through its Corporate Social Responsibility (CSR) efforts. The use of CSR has previously been established to encourage social interaction within the community, provide a link between participating in sport and positive health benefits, and establish a wider reach by appealing strongly to children and older adults.

All of the authors who have contributed an essay to this volume are invested in inclusion in one way or another. They also understand how sports could play positive role in realizing inclusion. The unfortunate reality is that we see so many examples of exclusion, prejudice, discrimination, and unfairness in sports. But we should not always be discouraged or dismayed. This introduction alone has already touched upon many efforts to bring about inclusion and equality in sports. When Mohamed Salah scores a goal for the Liverpool Football Club, fans go a little quieter for a short moment, allowing the Egyptian player to "[raise] his hands to the sky and then [kneel] on the field" to demonstrate his Muslim faith (Smith). The Right to Dream Academy in Ghana strives to achieve gender equality as it teaches youth about the importance of integrity, self-discipline, and other important values. Most of these students, without the academy, would not have the opportunity attend a school (Sidman).

On one level, this book is a testament to the fact that sport could encourage inclusion and fairness if we are intentional about how we organize it, play it, and talk about it. But on another level, it shows how complex the issue of fairness and inclusion is. Kayla Montgomery and Mack Beggs show that there are many nuances and intricacies associated with sports and inclusion.

WORKS CITED

Barone, Emily. "The Astronomical Cost of Kids' Sports." *TIME*. TIME. 24 August 2017. Web. 11 May 2018.

Bird, Liviu. "USWNT Team Doctor: Artificial Turf Takes Toll on Recovery Time, Bodies." *Sports Illustrated*. Sports Illustrated. 3 June 2015. Web. 7 May 2018.

Bogage, Jacob. "Youth Sports Study: Declining Participation, Rising Costs and Unqualified Coaches." *Washington Post* 6 September 2017. Web. 11 May 2018.

Crewdson, John M. "Cheering for the Cowboys." *New York Times*. New York Times. 19 April 1978. Web. 9 May 2018.

Crouse, Linsay. "For Runner with M.S., No Pain While Racing, No Feeling at the Finish." *New York Times*. New York Times. 3 March 2014. Web. 29 June 2018.

Das, Andrew. "Pay Disparity in U.S. Soccer? It's Complicated." *New York Times*. New York Times, 21 April 2016. Web. 7 May 2018.

_____. "U.S. Soccer Sues Union Representing the Women's National Team." *New York Times*. New York Times, 3 February 2016. Web. 7 May 2018.

DePauw, Karen P. "The (In)Visibility of DisAbility: Cultural Contexts and 'Sporting Bodies.'" *The Thirty-First Amy Morris Homans Lecture*, 1997, http://www.humankinetics.com/acucustom/sitename/Documents/DocumentItem/11338.pdf. Accessed 30 January 2018.

FIFA U-17 Championship Peru 2005. 2005. PDF file.

"Formula 1: 'Grid Girls' Will Not be Used at Races This Season." *BBC*. BBC. 21 January 2018. Web. 9 May 2018.

"Hamilton Backs Return of 'Grid Girls' in F1: Then Deletes Controversial Post." *Sky News*. Sky UK, 7 April 2018. Web. 9 May 2018.

Hoff, Eli. "Buying the Badge: The Inaccessibility of Soccer Officiating in Minnesota." *E Pluribus Loonum*. Vox Media, 4 April 2018. Web. 11 May 2018.

Lloyd, Carli. "Carli Lloyd: Why I'm Fighting for Equal Pay." *New York Times*. New York Times, 10 April 2016. Web. 7 May 2018.

Macur, Juliet. "Washington Redskins Cheerleaders Describe Topless Photo Shoot and Uneasy Night Out." *New York Times*. New York Times, 2 May 2018. Web. 9 May 2018.

McCarthy, Niall. "Soccer's Ridiculous Gender Wage Gap." *Forbes*. 28 November 2017. Web. 7 May 2018.

McDonagh, Eileen, and Laura Pappano. "Playing with the Boys: Why Is Gender Segregation in Sports Normal? Males and Females Should Play Together." *The Sun* 6 February 2008: A17. *ProQuest*. Web. 27 December 2017.

Pieper, Lindsay. *Sex Testing: Gender Policing in Women's Sports*. Champaign: University of Illinois Press, 2006. Print.

Schachter, Ron. "Title IX Turns 35." *University Business* 10.3 (2007): 44–50. Web. 29 December 2017.

Schilken, Chuck. "Transgender Boy Wins Texas Girls Wrestling Championship for the Second Year in a Row." *Los Angeles Times*. Los Angels Times. 26 February 2018. Web. 29 June 2018.

Shell, Adam. "Why Families Stretch Their Budgets for High-priced Youth Sports." *USA Today*. USA Today. 5 September 2017. Web. 11 May 2018.

Sidman, Amanda. "One-of-a-kind African School Gives Girls 'Right to Dream.'" *Today*. NBC Universal. 14 October 2016. Web. 29 June 2018.

Smith, Rory. "Mo Salah of Liverpool Breaks Down Cultural Barriers, One Goal at a Time." *New York Times*. New York Times. 2 May 2018. Web. 3 May 2018.

"There's a Sinister Side to Life in North Korea's Cheerleading Squad." Newswww.au. All Times AEST, 23 February 2018. Web. 9 May 2018.

"They're Pretty: Monaco Grand Prix Says 'Grid Girls' Are Here to Stay." *Fortune*. Time. 5 April 2018. Web. 9 May 2018.

Wallace, Ava. "Coach of WNVA Champs Says Lack of White House Invitation Reflects Trump's Views on Women." *Chicago Tribune*. 3 May 2018. Web. 9 May 2018.

Soccer Saves the World?

The Complexities of Using the Global Game for International Development

ANDREW GUEST

At the turn of the 21st century, United Nations Children's Fund regularly rated the sub–Saharan African nation of Angola as the worst place in the world to be a child. When I arrived there in 2002 to do research in conjunction with volunteering for an international non-governmental organization (NGO) using sports and play to facilitate child development in refugee camps, the country was just emerging from a 27-year civil war. The infrastructure was devastated. Outside the capital of Luanda, where oil and diamond money made for a surprisingly vibrant and expensive safe zone, education, health care, jobs, and roads were all in short supply. Angola was, in other words, a prime target for international development efforts.

My work took me on a daily drive in a rickety UN Land Cruiser from Luanda to long-term refugee camps ringing the far outskirts of the city. The drive passed a dystopian mix of gleaming new office buildings for oil companies and government ministries next to red dirt hillsides of tiny wood huts densely packed with gaps only for canals full of trash and debris. Amidst the intense inequality, there was just one constant. Any reasonably open and flat space would often be teeming with kids playing soccer.

The communities where I worked were mostly comprised of internally displaced Angolans and Congolese who had fled across the nearby border and been settled in Angola. Though life was hard, people were making it and, one of their great pleasures was soccer. Kids played constantly, young men had organized a semi-formal league, and nearly everyone had a favorite team from elsewhere in the world—in a nod to Angola's Lusophone culture, the Brazilian national team and Sporting Lisbon were particularly popular.

For my research work, after several months of familiarizing myself with the communities and working on coach training and youth programs, I spent several weeks undertaking surveys and learning about the daily lives of children. One day, as a group of Angolan assistants and I surveyed kids in an open-air tin roofed school block, one of the assistants pulled me aside and said, "There's a kid here I think you'll find interesting to talk to yourself." He introduced a boy I've called "Diego" in other academic writing (Guest, "Cultures of Play" 5) who distinguished himself from the crowd by a lack of functioning legs. I never quite learned why Diego's legs had no musculature, serving merely as stick-like props to balance his torso as he propelled himself about using his fists as levers, but the most realistic speculation was that he had been afflicted by polio.

Interviewing Diego about his life and love of soccer was interesting, but emotionally conflicting. Many of my research questions were about sports and play, and I did not want to make Diego feel bad about his disability. But for the sake of research protocol I asked, "How many days a week do you usually play sports and physical games?" And, I added quickly to lighten the blow, "It's ok if it's zero." Diego looked at me with uncertainty, sensing that I had a particular expectation. Tentatively, he replied (in Portuguese): "I play soccer every day." Now it was my turn to be uncertain. "Every day?" I probably did not mean to say it out loud, but how could a boy with no functioning legs play soccer every day? "Well," Diego tried again, "I guess there were a few days where I had a cold and couldn't play. So, almost every day?"

As it turns out, Diego and friends in this particularly desolate refugee community on the deep outskirts of Luanda had a daily "kick-about" on the bare patch of dirt that served as both local school yard and soccer field. Diego just used his hands to bat the ball when the other kids used their feet to kick, but he was nimble enough at dragging his legs on their thickly scabbed knees to keep up. Later, while undertaking a more in-depth case study of Diego's life inspired by that first research interview, I asked his friends whether Diego's participation in the game ever caused problems.

"Kind of," his friends told me.

"We sometimes disagree about what should happen when the ball hits his [non-functioning] legs. Some of us think that's just like a handball for the rest of us. But mostly we just play…"

My research ended up being largely about the psychological resilience and adaptability of children in difficult structural circumstances. Diego was an ideal case study for that, but his story here is also a vivid example of both the promise and peril of using soccer as a way of addressing global inequality and as a tool for international development. The trope of impoverished barefoot boys passionately engaged in dusty games of pick-up soccer amidst tight alleys of mud and stick houses has become a clichéd image of childhood in the global south—a version of that image was the cover for the May 24, 2010, issue of *Sports Illustrated* in the run up to the first ever World Cup on the African continent. Like most tropes, that image offers both grains of truth and assumptions to be approached with caution. The pervasiveness of children playing soccer for fun in the streets and on dirt fields in places like Angola, sights that are rare in American neighborhoods, evoke hopeful feelings of innocence and potential. Seeing Diego joyously batting a ball with friends during his daily "kick-about" made me feel emotionally connected through a shared love for the game and reminded me of the good that opportunities to play and learn could unleash. But those images also evoke more complicated questions about what a game can actually do. In the face of massive global inequality, what might soccer really offer to children like Diego?

In recent decades, there has been an explosion of domestic and international organizations trying to explore the good the game can do at a grass roots level under the broad label of Sports for Development and Peace (often abbreviated as SDP). While the organizations involved in SDP efforts use all types of sports and play activities as tools, as the only truly global game soccer holds a privileged place in the world of SDP. In fact, in one recent review of global SDP organizations soccer was by far the most popular single sport used by SDP programs—while 384 organizations used multiple sports (often including soccer), 236 focused exclusively on soccer (Svensson and Woods). Only 25 programs focused exclusively on the next most popular sport for SDP programs: basketball. Further, while SDP programs operate on every continent, most programs exist in sub–Saharan Africa.

The emotional appeal of these programs is understandable: the combination of the world's most popular game, the needs and potential of children in the world's poorest countries, and the belief that opportunities and joy should be more justly shared can easily trigger our best humanitarian instincts. In fact, a 2011 *Sports Illustrated* feature article on the growing popularity of SDP began with the grandiose headline "Sports Save the World." But that exuberance and emotional appeal comes with significant risks for oversimplification. In the same way that the heated intensity of a competitive soccer game can bring out either the best or the worst in us, either a magical stoppage time goal or an impetuous studs-up tackle, the use of soccer for international development brings both joy and complications. Scholars have thus increasingly been attending to ways the zeal of soccer fans and SDP practitioners can be informed by more rational and academic analysis.

Soccer will not save the world. But it does have an almost unrivaled emotional appeal that crosses cultural boundaries, and there are evolving ways of thinking carefully about how to take advantage of that appeal while also rationally analyzing realistic roles for soccer as part of international development. This essay offers such analysis through considering several diverse examples of soccer being used towards prominent international development goals: FIFA's 20 Centres for 2010 program affiliated with the World Cup in South Africa; Grassroots Soccer programs to combat HIV; the One World Play Project's "ultra-durable ball to bring the transformative power of play to the hundreds of millions of youth who don't even have something as simple as a ball"; and women's soccer to promote gender empowerment as described in several documentary films. The analysis here is based primarily on secondary sources and publicly available information. Although I have done empirical work with SDP programs in sub–Saharan Africa, I have not worked directly with any of these efforts. I have, however, selected these as examples for this essay because they demonstrate the broad range of ways soccer might both contribute to international development and reflect its limitations. Each illustrates ways that the emotional appeal of soccer needs to be leavened with careful considerations of the complexity of international development if the game is indeed going to contribute to a more just world.

The Peril and the Potential of Soccer for Development

The 2010 FIFA World Cup in South Africa, as the first mega-sporting event hosted in sub–Saharan Africa, was prime terrain for sports and development programs. Symbolically it was an opportunity for the "developing" world to earn its place in the global conversation, and practically it became a hub for international development projects piggy-backing on the games. Hundreds of SDP organizations tried to officially or unofficially leverage the World Cup to fulfill the oft-cited (by SDP organizations) words of South African freedom fighter, president, and icon Nelson Mandela: "Sport has the power to change the world. It has the power to inspire. It has the power to unite people in a way that little else does. It speaks to youth in a language they understand. Sport can create hope where once there was only despair" (Nelson Mandela Foundation).

This ambition for sport was even codified by FIFA through the 2010 World Cup's "official social responsibility campaign"—a program called 20 Centres for 2010 to create youth centers based on a mix of soccer, education and development programming. As I've written elsewhere (Guest, "What's the Legacy"), the logos for the 20 Centres for 2010 program were everywhere at the official venues in South Africa, taking a prominent place next to the brand marks of official corporate sponsors as if to say, "Look, we are not just shilling for multi-nationals; we are also doing good in the world." Unfortunately, in contrast to the polished PR campaign, something was missing: the actual youth centers. At the time of the tournament only one had been completed: a center in Khayelitsha township of Cape Town that provided a scenic backdrop for further promotional events. There were perhaps four more centers done within a month of the tournament ending, at least according to one of the few media sources to follow up on FIFA's promotional campaign (Kelto).

It is still hard to confirm the numbers and completion dates both because FIFA never publicized the actual 20 Centres as much as the concept, and because they were spread out across the entire continent of Africa. FIFA does have a final report available as a web resource, indicating 20 centers are being operated by non-governmental organization partners (FIFA, *20 Centres*). However, by early 2018, many of the links for "more information" about each center were no longer operational. While the few available pictures suggest that each individual center offers a nice community space with a small (often 40 meters by 20 meters) turf field and an accompanying small building with meeting spaces and offices, it is noteworthy that none seems to have a full-sized soccer field. Thus, as a legacy of a World Cup cycle that took in an estimated $3.89 billion in revenue and $2.17 billion in profit, from which FIFA, a non-profit organization, took $631 million to supplement its reserves (FIFA *FIFA Financial* 111), all of Africa was gifted 20 miniature fields—approximately one for every 50 million people on the continent.

In fact, the biggest problem with both the FIFA 20 Centres for 2010 program and many other efforts to use soccer for development is that they oversimplify the challenges of international development. They often say or imply that just a field and a ball can change lives and we can all feel good: "If the game can just make one child smile…" And while no one would object to the idea of making children smile, thoughtful analysis would point out several problems with this idea of how soccer can help. First, it assumes kids in developing communities would not play or smile without outside help. As Diego's story at the start of this essay suggests, that is a problematic assumption. In fact, in one of the few scholarly accounts of how communities received the 20 centers, Waardenburg et al. found that several years after its unveiling the turf field in Johannesburg's Alexandra township seemed less used (and less accessible) for soccer than the neighboring dirt streets. Second, and more subtly, the notion that soccer is important to development because it makes people happy may allow us to focus on the individual feelings of poverty and underdevelopment without taking seriously the broader social and structural forces that maintain inequality. Kids like Diego are indeed in need of help, but not in the form of another soccer game. They need their community to have decent schools and health care. They needed their parents to have access to jobs. They need to not live in stick-houses patched against weather by plastic United Nations High Commissioner for Refugees (UNHCR) tarps. If any of the 20 Centres for 2010 had been anywhere near Diego's community that would have been nice. But they were not. The closest was about 1800 miles away. Unfortunately, it probably would not have changed his life, anyway.

As scholars have started paying more attention to SDP endeavors, they often comment on this tension between the individual and societal levels of international development. David Black, for example, is a Canadian scholar of international development who has written several cautiously critical analyses of SDP, emphasizing that the endeavor does have the advantage of being "latecomers to the 'development enterprise,' with the opportunity to learn from some of the dangers and missteps that have befallen more 'mainstream' development practitioners through the chequered post–Second World War history of this enterprise" (122). One of Black's key cautions to SDP practitioners is to be aware that international development is both a "bottom-up" grass-roots community endeavor *and* a "top-down" political policy endeavor. It is nice to play a fun game of soccer with kids, but for that game to be meaningful it must relate to some kind of opening for broader policies offering opportunities and resources, such as for education, health, and recreational spaces. The 20 Centres for 2010 program was trying to provide those types of openings, but the scale of it was just too small to make a meaningful impact.

Black thinks this relates to the unease many have at thinking of sports as political. He writes: "No serious sport studies scholar would any longer defend the 'myth of autonomy'—the idea that sport is apolitical, 'above' or autonomous from politics. Nevertheless, it is very hard to develop the sort of contextualized understanding of the communities in and with which one is working that is necessary for successful and sustainable development interventions. This challenge may be compounded for many sportspeople, convinced as they are of the transcendent power of sport and often having been relatively disengaged from mainstream politics" (125). If soccer is going to do some good in the world, in other words, it cannot depend solely on how much we love the game.

This tension in stories of soccer and development, between the real emotional connection it offers and the structural inequalities it sometimes allows us to ignore, must be addressed if soccer is to contribute to international development. So what does it look like in (and on) the field? There are many possible examples of development programs leveraging soccer to do good, and none are perfect. But three further examples can help to illustrate the importance of balancing the emotional appeal of the game with more rational analysis.

Grassroot Soccer

While the idea of soccer as a universal language that brings people together is another cliché to be used with caution, the global popularity of the game does create serendipitous opportunities. Take, for example, the origin story of the prominent SDP program Grassroot Soccer—an organization that tries to leverage the appeal of soccer towards HIV education and health promotion. While Grassroot Soccer now spends millions of dollars a year in 45 participating countries, it started when Scotland's back-up goalkeeper in the 1978 World Cup became the coach of Highlanders FC in Bulawayo, Zimbabwe. The coach, Bobby Clark, brought along his 14-year-old son, who would go on to play for his father at Dartmouth College in New Hampshire, return to play for Highlanders and teach English in Zimbabwe, recognize the scourge of HIV in sub–Saharan Africa, go to medical school, and put it all together by creating a non-profit that "leverages the power of soccer to educate, inspire, and mobilize at-risk youth in developing countries to overcome their greatest health challenges" ("A Letter from"). As Tommy Clark explains it on the Grassroot Soccer website,

> Every day as I walked to practice [while playing for Highlanders in Zimbabwe], I was followed by a group of children who would abandon their own pick-up soccer games to join me on my walk. The bolder children would push to the front and walk next to me, practicing their English as I practiced my isiNdebele. Over time the group of children grew as word spread that a Mukiwa (white man) and professional soccer player was in their community. It was on these walks that I further realized the power and draw of soccer.
>
> Zimbabwe, however, had changed since I first arrived as a teenager. City squares that had teemed with artisans selling crafts and vendors selling food and staples were now empty. European tourists who had roamed the graceful streets of Bulawayo were conspicuously absent. Families were missing uncles, mothers, sisters, and grandparents.
>
> AIDS had struck.

Taking inspiration from his personal experience and his medical training, Clark along with several co-founders, hatched the idea of using professional soccer players to promote HIV prevention and other health messages in Zimbabwean communities. In 2002, the year of Grassroot Soccer's formal founding, the UNAIDS program estimated the adult HIV/AIDS prevalence in Zimbabwe to be around 33 percent. It was a crisis.

Clark notes "a chance meeting with Dr. Albert Bandura," a Stanford psychologist famous for articulating "social learning theory," as a prompt to wonder "if Michael Jordan could promote consumer products, why couldn't soccer stars promote health?" After focusing initially only on the familiar terrain of Zimbabwe, as of 2018, Grassroot Soccer identifies as an "adolescent health organization" and working with 35 implementing partners and reaching over 100,000 youth each year.

Grassroot Soccer has plenty of its own promotional material for the curious, and they have broadened their mission considerably over time (now addressing malaria, gender issues, youth development, and other development issues in addition to HIV). But their most basic method historically was to have coaches and mentors implement a "SKILLZ curriculum" that integrates information about HIV risk behaviors and prevention with soccer activities. For example, at least one version developed in conjunction with UNAIDS for use in South Africa offers 11 units including activities such as "Make a Choice." In this program, youth run around a field making choices of who to group with as a coach shouts questions progressing from "Who is your favorite soccer team" to "What is your favorite subject in school?" The activity would build to groupings that demonstrate that "for every 6 adults in South Africa, 1 had HIV" with an affirmation of the life "choices" we can make "to avoid getting or spreading HIV: Choose to abstain from sex; choose to stick to one partner who sticks only to me; choose to stay away from older partners; choose to always wear a condom if I do have sex" (USAID).

Has it worked? Does soccer offer a particularly compelling vehicle for these types of public health messages? Here is where the story requires more analysis and less emotional attachment. And here is where the story gets complicated.

Grassroot soccer, to their great credit, is one of the few SDP organizations who offer extensive public evidence about their programming. They take research seriously, offering a regular "research report" that as of 2016 offered summaries of "27 research studies since 2005 in over 20 countries, ranging from South Africa to the Dominican Republic. GRS has also conducted the largest school-based randomized controlled trial (RCT) evaluating a sport-based HIV prevention program, called the GOAL Trial." Using an RCT study, considered the gold standard for intervention research, in sport for development is exceedingly rare. Drawing from large school districts in South Africa, the Grassroot Soccer study found that their programs do indeed increase knowledge related to HIV prevention and rates of HIV testing. But the RCT trial also found that the group of youth exposed to the intervention were actually more likely than a control group to report multiple sexual partners and to perpetrate intimate-partner violence (Kaufman 3). This finding reinforces a finding that has long been known to social psychologists and that regularly stymies educators—in the realm of youth risk taking, knowledge does not always change behavior. Teens often know, for example, about the risks of driving too fast or of binge drinking. But when it comes to actual behavior, and especially teen behavior in group contexts, teens often prioritize emotional rewards over rational understandings of risk (Steinberg 55). While the Grassroot Soccer participants seemed to learn lots of useful information about HIV prevention, they also seemed inclined to engage in the kinds of behaviors that might bring some short-term pleasure at the expense of the health and safety of themselves and others.

To use another soccer analogy for the ways our emotions can override our rationality, we might take the famous example of the 2006 World Cup final when France's Zinedine Zidane headbutted Marco Materazzi of Italy. If you described this situation to Zidane that he is 19 minutes into extra time during a tied World Cup final, and an opposing player (supposedly) insults his sister for being a "whore," he would likely say the right thing to do would be to walk away and focus on winning the game. But in the heat of the moment, with his emotional system over-riding his rational thought, he took brief satisfaction in driving his forehead squarely into the chest of Materazzi. Zidane was sent off, and France went on to lose the game in kicks from the penalty mark.

It is not entirely clear why the GRS GOAL trial participants not only ignored their rational knowledge, but increased problem behaviors. Grassroot Soccer does not seem to have shared any detailed analysis of this randomized control trial's results publicly. It seems, however, that they have started to de-emphasize their SKILLZ curriculum and it may be that the randomized control trial results are at least part of the reason. If you have really randomized your intervention group and your control group, and you have the right sample sizes, then there is no other conclusion to draw than that participation in the soccer program contributed to risk behavior. This must have been a hard finding to confront, but Grassroot Soccer should be applauded for being willing to care about the evidence.

Grassroot Soccer should also be applauded for a variety of other ways they use soccer for development. In another program Grassroot Soccer administered and researched in Bulawayo, Zimbabwe, a separate randomized control trial found that a program to encourage voluntary male circumcision as a way of reducing HIV transmission had modest but significant effects. The program revealed that an hour-long informational session using the context of soccer was a cost-effective way to get young men to proceed with the voluntary circumcision. Grassroot Soccer has also been excellent about partnering with other relevant development players. They have teamed up with schools, with UNAIDS, with U.S. Peace Corps volunteers, and with the foundations for teams such as Arsenal and Manchester City. It is also worth noting that recent estimates of the adult HIV prevalence rate in Zimbabwe are approximately half what they were in 2002. The broader global effort towards HIV education and intervention seems to be working. Although exact role of soccer in that type of progress is something that would be very difficult to evidence, at least Grassroot Soccer recognizes that the game itself is not enough.

One World Futbol

If the game itself is not enough to make development happen, what about the ball? Soccer appeals to many in the development world because of its simplicity. You only really need a ball to play. This fact is part of the beauty of the game, and it has also been the font for many international service trips full of good-hearted travelers with extra luggage packed full of donated soccer balls. In many parts of the developing world, a ball is indeed a magical gift. Of course, the emotional pull of that gesture, like the emotional pull of the game itself, can be misleading amidst the complexities of international development.

In my own work as a Peace Corps volunteer in Malawi, I was actively discouraged from having people send large quantities of sports equipment because of huge import tariffs that would end up costing more than buying the equipment locally (which was exactly the point of the tariffs, to encourage people to buy local goods). And then, if the equipment did make it to schools or communities, it often would not last very long. Most manufactured soccer balls pop after significant use, particularly on fields of dirt and stone. The clichéd image of barefoot boys playing on dusty streets with an improvised ball is not just a product of poverty: the improvised balls made of collected plastic bags enmeshed in twine or rocks rolled in socks are sometimes the most functional way for kids to play the game in communities without unlimited access to turf fields and big box sporting goods stores. But being functional does not necessarily mean being optimal. And that image of the barefoot child with the twine ball feels so powerful emotionally that it practically begs for action.

At least that was the feeling that animates the origin story publicized by the One World Play Project, originally called One World Futbol, which is known in the world of soccer and development for inventing an "indestructible" soccer ball. As the story was explained by Gwen Knapp writing for *Sports on Earth* in 2013:

> The inventor, Tim Jahnigen of Berkeley, Ca., came up with the idea when he watched a 2006 documentary about Darfur refugees that showed children in a camp kicking a wad of trash bound by string. In Brazil, where billions have been spent on new stadiums, the game has become an impediment to basic needs. For children in a war zone, Jahnigen recognized that play was essential to their well-being. (The United Nations agrees and lists children's recreation as a human right.)
>
> Jahnigen learned that sending regular soccer balls would be pointless. Aid organizations had done it before, but the balls would quickly deflate or be destroyed on the hard ground. In one African village, he said, the nearest pump required a full day's walk at an adult's pace.

Jahnigen, according to multiple interviews and journalistic reports, was mostly an entrepreneur who did not know much about soccer, except that it is the most popular game in the world. But he came to see the issue of soccer balls as both a design problem to be solved and an opportunity for one of the fads in recent international development efforts: social entrepreneurship. In this model of development work entrepreneurial business endeavors, complete with degrees of a profit motive, offer an alternative to the traditional non-profit model of development that relies heavily on altruism and political will. The One World Play Project is officially a business, though one certified as a "B-Corp" for its emphasis on social responsibility.

On the design side, Jahnigen may have had an advantage by his lack of familiarity with soccer. He needed a material unlike the versions of leather and plastic that are intimately familiar to anyone growing up around manufactured balls. He found it in a type of synthetic foam most famous as the ingredient making Croc sandals cheap, durable, reasonably comfortable, and hugely popular. He then needed some seed funding to develop and test prototypes, and he found that from an old connection in the music industry: pop star Sting liked the idea and gave Jahnigen $300,000 to make it work.

After several iterations of design, and several forms of field testing (apparently including giving the ball to a Lion at the Johannesburg Zoo to make sure it was truly indestructible), One World Futbol was ready for business. And the business plan they chose involved a model made famous by TOMS shoes and Warby Parker glasses often referred to as BOGO: buy one, give one. The basic idea is that every time a (presumably affluent resident of the global north) consumer buys one of the product, another is given away to a (presumably poor resident of the global south) person in need. When I bought my then-three-year-old son a One World Futbol for Christmas a few years back, we got an indestructible soccer ball and we got thanked for donating an unseen other ball to someone somewhere else. We got a ball we could kick around in the backyard without worrying about leaving it out in the rain, and we got to feel good about ourselves for being philanthropic types.

The BOGO model is also rife with critics and complexities. Rothstein claimed that the model fits well with younger consumers who are concerned with how personal economic choices relate to broader social issues. He sees the model as one that is only likely to grow. But he also recognizes that, and his article was criticized for, perceptions that the BOGO idea is more about clever marketing than creating social change. Will charitable donations from successful Western companies really address global inequality? One of the founders of One World Futbol, Mal Warwick, actively chimed in on the issue through the comments section of the *Stanford Social Innovation Review* discussion, arguing that their model was distinctive because "1. We donate the same soccer ball as the one we sell to paying customers; and 2. The bulk of our donations are made possible through a generous sponsorship by Chevrolet."

In a separate comment on the same Rothstein article, Warwick goes on to argue the case for social value by using many of the standard arguments about the nearly miraculous power of soccer:

> The virtually indestructible One World Futbol—is more than useful to the young people who receive it. Because it enables them to play without fear that the ball will suddenly go flat and become useless, the One World Futbol helps promote health and wellbeing in communities where there may be no other opportunities for organized play. In a great many of these communities, the One World Futbol is employed in "sport for peace and development" programs undertaken by the UN, the national government, or NGOs—programs that teach conflict resolution, gender equity, HIV/AIDS prevention, and other critical subjects and skills.

In fact, that expansive vision of what a ball can do seems to be behind the change of the company's name from "One World Futbol" to the "One World Play Project." They see themselves as doing more than just giving away soccer balls, and they do indeed partner with a variety of sport for development organizations (including Grassroot Soccer) targeting diverse development goals.

At the same time, the ambitious rhetoric and emotional appeal associated with the One World Futbol should trigger the same degree of skepticism merited by the oversimplified claim that "sports save the world." For one thing, unlike Grassroot Soccer, the One World Play Project has very little publicly available data to support their claims. There does not seem to be academic literature comparing community levels of physical activity, health, or other measures of well-being before and after the introduction of One World Futbols. For another, that corporate sponsorship from General Motors may indeed make the business viable but it also means that most One World Futbols are emblazoned with a Chevrolet logo—mixing up a strong dose of corporate branding directed at children into what is framed as a social value endeavor.

Another complication of giving away soccer balls goes back to the logic of import tariffs imposed by countries such as Malawi. They have the potential to undermine local markets and fair-trade efforts. One World Futbols are manufactured in Taiwan and sold by a U.S. corporation, ensuring that any primary economic value accrues outside of the "developing" countries the balls are designed to help. As commenter Howard Brodwin noted in Rothstein's work, "There are a few BOGO soccer ball companies, and the mission of providing a free soccer ball to disadvantaged communities abroad is excellent. But there are also a several fair trade soccer/sports ball manufacturers, and the BOGO competitors can have a negative impact on their ability to sell and thereby meet their mission of providing fair wage/working condition employment. No easy answers here, and since this entire space is still evolving, I'm sure we'll see a shift in how this model can be applied."

In short, if the miraculous power of giving away indestructible soccer balls seems too good to be true then it probably is. Hower cited the then-President of Malawi Joyce Banda whose foundation received and distributed 11,000 One World Futbols as claiming on national television that "the balls would go to support the first nationwide youth soccer and netball tournaments, which was previously impossible due to a lack of durable balls." My experience of working with school soccer in Malawi for two years between 1997 and 1999 hints that soccer did not need "saving"—kids and schools were playing it constantly. I suspect, however, the honorable President Banda is making a semantic distinction here, because while there may not have been national school tournaments there were always enough balls to have a game.

Yet, even the questions we need to ask in an academic analysis should not negate the reality that in places like Malawi a soccer ball is indeed a magical and welcome gift. So while One World Futbol proffers many of the reasons to worry about soccer as a tool for development including the pandering to stereotypes of deficiency, the reliance on celebrity promoters who know little about development, the ulterior motives of global corporations, the failure to address structural inequalities, and the lack of clear and public evidence for its grand claims, it also ultimately embodies why soccer may have something to contribute to global development. There is something about a soccer ball, and about the game itself, that represents potential. The potential for joy, for social connection, for achievement, and maybe for development itself if it can be used in the right way. So, what might that look like?

Women Fighters

While Grassroot Soccer and the One World Play Project are variations on the development theme of Westerners perceiving needs in the developing world and exporting ways to address those needs, development experts often emphasize the importance of local solutions to local problems. What would it look like for local communities to make their own soccer for development program? One intriguing possibility is illustrated by a 2007 documentary film titled *Zanzibar Soccer Queens* and its 2016 follow-up *Zanzibar Soccer Dreams* (there is also a 2015 film *New Generation Queens* documenting a very similar version of the same story, but the production of that film seems independent of the other two). The filmmaker, a Cameroonian academic working at the University of South Wales named Florence Ayisi, explained to the *Mirror* that when she made the film she was specifically looking for ways to counter negative stereotypes of sub–Saharan Africa: "It was the era of Live Aid and Bob Geldof. I wanted to show the other Africa beyond the headlines" (Wightwick). She came upon the story of "Women Fighters FC" on Zanzibar

Island off the coast of Tanzania, a team inspired by a Swedish women's team traveling through Zanzibar in 1988 but taken up largely by local women in the decades since.

The name "Women Fighters" is entirely intentional—the women are very conscious of having to fight against not only the argument that soccer is a men's game, but also Zanzibar's predominantly Muslim population and its interpretation of religious strictures against women playing sports. They are very consciously using soccer to fight for their own development. Though not a glossy big-budget film, the documentary offers a rich analysis from local perspectives on the issue at hand. The Women Fighters talk about how much the game means to them as a chance to express themselves and their strengths, while critics speaking in the films (including a female university student, a male teacher, a female teacher, and some parents) argue that Islam prohibits the display of the body and discourages the female assertiveness inherent to soccer. This tension is central to the film's intent, with an academic reflection on the filmmaking arguing that the local women "metaphorically reveal their inner selves beneath traditional restrictions. This dichotomy of transgression vs. conformity in these women's identities is synecdochal for all women in Ayisi's films" (Ayisi and Brylla 131).

Soccer for development in this case thus becomes both a "transgression" and a complicated driver of social change. The process is not easy; several of the players become visibly emotional when explaining what it is like to see one's name on the back of a real jersey for the first time, or when describing their sadness at being forced to quit the game by a new husband. But watching video of their exuberance during games against men on slippery village fields, or against women in bumpy city parks, it is hard not to feel that soccer can indeed be empowering. The team's local critics, on the other hand, articulate an argument that mostly serves to highlight its own limits—their concerns that women in soccer uniforms might throw the whole community into disarray seems more about male fantasies and patriarchal control than it is about respecting "local culture."

The challenge of navigating "local culture" in using for soccer for development, however, is a real one. One of the classic issues for many development workers interested in gender equity as part of social change is to reconcile conflicting ideas about women's rights with a respect for local (often patriarchal) value systems. This challenge can be particularly pronounced in many parts of the developing world, and many parts of sub–Saharan Africa, where soccer is gender typed as masculine in local cultural discourse. In this case, however, there is some good evidence that the idea of "African culture" prohibiting women's soccer is another oversimplification.

Martha Saavedra, for example, wrote case studies of "football feminine" in Senegal, Nigeria, and South Africa finding that the boundaries of who can play and who cannot is always more about power than it is about "indigenous culture." In Senegal, for example, women's basketball is among the most popular sports—third only to men's soccer and wrestling in Dakar. And the Senegalese whom Saavedra talked to claim that is partially because basketball is a more graceful, feminine sport than the "brute" game of soccer. Of course, the fact that argument is nearly a complete inversion of how the games are perceived in other cultures (including in the United States) demonstrates that it is less about the sport and more about protecting territory.

But even beyond the "traditional culture" argument, there are a constellation of other challenges to the women's soccer in Africa—so much so that when Saavedra went on her research trip to Senegal in 1998–1999 to study women's football, she never actually got to see a women's match. They simply were not playing. Some of the obstacles are relatively obvious. Saavedra points out that men are usually well-embedded in the power structures and national federations that oversee the game, that women in many African communities have less leisure time than men, that there are many other social issues that may necessarily be priorities for African women's activists more than sports equity (e.g., violence against women, HIV, limited access to education, malnutrition).

The story of women's soccer in Zanzibar is important to understanding soccer and development precisely because it shows locals trying to renegotiate those power structures. One of the key figures in the films is a local woman named Nassra Mohammed, who founded Women Fighters FC after participating in the 1988 friendly match against the visiting Swedish women's team. In the initial 2007 film Mohammed, who has a career in the civil service, uses her forceful personality and ingenuity to both train the team and make it sustainable, even organizing the team to open a small provision store to help fund its endeavors. The film "was screened in Zanzibar in 2007 to an audience of more than 1,000, including the country's vice sports minister and secretary general of the Zanzibar Football Association" (Wightwick). Not coincidentally, the government since "changed official policy to encourage schoolgirls to play the sport." As Ayisi explained in the Wightwick article: "Something great has happened to girls…. Islam, soccer, and womanhood now seem to converge and coexist in harmony as women experience a significant transformation of their identities—from being 'hooligans' and 'street kids' to being regarded as cultural ambassadors."

Thus, in the 2016 film, we see Mohammed shifting her focus to the new programs in schools. She is now a coaching instructor affiliated with the Confederation of African Football (CAF), training both men and women while helping teachers instantiate soccer for girls in the local school system. There are at least two key lessons here that are surprisingly rare in the use of soccer for development and gender empowerment. First, targeted efforts to spread women's soccer are most likely to lead to social change only when they filter into ongoing social structures such as schools. Second, soccer for development needs local champions to have any hope of making a difference. In combination, this is a small-scale example of David Black's emphasis on the importance of both top-down public policy and bottom-up grassroots community in successful development projects

The importance of local, bottom-up endeavor to making soccer relevant in development does not, however, mean that international forces are irrelevant. The 2007 film, for example, led to Women Fighter's FC being sponsored for a cultural exchange in Potsdam, Germany, a trip that the women in the 2016 film describe as paradigm shifting. More abstractly, in a short version of the film labeled as an "impact study," Coach Nassra Mohammed notes that "this current situation of globalization, with people moving freely has helped us a lot. People from different places have interacted, improving understanding. Society in Zanzibar has now accepted that football can be played by women and men. Even when walking down the street, people stop me and ask 'how is your team,' 'how is the game going?'" (*Zanzibar Soccer Queens Impact Study*).

Ultimately, however, as much as those of us soccer fans in the Global North want the game to be something *we* can use as a development tool, the Zanzibar examples makes clear that nothing will do more good than strong women (and men) empowered to work in their own communities with the support of structures such as the education system. This idea was driven home powerfully by the final scene of *Zanzibar Soccer Queens*—a simple shot panning slowly across the faces of Women Fighters FC as they line up in their crisp white uniforms for a game. It is a shot familiar to any soccer fan anywhere, the pre-game line up, but amidst the usual mix of intensity and anxiety these faces also vividly convey the sense of purpose that has the potential to take soccer beyond emotional appeal and towards documented empowerment.

Soccer for Development?

In arguing for the importance of balancing the raw emotional appeal of soccer with more analytic lenses when thinking about the game's potential contributions to international development, the intention is not to undervalue emotion. After all, organizations such as Grassroot Soccer, the One World Play Project, and Women Fighters FC are only on the radar of soccer fans when they see an occasional promotional video or blog post that is designed to make us feel good about the game. And that good feeling we are supposed to get when we learn about soccer and development is important. It taps a deep and often unconscious hope that the game we love is not just a hedonistic entertainment; a hope that it might be a force for good in the world. That hope is closely related to the feelings evoked by the clichéd image of children playing soccer with a rag ball in the streets—the feeling that the game offers human connection. Soccer for development efforts, in other words, tap our hopes that the love of soccer is meaningful.

It is, however, wise to balance the emotional tug of soccer and development with a return to a basic and critical analytical question: what do people in marginalized communities, kids like Diego, really need? Despite being physically disabled and living in an impoverished refugee community, Diego did not really need mere exposure to the game. He already played more robustly than many children in more privileged circumstances. He also did not really need the game to teach him "life skills." His ability to adapt and persevere was beyond what most curricula could teach. But he did need the types of opportunities and supports that many Western soccer fans take for granted: education, health care, living-wage jobs, decent shelter. And while soccer cannot really provide those things, no other single development tool can either. Soccer might, instead, be one small part of chipping away at the underlying problems of global inequality, if used intelligently.

While part of the appeal of soccer as a development tool is its universality and its emotional tug, the magic of the game, that appeal must build upon what we have learned about international development. Development works best when based on reasonably objective evidence. Development works best when it combines emotion and engineering. Development works best when it empowers people to work for social change in their own communities. Soccer and development, much like the game itself, is never as simple as it seems.

Works Cited

Ayisi, Florence, and Catalin Brylla. "The Politics of Representation and Audience Reception: Alternative Visions of Africa." *Research in African Literatures* 44.2 (2013): 125–141. Print.
Black, David R. "The Ambiguities of Development: Implications for 'Development through Sport.'" *Sport in Society*. 13.1 (2010): 121–129. Print.
Clark, Tommy. "A Letter from Tommy Clark." *Grassroots Soccer*. Grassroot Soccer, 2018. Web. 21 April 2018.
FIFA. *FIFA Financial Report 2010*. Zurich: FIFA, 2011. PDF file.
_____. *20 Centres for 2010 Football for Hope: Final Report of the Official Social Campaign of the 2010 FIFA World Cup*. Zurich: FIFA, 2010. PDF file.
Guest, Andrew. "Cultures of Play during Middle Childhood: Interpretive Perspectives from Two Distinct Marginalized Communities." *Sport, Education and Society* 18.2 (2013): 167–183. Print.
_____. "What's the Legacy of the 2010 World Cup?" *Pacific Standard*. The Social Justice Foundation, 10 June 2014. Web. 21 April 2018.
Hower, Mike. "One World Futbol: Saving Soccer in the Developing World." *Sustainable Brands*. Sustainable Life Media, 7 March 2013. Web. 21 April 2018.
Kaufman, Zachary A. "The GOAL Trial: Sport-based HIV Prevention in South African Schools." Diss. London School of Hygiene & Tropical Medicine, 2014. Print.

Kelto, Anders. "FIFA Hits Snags in Fulfilling World Cup Vow in Africa." *NPR*. NPR, 27 July 2010. Web. 21 April 2018.
Knapp, Gwen. "The One World Futbol is a Marvel of Indestructibility." *Sports on Earth*. MLB Advanced Media, 19 June 2013. Web. 21 April 2018.
"A Letter from Tommy Clark." *Grassroot Soccer*. Grassroots Soccer. Web. 5 June 2018. 1 Apr.
Nelson Mandela Foundation. "Speeches." Nelson Mandela Foundation. *Nelson Mandela Foundation*, Web. 5 June 2018.
Rothstein, Nathan. "The Limits of Buy-One Give-One (SSIR)." *Stanford Social Innovation Review*. Stanford University, 28 January 2014. Web. 21 April 2018.
Saavedra, Martha. "Football Feminine–Development of the African Game: Senegal, Nigeria and South Africa." *Soccer & Society* 4.2–3 (2003): 225–253. Print.
Steinberg, Laurence. "Risk Taking in Adolescence: New Perspectives from Brain and Behavioral Science." *Current Directions in Psychological Science* 162 (2007):55–59. Print.
Svensson, Per G., and Hilary Woods. "A Systematic Overview of Sport for Development and Peace Organisations." *Journal of Sport for Development* 5.9 (2017): 36–48. Print.
USAID. *Generation SKILLZ: Coach's Guide*. PDF file.
Waardenburg, Maikel, Marjolein van den Bergh, and Frank van Eekeren. "Local Meanings of a Sport Mega-event's Legacies: Stories from a South African Urban Neighbourhood." *South African Review of Sociology* 46.1 (2015): 87–105. Print.
Wightwick, Abbie. "These Female Footballers Were Once Labelled 'Hooligans' and Beaten with Sticks." *Mirror*. MGN Limited, 23 May 2016. Web. 21 April 2018.
Wolff, Alexander. "Sports Save the World." *Sports Illustrated* 115.12 (2011):62–74. Print.
Zanzibar Soccer Queens. Dir. Florence Ayisi. Filmmakers Library, 2007. Film.
Zanzibar Soccer Queens Impact Study. Dir. Florence Ayisi and Catalin Brylla, 2016. Film.

The CONIFA World Cup for Unrecognized States

GLEN DUERR

Statehood is an important feature of life in the 21st century. Whether recognized or not, citizenship within a specific country is an important formality, such that people are connected to recognized countries exist throughout the world. However, the reverse is also true where a significant number of people within a territory seek independence for their entity away from their formally recognized state. These, unrecognized states, exist all over the world and include examples such as Québec (Canada), the Basque Country (Spain/France), Zanzibar (Tanzania), and Tamil Eelam (Sri Lanka) among others.

This essay investigates a core advantage in international politics: state sovereignty. Obviously, state sovereignty is also a major disadvantage to an out-group, people who are not represented by a recognized independent country. There is a clear distinction between people that have state sovereignty, and those that do not feel like they are represented in world affairs under the state-centric model. Statehood provides the benefit of institutional protection on the world stage, which makes genocide and loss of culture less likely. The core difficulty here is that the vast majority of people in the world are represented in international organizations, but this is not true amongst all people. Thus, an investigation of stateless peoples is useful in a discussion of representation.

On the soccer pitch, players are all equal at the start of the match: there are no specific advantages that any one player has over another. Jerseys cannot win matches. Also, on the soccer pitch, state sovereignty is not an obvious disadvantage since the best players can participate—and get paid copious amounts of money—playing for the top teams regardless of their respective national backgrounds. In fact, for some clubs, not playing for one's national team is an advantage because the player faces no risk of injury whilst away playing on international duty. For example, when former England international, Paul Scholes, retired from international competition in 2004, it was perceived that he lengthened his career at Manchester United (he played until 2013, just shy of his 39th birthday).

For most players in the world, their maximalist goal is to represent their country at major tournaments, especially the Fédération Internationale de Football Association (FIFA) World Cup. FIFA aligns closely to the geopolitical reality of the world. The United Nations has 193 members, whilst FIFA (in 2018) has 211 member associations. FIFA does not deviate dramatically from the United Nations, but typically allows for colonial and territorial possessions of the United Kingdom, France, the Netherlands, and the United States to participate separately within the FIFA system. For example, Bermuda is a member association of FIFA, but formally belongs to the United Kingdom in the UN system. In fact, many of these non–UN members associations of FIFA are in the Caribbean and compete under the Confederation of North, Central American and Caribbean Association Football (CONCACAF) regional system of North and Central America and the Caribbean.

There are some idiosyncrasies, as well. For example, the Home Nations of the United Kingdom—England, Scotland, Wales, and Northern Ireland—despite being part of one country, each have independent associations, and can thus participate separately (MacClancy). Effectively, since each association was formed in the 1870s and 1880s, each of the Home Nations were grandfathered in when FIFA was created. The political status of Kosovo is still heavily contested after their declaration of independence of 2008 (Montague, but the territory was granted entrance into FIFA and UEFA (Union of European Football Associations, which serves as the European continental association) in 2016. Thus, territories like the Home Nations are grandfathered in to the FIFA system, and some territories like Kosovo have de jure recognition through football, but not in geopolitics.

Despite these additional accommodations, there are still millions of people around the world who seek to play, or support, another entity that is not recognized as an independent state under the United Nations, or as a member association under FIFA. Take, for example, the region of Catalonia in northeastern Spain. There is an extensive movement seeking independence for this territory. The people of Catalonia are represented under FIFA through their national association, Spain, but they decry the lack of opportunities to play soccer as an independent country/association. Catalonia recently declared independence, so it is possible that the region will gain FIFA and UEFA membership at some point, but, because of the contestation by Spain, this reality is extremely unlikely (Foer). There is a caveat to this discussion: once per year, usually around Christmas/New Year's Day, some of the autonomous communities of Spain can play an "international" match. Thus, Catalonia has played against a range of different international opposition (Duerr, "The Goal"). For example, Catalonia competed against Tunisia in 2016, Nigeria and Cape Verde in 2013, and Argentina in 2009, among others. Catalonia also played against the Basque Country in both 2014 and 2015 as an intra-Spanish friendly match.

There is a rich history of sporting separateness in Spain. In the Basque Country, for example, Athletic Bilbao play in La Liga and maintain a policy of homogeneity for its players (MacClancy 182; Duerr, "The Goal"). Founded in 1898, Athletic Bilbao only uses players of Basque ancestry, with at least one parent. The team even uses the English term, Athletic, rather than the Spanish, Atletico. Yet, the Basque Country is not a member of FIFA, and does not participate against the other states of the world.

This essay investigates the themes of inequality and justice in the international football arena with an emphasis on the Confederation of International Football Associations (Confederation of International Football Associations), a governing body for stateless nations in the world. The focus is to examine the role of CONIFA is conferring some level of recognition on stateless nations and to assess the political role of the organization. Two other ethereal questions are also secondarily assessed here. Justice is typically a concept widely linked to law, in this case, international law. The first theoretical question in the background of this essay is, at what point is the system of sovereign states just? There are many regions of the world in which statehood could be applied, but, for a range of reasons, is not granted to a group. The idea of secessionism is also applied in a limited sense by much of the international community for fear that some largescale contagion effect will occur increasing the number of states. A growth in the number of secessionist movements could also enflaming fissiparous enmities across the globe. Thus, the second background question is one of the legitimacy to secession. At what point is secession reified by participation in international soccer?

Self-Determination

The idea of self-determination is a relatively new one. Principally popularized by American president Woodrow Wilson in his famous *Fourteen Points* speech in 1918, the concept of self-determination illuminated stateless nations throughout Europe, as well as the colonized world (Wilson). Put simply, self-determination describes the ability for people groups, or nations, to organize themselves politically within a specific territorial boundary, form a government, and gain recognition from other independent states.

The era from the Crimean War (1853–56) to World War I (1914–18) is littered with attempts to create new states throughout southeastern Europe—

a region of the world where self-determination movements grew most dramatically in this period. For example, the "anti–Hapsburg Congress for Oppressed nations—Czechs, Croats, Slovenes, and Poles—convened in Rome" as a mechanism to strategize for recognition (Mazower 47). Several states were created in southeastern Europe in the late 19th and early 20th centuries including Romania, Bulgaria, Albania, Serbia, and Montenegro. Greece was newly reconstituted in 1821 following a war of independence with the Ottomans. The creation of new countries in Central and Eastern Europe such as Czechoslovakia and the Kingdom of Serbs, Croats, and Slovenes (later the Kingdom of Yugoslavia). Poland was recreated in 1918 after more than a century-long absence from the world stage. Various British and French mandates were created out of the ashes of the Ottoman Empire's dissolution post–World War I.

Self-determination grew as a political concept in the aftermath of World War I. The number of states continued to grow, especially in the after of World War II (1939–1945). Decolonization created over a hundred new states on the world stage, specifically between 1945 and 1975 (Fazal and Griffiths). New countries like Algeria in North Africa, India in South Asia, Israel in the Middle East, and Indonesia in Southeast Asia all gained their independence during this period. Of course, vast sections of the world like Europe, East Asia, and the Americas already had statehood, but this period between 1945 and 1975 was when many new states (former colonies) gained formal, de jure recognition on the world stage.

The term self-determination is strongly tied to the concept of secession, effectively creating a new country out of an existing state. A definition of secession is "a self-determination movement on the basis of an ethno-nationalist identity that encompasses claims ranging from increased cultural and political rights to struggles for territorial independence" (Pokalova 430). Also, "secession, then, represents an instance of political disintegration, wherein political actors in one or more subsystems withdraw their loyalties, expectations, and activities from a jurisdictional centre and focus them on a center of their own" (Wood 111). Secession is a possible outcome of a movement for self-determination; some movements seek greater autonomy, others may seek political disintegration.

The idea of the CONIFA World Cup is similar in spirit to these earlier conferences and conflicts as a mechanism to gain wider recognition throughout the world to one day join the community of states within the United Nations. Since the UN General Assembly (UNGA) equally treats non–Permanent five members, there is no formal discrimination based on size. Most CONIFA members are small in terms of population, and thus seek greater representation on the world stage through available power channels like CONIFA. For example, India and Nauru have the same voting power in the UNGA despite a population difference of over 1.2 billion people between the two countries. In soccer and in geopolitics, larger and wealthier countries perform better and are more protected on the world stage (Kuper and Syzmanski 277). CONIFA plays a subsidiary role of representing stateless peoples that do not fit the powerful mold.

CONIFA is strongly tied to the intertwined concepts of self-determination and secession, such that all member associations seek recognition on a grander stage. Since CONIFA represents the aspirations of stateless nations that do not have recognition in either the UN system, or FIFA, teams can play against one another, and raise awareness to their own causes—even if CONIFA simply acts like a support group for non-recognized entities.

Sports in general, and soccer specifically, have transformative political powers. Although sports have limitations, there are political facets that spillover into the political arena. The historian Eric Hobsbawm, utilizing the famous work of Benedict Anderson, said that "the imagined community of millions seems more real as a team of eleven named players" specifically inferring a team on a soccer pitch (143).

The geographer David H. Kaplan notes that "modern 'stateless' nations accommodate themselves to a state-centric order to gain recognition as states in the making" (Herb and Kaplan 33). Kaplan, and his co-editor Guntram Herb theorize that identities are layered, nested alongside one another. In effect, the notion of the CONIFA World Cup is for stateless nations to gain some level of international recognition, even if it is only amongst other stateless nations. An interesting component of the debate on stateless nations is the use of banal symbols that reinforce nationalism in most cases around the world; banal items like a flag and an anthem to which people pay allegiance (Billig). In the case of stateless nations, however, seeing one's flag flown, and anthem played, on a football field somewhere across the world has an emotive element of being de facto recognized, at least for the duration of the tournament, amongst other peoples of the world. There is a sense of representation despite the political dilemma facing many of these stateless nations.

In recent years, the academic literature on non-state actors and stateless nations in relations to sports, has grown impressively. Sack and Suster, for example, investigate the role of soccer in the advance of Croatia's aspirations for independence in the early 1990s. The former Yugoslavia, Palestinian territories (Montague), and Taiwan, have all become focal points of scholars in an investigation of subnational issues in sports.

The CONIFA World Cup

The CONIFA World Cup is the main global football competition for unrecognized states (Demytrie). In 2014, 2016, and 2018, the tournament was held in Sápmi (Sweden), Abkhazia (Georgia), and London on behalf of Barawa (Somalia). Preceding the CONIFA World Cup is the VIVA World Cup, which was held in 2006, 2008, 2009, 2010, and 2012 before disbanding. The scheduled 1988 Alternative World Cup was the predecessor of the VIVA World Cup.

On the specific subject of the CONIFA World Cup, much of the scholarship is underdeveloped. Several promising theses and papers have been written on the subject, but it has not yet attracted scholars in major academic journals about soccer, and sports more generally. Of course, the CONIFA World Cup is a minor tournament on the world calendar, but its political resonance is much greater than the on-field product—and that is the intention. Sascha Düerkop, General Secretary of CONIFA, noted that some matches for the 2014 tournament had zero people in attendance (Shemetov). In Abkhazia in 2016, the average attendance was around 1,000 fans, at least when the home side was not playing (Shemetov).

Table 1. History of the CONIFA World Cup

Continent/CONIFA World Cup	Sápmi 2014	Abkhazia 2016	Barawa (London) 2018
Europe	Abkhazia	Abkhazia	Abhazia
	Artsakh	Northern Cyprus	Ellan Vannin
	County of Nice	Padania	Felvidék
	Ellan Vannin	Raetia	Northern Cyprus
	Occitania	Sápmi	Padania
	Padania	Székely Land	Székely Land
	Sápmi	Western Armenia	Western Armenia
	South Ossetia		
Africa	Darfur	Somaliland	Barawa
			Kabylie
			Matabeleland
Asia	Arameans Suryoye	Chagos Islands	Tamil Eelam
	Iraqi Kurdistan	Iraqi Kurdistan	Tibet
	Tamil Eelam	Panjab	Panjab
		United Koreans of Japan	United Koreans of Japan
Oceania	—	—	Tuvalu
Americas	—	—	Cascadia

CONIFA is an organization that exists outside of the jurisdiction of FIFA as a means of bringing together unrecognized states and territories. As of May 2018, CONIFA's Facebook page maintained over 20,000 followers from around the world, with some level of interest in the tournament. This indicator shows that CONIFA is still a relatively small entity in world soccer, but its popularity suggests an opportunity to push against the state-centric model of sports outlined under FIFA. According to the CONIFA website: "CONIFA aims to build bridges between people, nations, minorities and isolated regions all over the world through friendship, culture and the joy of playing football. CONIFA works for the development of affiliated members and is committed to fair play and the eradication of racism" (Confederation of International Football Associations). In 2018, CONIFA claimed membership of 47 associations spread throughout the world. CONIFA seeks to join various "nations, de-facto nations, regions, minority peoples, and sports isolated territories" (Confederation of International Football Associations). From their own definition, the terminology is quite broad, as well as the acceptance of groups who wish to join CONIFA. Some member organizations have well-known pro-independence groups and political parties purporting their sovereignty. Tamil Eelam, for example, is a region of Sri Lanka populated mainly by Tamils who long sought independence from the 1980s through the 2000s, and although the movement no longer fights in a civil war, the goal of independence remains pertinent. Other associations, however, are not well-known. In Europe, for example, Délvidék (in southern Hungary/northern Serbia) and Yorkshire (northern England) have very low intensity movements and groups in support of independence, but very little recent political activity.

The CONIFA World Cup is also a mechanism to rebuild an identity, perhaps one in which the linguistic and culture identity has been enveloped due to globalization or the forces of powerful states. For example, Natalie Fertig's thesis demonstrates how the Manxian national team of Ellan Vannin was built on developing their historic identity: "In the weeks prior to leaving the Isle of Man, Blackburn had tested the Manx players on Manx history. It was important to him that the team was representative of the Manx culture, because it is a culture in jeopardy. The last native speaker of Manx Gaelic, the Isle of Man's official language, died in the 1970s, and youth growing up" (Fertig). The political scientist Britt Cartrite has documented this concept of "rediscovering" one's shadow (1). Cartrite's study examines numerous "lesser-known" cases of secessionism and subnational identity across Western Europe. He found that many of these regions are essentially rediscovering their past and awakening from a dormant state wherein the local language eroded under the forces of a powerful state, or the need to develop trade in a globalizing world. He wrote, "Across Western Europe ethnic groups seek to 'reclaim their shadow,' actively seeking special accommodations or, in a handful of cases, their own country. Ethnic groups increasingly reject their assimilation into larger national identities, occasionally even turning to terrorism to advance their cause" (7). Another political scientist, Seth Jolly, demonstrates the role of the European Union in furthering subnational movements in regions across member states. The existence of the EU has decreased the power of the state, and emboldened regional identities through the resurgence of languages, and cohesion funds distributed to poorer areas of Europe.

In some ways, the CONIFA World Cup is facilitating the growth of viable subnational actors. In tandem with the rise of intergovernmental organizations that weaken the power of the state, CONIFA's position provides a sporting outlet to subnational units with a desire for greater autonomy and recognition across the world. What is noteworthy is the existence of a World Cup of soccer/football for unrecognized countries that have not been able to obtain membership in the world governing body of soccer/football, FIFA. Writ large, this is a means for all these subnational entities to showcases themselves in an organized fashion, which may help to propel the overarching political goals.

CONIFA hosts the biennial soccer tournament in a range of different locations. The first tournament, hosted by the Sápmi (Sweden) in 2014, then a second a tournament in Abkhazia (Georgia) in 2016, and then a third tournament hosted in London (United Kingdom) on behalf of the Barawa people from southwestern Somalia in 2018. The expectation is that CONIFA tournaments will be played into the future as a mechanism of representing stateless nations in the world.

The 12-team tournament in 2014 included Abkhazia, Arameans Suryoye, Darfur, Ellan Vannin, (Iraqi) Kurdistan, Nagorno-Karabagh, Nice (County of Nice), Occitania, Padania, Sápmi, South Ossetia, and Tamil Eelam. The tournament represented five teams from Western Europe, one team from South Asia, one team from Africa, three teams from the Caucasus, and one team from the Middle East. Given the nature of the tournament, it is perhaps not surprising that the geographical makeup of the representatives was lopsided towards Europe, especially if eight of the 12 teams would be in the UEFA zone. This was a shortcoming of CONIFA—one that they have worked to correct.

For the 2014 CONIFA World Cup, the 12 teams were divided into four groups of three teams. Each team played against the two other teams within the same group. The top two teams in each group then emerged into the quarterfinal stage where they played a knockout elimination tournament to decide the winner. Remaining teams also contested a placement contest to decide the final rankings from first through twelfth. The 2016 CONIFA World Cup followed the same format as 2014. However, for the 2018 CONIFA World Cup, the field was expanded to include 16 teams, each divided into four groups each consisting of four teams: Abkhazia, Barawa, Cascadia, Ellan Vannin, Felvidék, Kabylie, Kiribati, Matabeleland, Northern Cyprus, Padania, Panjab, Székely Land, Tamil Eelam, Tibet, Western Armenia, and United Koreans of Japan. Thus, in comparison to 2014, the 2018 tournament featured seven teams from Europe (including three from the Caucasus), four from Asia, three from Africa, and one from North America and Oceania.

CONIFA World Cup Hosts

For any territory, hosting a "Mega-Event" is a special occasion in that a city, region, or country welcomes people from all over the world. It is an opportunity to showcase one's infrastructure, situation, and hospitality to those from elsewhere. It is also a responsibility to secure the venues and provide a great spectacle for spectators to enjoy. The politically volatile backdrop to any of these tournaments makes hosting a strong competition important for the future of CONIFA and for some of the member associations participating.

The 2014 CONIFA World Cup was hosted by the Sápmi in Östersund, Sweden. All matches were played at the Jämtkraft Arena, a venue with seating for over 6,000 fans (Confederation of International Football Associations). Based on the centrality of the tournament in one stadium, all teams were able to watch each other play, and to develop a spirit of camaraderie surrounding their shared political grievances. The model is an interesting one in comparison to modern Mega-Events, which are enjoyed by hundreds of thousands of spectators over several weeks; overall, CONIFA is a small tournament so one small stadium makes sense, but also builds a greater connection because of the use of only one stadium.

The 2016 CONIFA World Cup was hosted by Abkhazia in Sukhumi and Gagra, two cities in the region of Abkhazia, belonging to Georgia under international law, but de facto self-ruled since Russian military intervention in 2008 (Rukhadze and Duerr 31). In Sukhumi, Dinamo Stadium was used as the venue, seating 4,000 fans; in Gagra, Daur Akhvlediani Stadium was used seating 1,500 fans (Confederation of International Football Associations). The model used for 2016 was more spread out to two stadiums reducing the intimacy of the 2014 tournament, but also expanding the scope of the competition. In 2016, the region of Abkhazia hosted the most recent iteration of the tournament. From a security standpoint, Abkhazia was an odd choice because of the recent violence in the region, and the disputed status on the world stage. Given Russia's protection and recognition, however, Abkhazia maintains significant stability despite recent contestation over the region. Abkhazia serves as a puppet state of the Kremlin and may informally be considered part of Russia's territory by some within the government.

The 2018 CONIFA World Cup was hosted by the Barawa (a region of southwestern Somalia), but all games were played in London. Three small stadiums, in the range of 2,500 to 5,500 fans were utilized in Sutton, Bromley, and Enfield. Like the 2016 tournament, the use of multiple stadia reduces the intimacy of the tournament replete with personal connections amongst all participants, but this is sacrificed for a greater appeal to more people in different places. On January 11, 2018, the draw for the CONIFA World Cup took place in Northern Cyprus assigning the 16 teams into four groups, each with four teams. Like the FIFA World Cup, only two European teams can be in the same group. And, with that exception, a specific team from one continent cannot be drawn into a group with another team from the same continent. The timing is also intriguing in that it precedes the FIFA World Cup in Russia by a few weeks. One of the core challenges for CONIFA is to garner sufficient international attention to draw people to view the larger political component behind the existence of CONIFA.

The Member Associations of the CONIFA World Cup

The following teams, in alphabetical order, participated in one or more of the 2014, 2016, and 2018 CONIFA World Cups: Abkhazia, Arameans Suryoye, Artsakh (Nagorno-Karabagh), Cascadia, Chagos Islands, Darfur, Ellan Vannin (Isle of Man), Felvidék, Kabylie, Kiribati, Northern Cyprus, Occitania, Iraqi Kurdistan, Matabeleland, (County of) Nice, Padania, Panjab, Raetia, South Ossetia, Sápmi, Somaliland, Székely Land, Tamil Eelam, Tibet, Western Armenia, and United Koreans of Japan. Given this eclectic list of competitors at the CONIFA World Cup, a brief discussion of each situation is useful to draw out the secondary themes of justice and recognition in the world through soccer. Some regions are de facto independent states in that they govern themselves; some regions aspire of statehood; other regions simply want greater global recognition for their history and language without desires of sovereignty.

To start, two of the regions, Abkhazia and South Ossetia—officially part of Georgia—were invaded by Russia in 2008. Both have been declared independent but have been scarcely recognized in the world community. Although a decade since their respective declarations of independence, they have been recognized by Russia, Nicaragua, Venezuela, and Nauru. Both Tuvalu and Vanuatu, UN member states in the South Pacific, recognized Abkhazia and South Ossetia, but withdrew their support for official recognition. Both Abkhazia and South Ossetia hold de facto independence, but their status in the international community is heavily contested as the Republic of Georgia, under international law, still holds the rights to both territories (Rukhadze and Duerr 42). Participating in the CONIFA World Cup could serve to challenge the sovereignty of Georgia, especially since Abkhazia hosted the 2016 tournament.

The next group of regions are all small, or have no serious claim on independence; yet, all regions seek greater recognition across the world. Arameans Suryoye represents Syriacs around the world—in some senses, it is a team based around ethnicity rather than statehood. Syriacs trace their historical homeland to the Levant region of the Near East. There is no major secessionist movement, but more a desire to protect historic Syriac culture. Artsakh, better known as Nagorno-Karabagh, is a predominantly Armenian region within Azerbaijan—both countries in the North Caucasus neighboring Georgia. Like Abkhazia and South Ossetia, Nagorno-Karabagh is a de facto independent state (Kaufman; Jaksa). Cascadia is a region in the northwest of the United States; there is a low intensity movement for independence in Cascadia, but one that has never tested the ballot box (Shobe and Gibson). The Chagos Islands are officially an Overseas British Territory within the Indian Ocean south of the Indian Subcontinent. The case of the Chagos Islands is very contemporary because of rising sea levels that have increasingly threatened the mere existence of the islands. The Chagos Islands team represents the Chagos Archipelago, a British Overseas Territory in the Indian Ocean—seven small atolls spread across over 60 islands. Most of the team members come from the Chagossian diaspora around the world since very few people still live on the Chagos Islands. Darfur is a region in western Sudan, which is predominantly black African as opposed to ethnically Arab as are most members of the Sudanese government in Khartoum. The region has been subject to a brutal genocide since 2004 with the Sudanese government seeking to stave off another independence movement—South Sudan became an independent country in 2011. Ellan Vannin represents the Isle of Man, an island with some autonomy in the United Kingdom, located in the Irish Sea between the UK and the Republic of Ireland. There is no serious secessionist movement in the Isle of Man, but the Manxian identity remains a prominent source of identity for many people on the island (Fertig; Cartrite). In some senses, the goal is to revive Manxian identity through the existence of an independent football team.

Felvidek and Székely Land both represent ethnic Hungarians in adjacent territories. The 1920 Treaty of Trianon—one of the major treaties signed in the conclusion of World War I—still overlays some of the political tension for two of the cases: Felvidék and Székely Land. Both regions are majority ethnic–Hungarian but reside within Slovakia and Romania respectively. The Treaty of Trianon, which effectively dissolved the Austro-Hungarian Empire in the aftermath of World War I, also reduced the size of the Hungarian state at least as a state aligns with ethnic identity. Significant ethnic-Hungarian regions were drawn outside of Hungary in Slovakia, Serbia, and Romania. Although both movements are fairly low-intensity, they could grow into something more volatile with greater demands for more autonomy, and perhaps independence. The Kabylie are a Berber speaking people in northern Algeria. Geographically, Kabylie is a very small region next to the Mediterranean Sea. Historically, Berber peoples have sought independence, so participation in CONIFA is a mechanism to retry claims for sovereignty. Kiribati is an independent country with membership in the United Nations since 1999. The population is a little over 100,000 people. Strangely, Kiribati is not a member of FIFA, despite de jure international recognition, and only an associate member of the Oceania Football Confederation. Thus, despite enjoying the privileges of UN membership, Kiribati participates in the CONIFA World Cup. Northern Cyprus is an ethnically Turkish region in the north of Cyprus. The civil war in Cyprus in 1974 resulted in a "frozen" end to the conflict leaving the Mediterranean island separated between Greek and Turkish populations. The Greek half of Cyprus belongs to the United Nations and to the European Union. Occitania is a historic region covering all southern France replete with a mutually unintelligible language. This area once supported the idea of independence, but now desires greater recognition within France. The city of Nice—winners of the 2014 CONIFA World Cup—in southeastern France is in an interesting geographic position sitting on the border with Italy. In fact, Nice used to belong to the Kingdom of Piedmont-Sardinia (a precursor to modern day Italy), but was given to France in exchange for support in a war against the Austrian Empire. Interestingly, the boundaries of Occitania and the County of Nice overlap such that both regions contest the same territory. If either movement gains sufficient strength, CONIFA may have to play the role of mediator in international competitions.

Iraqi Kurdistan is possibly the most recognizable region in the CONIFA World Cup because that the region is probably most likely to realize its maximalist goal of independence. This is not to say that Iraqi Kurdistan will become independent, just that the region has significant momentum towards increasing their autonomy. The interesting compilation of teams draws some that are viewed with some legitimacy in the international community—such as Kurdistan—to others that have limited ability to ever gain independence. The Kurds are the world's largest ethnic group without the institutional protection of statehood. This lack of support has a long history. In 1920, under the Treaty of Sèvres, one of five major treaties signed at the end of World War I, promised the Kurds an independent state. This promise was later reneged with the Treaty of Lausanne in 1923, which created a formal country of Turkey out of the embers of the collapse of the Ottoman Empire. The problem for the Kurds is that a Kurdistan was no longer part of the plan for the international community—leaving Kurds in Turkey, Syria, Iraq, and Iran without statehood. The Kurds have long desired independence, so the CONIFA World Cup is a mechanism to stay pertinent on the radar of international actors across the world.

The next few regions also possess low intensity movements. Matabeleland is a region of western Zimbabwe in southern Africa. It is home of the ancient Rozvi Empire and home to the Ndebele people. Panjab (also called Punjab) is a region between eastern Pakistan and northern India in South Asia. There are no formal geographical regions depicted in either India or Pakistan, but the Punjabi language spoken by over 100 million people. Raetia is a historic region that existed under the Roman Empire. It encompasses several German-speaking countries in Central Europe today—Austria, Germany, Switzerland, and Liechtenstein (including a small section of Italy). Given that the territory of Raetia crosses so many international borders, independence is unlikely. However, there is a greater recognition of an ancient identity, which is valued by some members of the community.

The Sápmi population is an interesting point of discussion within CONIFA given that the population resides across several different countries across Scandinavia—as noted earlier, the Sápmi hosted the 2014 CONIFA World Cup. The Sápmi are an indigenous population much like First Nations peoples in Canada, Native Americans in the United States, the Aboriginal and Torres Strait Islander peoples of Australia, and the Maori of New Zealand among other groups. The Sápmi have a level of institutional autonomy within Scandinavia possessing a direct parliament. This opportunity to participate on the world stage within a broader tournament creates for the indigenous peoples of Scandinavia an opportunity to realize independence in a limited sense, whilst remaining tethered to the economic power of their respective countries with high levels of life expectancy, health care, and other metrics.

Somaliland is, for all intents and purposes, an independent entity with a functioning government, economy, and civil society. Located in the northern section of Somalia, it shares a border with both Ethiopia and Djibouti. The claim for independence is also based on differing colonial rule. French Somaliland, for example, is now Djibouti. CONIFA is a mechanism for Somaliland to display its stability despite ties to Somalia, and the inherent weaknesses of government that have plagued Mogadishu since 1991.

The case of Tamil Eelam is another politically interesting example. The civil war in Sri Lanka started in 1983 and lasted until 2009. Most notoriously, the Liberation Tigers of Tamil Eelam, a noted terrorist organization by many governments, and freedom fighter organization according to their own frame, conducted hundreds of guerrilla style attacks in the country. Even though the civil war has ended, the proposition of Tamil independence remains a major consideration in Tamil-majority areas of Sri Lanka. Participating in the CONIFA World Cup provides a mechanism through which this dream of independence remains plausible. The Tamil diaspora is significant in the United Kingdom and Canada, such that the London-based 2018 tournament will likely attract significant members from the Tamil community.

Tibet is a contentious region of western China renowned as the spiritual birthplace of Buddhism. As with the One China policy, secession is forbidden away from Beijing, and the expectation is that Hong Kong, Macau, and Taiwan will all become part of China. This also extends to the South China Seas, and possible the Senkaku Islands that belong to Japan. Western Armenia is an indigenous region in the east of Turkey wherein historic Armenians resided. It is a contentious area, especially since the Turkish government has acted so forcefully against the Kurds in the southeastern portion of the country.

Another case is the United Koreans of Japan. Since the Japanese invaded the Korean peninsula in 1905, and then formally annexed the territory in 1910 as a colony, the relationship between Koreans and Japanese has been strained. The actions of the Japanese government and soldiers during World War II is the central reason for this bitter relationship. Thousands of ethnic Koreans reside in Japan and have done so for decades. Yet, for many of those decades, ethnic Koreans were not eligible to gain Japanese citizenship because strict ethnic guidelines that existed historically. In the 1990s, citizenship laws were loosened provided that the applicant understood the Japanese language and adopted a Japanese name. It is now easier to gain Japanese citizenship, but the historically Korean areas of Japan still feel a sense of distinction from the rest of the country. There is no serious movement to gain independence, especially since the geographic dispersion of Koreans makes it difficult to claim a contiguous territory, but recognition through soccer is an important marker for some ethnic Koreans in Japan.

Although this section is quite encyclopedic in nature, the comparison of numerous cases highlights the potential for independence of some regions, alongside others that seek greater justice and recognition for language and culture in the world. CONIFA, then, is a catch-all entity that can provide the pedestal for any and every movement, even those with contradictory positions on the world stage.

VIVA World Cup

The CONIFA World Cup was preceded by the VIVA World Cup, which functioned as a precursor to the current tournament. Five tournaments were held from 2006 to 2012, in 2006, 2008, 2009, 2010, and 2012. The following teams participated in one or more of these tournaments: Arameans Suryoye, Darfur, Gozo, Iraqi Kurdistan, Monaco, Northern Cyprus, Occitania, Padania, Provence, Raetia, Sápmi, Southern Cameroons, Tamil Eelam, Two Sicilies, Western Sahara, and Zanzibar. Much of the same discussion surrounding the CONIFA World Cup applies to the VIVA World Cup as a mechanism to garner greater international sympathy and support for the territorial positions of the participating entities.

Regions not discussed earlier in this essay include Gozo, Monaco, Provence, Southern Cameroons, Two Sicilies, and Western Sahara. Gozo belongs to the archipelago of the small Mediterranean country, Malta. Monaco is an independent country located between France and Italy without FIFA membership due to its small size. But, unlike many of the other federations, Monaco is an independent state with UN membership; it is also home to a Formula 1 race. Provence is a region in France, much like Occitania. Southern Cameroons references a part of the West African country of Cameroon, which had different colonial ties. Two Sicilies references part of modern-day southern Italy that historically was an independent kingdom including the island of Sicily, as well as much of the southernmost portion of Italy. Two Sicilies in Italy is the name of one of the former states that existed prior to the unification of Italy in 1861. The Kingdom encompassed most of southern Italy as well as the island of Sicily. Finally, Western Sahara is a region in the southern portion of Morocco that has long made claims for independence. The region covers significant desert area and was occupied by Spain through much of the 20th century giving it some distinction from Morocco.

In the VIVA World Cup, Padania won the 2008, 2009, and 2010 versions of the tournament. Iraqi Kurdistan won in 2012 when the region hosted the tournament. Sápmi won the inaugural version of the VIVA World Cup, in 2006. This tournament served as a movement to build momentum for the CONIFA World Cup such that many of the same member associations still participate against one another.

No Shows

Given an overview of all member associations that have competed in the CONIFA and VIVA World Cups for unrecognized states, there are distinctions between different teams. Some entities could become independent states and UN members in the relatively near future. However, many of the most serious secessionist movements in the world do not send teams. Obviously, Scotland is a member of FIFA, but it does not entertain a discussion with CONIFA, nor do Catalonia, the Basque Country, Flanders, and Greenland—some of the most prominent pro-independence movements in Europe (Jolly).

Interestingly, some of the most likely entities to gain recognition at the United Nations—the Taiwanese, Kosovars, Palestinians—do not participate in the CONIFA World Cup. These are political movements with larger goals. Thus, the expectation is that a group should not gain membership in CONIFA is they aspire to join FIFA. All three territories have formal associations within

FIFA. Taiwan has to fall under the name, Chinese Taipei, in order to participate amongst other members associations.

The major shortcoming of the 2014 CONIFA tournament was the withdrawal of the teams from Québec and Zanzibar. The inclusion of these two teams—from North America and East Africa respectively—would have significantly improved the geographic representation of the tournament. Zero teams represented the Western Hemisphere. Given the importance of this shortcoming for CONIFA, the case of Québec deserves a little more attention.

Québec, one of ten provinces in Canada, is linguistically and culturally different from the rest of the country as the only Francophone-specific territory. In 1980 and 1995, the people of Québec voted in independence referendums on the status of the province within, or outside of Canada. Of note, the 1995 referendum was supported by 49.4 percent of voters; potentially meaning that Québec could have become independent at that juncture had negotiations favored full independence (Hébert and LaPierre xiii).

Officially, Canada is a bilingual country, and New Brunswick a bilingual province. But Québec still possesses a distinction from the rest of Canada despite significant Franco-Ontarian, and other Francophone communities throughout the other Anglophone prominent provinces. Québec's leaders, specifically former Bloc Québécois leader, Gilles Duceppe, once promoted the idea of Québec joining FIFA and CONCACAF as a mechanism of building greater international autonomy (Duerr, "The Goal"). Thus, for Québec to compete within CONIFA might be considered an admission of decreasing seriousness for Québec's sovereignty movement.

Political, Not Political?

Although the FIFA World Cup attempts to remain apolitical, it is an impossible task to remain devoid of political decisions. Likewise, the CONIFA World Cup is similarly plagued with decisions of a political nature. Yet, there is an inherently political side to CONIFA since they aspire to be independent, and to compete, like any other state, on an international stage. CONIFA cannot avoid politics, and thus provides a platform for unrepresented or underrepresented groups. In doing so, however, there is the potential to reify secessionist beliefs, which could lead to violent outcomes.

Ultimately, the international community is loath to recognize differ regions around the world. The issue of state sovereignty as a protected right. Membership creates in-groups and out-groups. Thus, the reasoning for CONIFA is to fill a gap between the in-group and out-group in world affairs.

State sovereignty should remain an international norm, but there are few opposing reasons as to why some regions should not be recognized as independent states. In Somalia, for example, the country has largely been without government since 1991. Successive governments, while they have worked hard to extend the power of the state have had difficulty extending jurisdiction beyond certain sections of Mogadishu. In cases where governance has been stifled for years, or cases of ongoing civil war, membership in international bodies should be extended to groups like Somaliland. In a situation like Somalia, people in Somaliland and other regions of the country are associated with Mogadishu and therefore have difficulty obtaining credit and trading partners. International recognition for Somaliland would help to change this dynamic. Somaliland could then build its own reputation, and potentially increase its GDP per capita through hard work, negotiation, and specialization in a global economy; its people could flourish under a change of system. CONIFA provides a backdrop to greater representation.

There are, of course, pitfalls to avoid. Opening sovereignty could encourage secession, so very specific criteria should be followed. If a particular group provokes a conflict, sovereignty should not be the reward at the end of the conflict. But, providing sovereignty is a mechanism is to punish states that wallow in a civil war for decades; some states, after all, are enveloped in never ending wars (Hironaka). Using the norm of international recognition is a means through which longstanding civil wars can be mitigated and/or discouraged.

Another potential pitfall is the case of South Sudan. After a long process of gaining independence from Sudan through a referendum in January 2011, the new state gained formal recognition in July 2011. However, since independence, South Sudan has been mired in a state of civil war with multiple factions fighting to wrestle control of the governing structures of the country. The example of South Sudan has frightened members of the international community from introducing secession as an option for conflict resolution. Yet, when considering other cases, many are successful. Montenegro, which gained its independence in 2006, has been peaceful, and Serbia, the entity from which the Montenegrins seceded, has also continued to build its democratic governing structures and could be considered for membership in the European Union in future years. In East Timor, a Southeast Asian country with independence in 2002, peace has returned to the segment of the island of Timor, which it occupies. Although Ethiopia and Eritrea engage in periodic skirmishes, the 1993 division of the countries has held as a model for conflict resolution. Dividing the states of the former Yugoslavia has also demonstrated some value as a mechanism to implement peace in the once volatile region of southeastern Europe.

Secession is a useful tool in the diplomatic tool belt. Although most countries like to protect sovereignty, and abhor the thought of their own division, there are places where people could better flourish with greater freedoms. If there is a level of stability within the contender state, secession should be a broad option.

Assessing the CONIFA World Cup

The subnational entities represented at the CONIFA World Cup run a spectrum from those with de facto independence in which a functioning government operates a state-like entity just devoid of formal international recognition. Others, however, are very much aspirational in nature, seeking independence as a minority of the population even within the region being represented. Some members of CONIFA do not seek any form of territorial recognition, rather a recognition that comes from participating on the world stage. Recognition of minority status within the framework of another state.

Like FIFA, CONIFA also has a "World Rankings" points system, which provides a means of comparison amongst member associations across the world. This provides some evidence that CONIFA is building a model that represents stateless nations, such that it is increasingly viable. The popularity of CONIFA has also grown over time with more member associations joining the organization. Finally, it serves as a place to fit when the state sovereignty structures of the world do not comply with the political desires of some people in different stateless nations throughout the world.

As a world body, CONIFA is growing in stature. Not only did the size of the tournament expand in 2018, but the CONIFA World Cup also gained a sponsor. Paddy Power, based in the Republic of Ireland, is a gambling company with storefronts in both Ireland and the United Kingdom. It is also the sponsor organization of the CONIFA World Cup and will allow people across the world to bet on winners and losers of the tournament.

The CONIFA World Cup also attempts to provide global representation in its tournaments. In some cycles, this geographic diversity is a stretch, which is a reason why some entities are included across a spectrum of likeliness to gain independence. The distribution of teams around the world is much more equitable in 2018 than it was in 2014. There is still no geographic representation from South America, and very little in North America, but the expanse of territory covered has grown.

The success of the CONIFA World Cup is to allow citizens of the world to participate in a recognized competition outside of the constraints of the UN international recognition system. It is a mechanism of participating outside of the known boxes in international relations. The obvious challenge with such a system is to assess the utility of such actions. Does the existence of CONIFA undermine state sovereignty? Does it matter? Should the status quo be challenged by an outside actor like CONIFA? The answers to these questions depend largely on where one is located. Very few world leaders wish to see their states divide into new states. After all, only two countries in the world—Ethiopia, and St. Kitts and Nevis—provide provisions for secession within the respective constitutions. Yet, most leaders want a reasonable "safety valve" for minority identities within a state—playing soccer is a much better outlet than starting a civil war.

Conclusion

As noted in the introduction, the state-centric model of the world is one that is somewhat flexible in global football. Since FIFA, in 2018, has 211 members as compared to the 193 member states of the United Nations, some subnational entities and overseas territories have formal permission to play on the international stage. For all the other soccer playing regions, territories, and stateless nations, however, there is no outlet to play football on the highest stage. Thus, the CONIFA World Cup is intriguing because it presents an opportunity for many of these regions to come together to participate against one another.

The state-centric model remains an important facet in international norms. Advances to remove borders and eliminate statehood are unlikely to succeed, and borders provide a sense of control over trade and citizenship. However, one mechanism could be to open the process of creating more countries. There is no moratorium on the number of member states that can fit into the UN General Assembly.

Of course, strict guidelines should be utilized before more members are granted entrance into the organization. Stateless nations should have a recognizable culture and language to be considered for statehood. They should also possess a reasonable chance of economic success to provide for its citizens. These movements must also make a commitment to peace, otherwise the idea of secession as a tool for conflict resolution is not a preferable outcome in the world.

The utility of the CONIFA World Cup is that it provides an outlet for sets of people across the world to express an alternate national identity. For some, there is a clear attachment to territory, language and/or culture that is not appropriately refined at the state level. This is a difficult discussion because the propensity for political violence is palpable in cases where there is a desire to divide the state. In large measure, however, participating in the CONIFA World Cup is a benign gesture, designed to provide recognition without an overt political movement in support of widespread petitions for independence. The CONIFA World Cup is designed to bring greater attention to unrecognized subnational units across the world through peaceful means. There are dangers in advancing secessionist causes, which could develop into violent revolutionary movements. The academic literature is split on this topic because many autonomist organizations seek greater rights and recognition through peaceful means. It is possible that the existence of CONIFA could reify existing secessionist movement, which, in turn, could lead to violence. However, scholarship suggests that the literature is split on this point; autonomy gained through membership in organizations like CONIFA in some regions reify secessionist demands, in other cases autonomy is satisfactory as a means of representation (Bird and Vaillancourt).

Equality in this case is a double-edged sword in that there is an inherent desire on the part of many regional governments and their supporters to gain independence, yet the idea of advancing secessionism to the point of absurdity has its dangers. For example, in the case of Québec in Canada, the people twice voted in independence referendums to decide the constitutional fate of the province. During the second sovereignty referendum campaign, the Cree nation—a First Nations indigenous people living in northern Québec—openly discussed the possibility of seceding from Québec if it gained independence. Likewise, some Anglophones in western Montreal discussed staying within Canada as well. In effect, the Cree could secede from Québec, which seceded from Canada. At what point does secession occur to absurdity?

The CONIFA World Cup has also struggled to attract the high-level independence movements. Kosovo, for example, opted not to join CONIFA and eventually gained membership in FIFA and UEFA in 2016. Movements like Québec and Zanzibar have also declined invitations to play within the CONIFA system. Major, semi-recognized entities like Palestine and Taiwan do not play within the system, either. Thus, even amongst secessionist movements around the world, CONIFA remains, unwittingly, unrecognized.

As with any nascent tournament or organization, the future depends on success in the present. The CONIFA World Cup could easily disband if there is some form of existential threat or situation, which forces the organization to stop its work. Yet, the reverse is also true. If the 2018 CONIFA World Cup is seen as successful, much momentum could carry the tournament to 2020 and beyond.

While the CONIFA World Cup is unlikely to change the dynamics of state sovereignty in the modern world, the existence of the tournament raises some important questions on self-determination and national identity. As the political scientist, Britt Cartrite noted, some ancient nations are "rediscovering their shadow" (Cartrite 1) and through CONIFA there is an opportunity to again see the national flag flown alongside the national anthem. This provides a level of recognition, but one that fills a gap in the state sov-

ereignty system, rather than one that reifies old hostilities—CONIFA needs
to be wary of this challenge, lest its good work representing stateless nations
be lost.

Works Cited

Bird, Richard, François Vaillancourt, and Édison Roy-César. "Is Decentralization 'Glue' or 'Solvent' for National Unity?" *International Studies Program Working Paper 10–03.* 2010. PDF file.
Billig, Michael. *Banal Nationalism.* Los Angeles: Sage, 1995. Print.
Cartrite, Britt. "Reclaiming their Shadow: Ethnopolitical Mobilization in Consolidated Democracies." Diss. University of Colorado, 2003.
Confederation of International Football Associations. "About Us." *CONIFA.* CONIFA, Web. 23 April 2018.
Demytrie, Rayhan. "A World Cup for Unrecognized States" *BBC News.* BBC. 2 June 2016. Web. 16 May 2018.
Duerr, Glen. "The Goal of Independence: Secessionist Movements in Europe and the Role of International Soccer." Thesis. The University of Windsor, 2005.
_____. "Civic Integration or Ethnic Segregation? Models of Ethnic and Civic Nationalism in Club Football/Soccer." *Soccer & Society* 18.2–3 (2017): 204–217. Print.
Fazal, Tanisha M., and Ryan D. Griffiths. "Membership Has its Privileges: The Changing Benefits of Statehood." *International Studies Review* 16.1 (2014): 79–106. Print.
Fertig, Natalie. "The Secessionists Played Soccer" *CUNY Academic Works.* Web. 23 April. 2018.
Foer, Franklin. *How Soccer Explains the World: An Unlikely Theory of Globalization.* New York: HarperCollins, 2004. Print.
Griffiths, Ryan D. *Age of Secession: The International and Domestic Determinants of State Birth.* Cambridge: Cambridge University Press, 2016. Print.
Hébert, Chantal, and Jean Lapierre. *The Morning After: The 1995 Quebec Referendum and the Day That Almost Was.* Toronto: Vintage Canada, 2015. Print.
Herb, Guntram Henrik, and David H. Kaplan, eds. *Nested identities: Nationalism, Territory, and Scale.* Lanham, MD: Rowman & Littlefield, 1999. Print.
Hironaka, Ann. *Neverending Wars: The International Community, Weak States, and the Perpetuation of Civil War.* Cambridge: Harvard University Press, 2005. Print.
Hobsbawm, Eric J. *Nations and Nationalism since 1780: Programme, Myth, Reality.* Cambridge: Cambridge University Press, 2012. Print.
Jaksa, Urban. "South Caucasus: Nagorno-Karabakh between a Contested Territory and a Small State." *Center for Small State Studies.* 2015. PDF file.
Jolly, Seth K. *The European Union and the Rise of Regionalist Parties.* Ann Arbor: University of Michigan Press, 2015. Print.
Kaufman, Stuart J. *Modern Hatreds: The Symbolic Politics of Ethnic War.* Ithaca: Cornell University Press, 2001. Print.
Kuper, Simonn, and Stefan Syzmanski. *Soccernomics: Why England Loses, Why Spain, Germany, and Brazil Win, and Why the US, Japan, Australia and Even Iraq Are Destined to Become the Kings of the World's Most Popular Sport.* New York: Nation Books, 2014. Print.
MacClancy, Jeremy, ed. *Sport, Identity and Ethnicity.* Oxford: Berg, 1996. Print.
Mazower, Mark. *Dark Continent: Europe's Twentieth Century.* New York: Vintage, 1999. Print.
Montague, James. *Thirty-one Nil: On the Road with Football's Outsiders: A World Cup Odyssey.* London: Bloomsbury, 2014. Print.
Pokalova, Elena. "Framing Separatism as Terrorism: Lessons from Kosovo." *Studies in Conflict and Terrorism* 33 (2010): 429–447. Print.
Rukhadze, Vasili, and Glen Duerr. "Sovereignty Issues in the Caucasus: Contested Ethnic and National Identities in Chechnya, Abkhazia, and South Ossetia." *Sprawe Narodowsciowe (Issues of Nationality)* 48 (2016): 30–47. Print.

Sack, Allen L., and Zeljan Suster. "Soccer and Croatian Nationalism: A Prelude to War." *Journal of Sport and Social Issues* 24.3 (2000): 305–320. Print.

Shematov, Maxim. "Who Plays in a World Cup of Unrecognized States?" *Newsweek*, 6 May 2016. Web. 23 April 2018.

Shobe, Hunter, and Geoff Gibson. "Cascadia Rising: Soccer, Region, and Identity." *Soccer & Society* 18.7 (2017): 953–971. Print.

Sputnik Abkhazia. "Participating Teams in the CONIFA World Football Cup 2016 Abkhazia." *#ABKHAZIA2016*. 29 March 2016. Web. 10 March 2018.

Wilson, Woodrow. "President Woodrow Wilson's Fourteen Points." *Yale Law School*. Lillian Goldman Library. Web. 15 May 2018.

Wood, John R. "Secession: A Comparative Analytical Framework." *Canadian Journal of Political Science/Revue Canadienne de Science Politique* 14.1 (1981): 107–134. Print.

Homophobia in Sport

Who Can Play?

Cedrick Heraux

"Labels are for filing. Labels are for clothes. Labels are not for people."—Martina Navratilova

The decision to come out as gay[1] is an intensely personal one. While a private decision, gay professional athletes must also reckon with the fact that their role as prominent public figures means that coming out carries the burden of being seen as representatives of the gay community. Traditionally, they also faced "a persistent pattern of homophobia in all sports, regardless of whether the activity was a team sport, individual sport, contact sport, or noncontact sport" (Anderson, "Openly Gay Athletes" 863–864). This has meant that, to date, most gay professional athletes have only come out after retirement from their sport. As of this writing, there are no openly gay male athletes active in any of the "Big Five" top-tier professional sports leagues in the United States (National Football League [NFL], National Basketball Association [NBA], National Hockey League [NHL], Major League Baseball [MLB], and Major League Soccer [MLS]) during the 2018 seasons. While there are fewer equivalent top-tier professional sports leagues for female athletes, the number of openly gay women in competition is substantially higher (Zeigler, *Fair Play*).[2]

When in 1975, three years after his retirement from the NFL, David Kopay came out in an interview with the *Washington Star*, he did not realize that he was stirring the beginnings of a social movement. As the first former professional team-sport athlete to acknowledge being gay, Kopay simply appeared to have stopped caring about the potential ramifications of his announcement. In describing his relationship with a teammate,[3] he merely sought to demonstrate that it was possible to compete in the ultra-masculine world of American football while being gay (Kopay and Young). What followed was not a spontaneous explosion of coming out announcements by professional athletes, but silence. Over the next 40 years, numerous women, active and retired, in a variety of sports, both individual and team, came out; a relatively large number of men, both active and retired, in individual sports came out as well. However, the number of male professional team-sports athletes who came out remained incredibly low, with virtually all of those only coming out after retirement. Only very recently has that trend started to turn.

The Prevalence of Hegemonic Masculinity: What Makes a Man a Man and a Woman a Woman

While the idea of gender roles (i.e., how "men" and "women" should behave) has been around for quite some time (Collins), the idea of "doing gender" as "socially-guided ... activities that cast particular pursuits as expressions of masculine and feminine 'natures'" (West and Zimmerman 126) is a relatively recent convention. That conversation has been centered around the concept of hegemonic masculinity, "defined as the configuration of gender practice ... which guarantees (or is taken to guarantee) the dominant position of men and the subordination of women" (Connell 77). More specifically, given the emphasis on "overt displays of force and power, on patriarchy ... [t]wo groups positioned as anathema have been women and gay men" (Hardin et al. 184). Put more simply, sports are presumed to be the domain of normative (i.e., male heterosexual) behavior, and thus the presumption is that gay men, due to their association with femininity, do not participate in sports. Likewise, sports participation by women must mean that they are gay, and thus associated with masculinity (Elling and Janssens 72–73; Hardin et al. 185–186). West and Zimmerman articulate this phenomenon as well, noting that "[we] use the category [of sexuality] that seems appropriate, except in the presence of discrepant information or obvious features that would rule out its use" (133). That is, given normative assumptions about sports and gender, we assume that male athletes are straight and female athletes are gay.

It is important to note that the dominance of the *concept* of hegemonic masculinity does not require large-scale active participation. Indeed, research notes that "[it is] not assumed to be normal in the statistical sense; only a minority of men might enact it. But it [is] certainly normative" (Connell and Messerschmidt 832). Yet, sports experience overt displays of masculinity by default, and thus participation by athletes, and male athletes in particular, is presumed to be higher than in the non-athlete population. Notably, Anderson argues this persists throughout the "masculine hierarchy" of sports (i.e., that with football and hockey as the most masculine sports, and marginalized pursuits, such as cross-country running, as decreasingly masculine) ("Openly Gay Athletes" 862).

Sexuality and Professional Sport: A History of Homophobia

Teammate and Competitor Concerns

The primary emphasis in any sports competition is to win. In that context, sports have been idealized as a place where nothing else matters aside from an athlete's ability to play the game. The belief that "winning solves everything," however, is put to the lie by the amount of discrimination that has historically occurred amongst teammates in various sports leagues. As mentioned previously, sports are the presumed domain of heterosexual men, and thus athletes have operated within the framework of their teammates being heterosexual. This is particularly important given the large amount of homosocial activity present within sports. Locker rooms are, by necessity, intimate environments, as athletes are dressing/undressing and showering with one another (Elling and Janssens). Beyond that, however, athletes often make physical contact with each other (e.g., slapping other athletes on the buttocks), even going so far as to mimic sexual activity. Importantly, Demetriou notes, this homosocial activity serves to reinforce, legitimate, and reproduce concepts of masculinity and patriarchy. When all team members are presumed to be heterosexual, this homosocial behavior is ironically considered normal and acceptable. However, when the possibility exists that one or more teammates may be gay, this behavior becomes "risky" in the sense that it may encourage actual sexual activity from those teammates. Thus, the "homosocial undertones of the locker room depend on the assumption that no one is gay" (Buzinski and Zeigler 143). It is so important to sustain this assumption, in fact, that New York Mets catcher Mike Piazza held a press conference in 2002 to announce that he was not gay (Rubin and Goldiner).

The earliest concerns, then, about gay teammates, stem from the belief that these non-normative individuals are likely to act in a predatory manner. Indeed, Cox and Thompson note that female soccer players "revealed that much of the construction of the lesbian player as the 'bogey' ... is centered around an assumption [that lesbian teammates] will exhibit 'male-like' predatory behaviors amongst other women and be sexually aggressive" (16). This adherence to stereotypical thinking is reinforced by more overt homophobia, such as the use of homophobic language and slurs, which, in turn, results in gay athletes remaining closeted (Anderson "Openly Gay Athletes"). This is clearly a well-founded fear, as evidenced as recently as 2013 when San Francisco 49ers player Chris Culliver, in a radio interview, stated, "We ain't got no gay people on the team. They gotta get up out here if they do. Can't be with that sweet stuff…. Nah, can't be … in the locker room, man" (Strauss). While chastised for his comments, Culliver was following in a long tradition established by others such as New York Giants player Jeremy Shockey, who in 2002 stated that he "wouldn't stand for it" if he had a gay teammate (Vacchiano), and retired NBA player Tim Hardaway,[4] who in 2007 noted, "I don't like gay people and I don't like to be around gay people. I am homophobic" (Alfano).

Athletes also use homophobic slurs during competition to denigrate opposing players, based on the presumption that the latter would find it offensive to be thought of as gay. One of the earliest, and most notable, examples comes from the ultra-masculine sport of boxing. In 1962, the closeted Emile Griffith was taunted with a particularly strong Spanish homophobic slur by his opponent, Benny "Kid" Paret, during the pre-match weigh-in. Enraged to the point of having to be taken outside to cool off by his manager, Griffith eventually battered Paret into unconsciousness in the ring, resulting in the latter's death ten days later (Pugmire). Another example comes from English soccer. In 1999, Graeme Le Saux was continually taunted by international teammate Robbie Fowler,[5] who derided Le Saux for his "unmanly pursuits" (such as antiquing) and education, with Le Saux contemplating quitting the sport because of his continual abuse by opponents and fans (Chaudhary). Similarly, in 2004 NFL wide receiver Terrell Owens, in an interview with *Playboy* magazine, implied that his former teammate, quarterback Jeff Garcia, was gay. The former, having recently moved to the Philadelphia Eagles from the San Francisco 49ers, where the two had been teammates, was asked if Garcia was gay and responded by noting, "Like my boy tells me: 'If it looks like a rat and smells like a rat, by golly, it is a rat'" (Buzinski "Owens, Garcia and Gay").

Fan Abuse and Use of Stereotypes

While teammates and competitors may have more information regarding the private lives of their fellow athletes, professional sports do not exist in a vacuum. Thus, it is instructive to examine how fans (and the industry of sports journalism) have behaved towards out or suspected gay athletes. Here it is important to note that many athletes have stated that another compelling reason for remaining closeted was the belief that their fans would not be accepting. This is supported by a large-scale research project conducted by Denison, who found that 41 percent of participants felt that homophobic abuse was most common in the spectator stands (50). Interestingly, 60 percent of the straight participants in the study believed that the stands were not safe for openly gay spectators due to the prevalence of homophobic abuse. Thus, athletes have been more likely to come out after the end of a playing career due to the belief that fans care less about the personal lives of players who are no longer active. Buzinski and Zeigler confirm this, noting that "the fear of having their athletic careers destroyed is the biggest motivator in keeping athletes closeted" (13). Retirement frees an athlete from the concern of a ruined career, thus easing their burden in coming out.

Sports fans have a long history of using homophobic slurs to call into question the masculinity or femininity of opposing players (Zeigler, *Fair Play*). Yet, it is not only opponents who may be subject to these attacks, but their own players and fellow fans as well.[6] While the average fan may be unable to attend a sporting event due to costs or time constraints, the ability to provide commentary and interact with other fans is readily available in the form of sports talk radio and internet chatrooms/message boards. Nylund, for example, in an analysis of the massively popular Jim Rome Show, finds that "much of the discourse on the show contains themes of misogyny, violence, and heterosexual dominance including themes that reinforced sexism and lesbian-baiting" (146). That is, the conversation between Rome and his listeners often developed in a way that reinforced the masculinity of the speakers, while calling into question the masculinity of under-performing male athletes or the femininity of "superstar" female athletes. In looking at how sports media handled the coming out of former NBA player John Amaechi in 2007, Hardin et al. note that while newspaper coverage appeared progressive at first glance, many sportswriters "seemed to throw up their hands at the daunting prospect of changing [homophobic] attitudes, thereby reinforcing homophobia as an inherent part of men's sports" (192). This same phenomenon occurs on the internet, with Cleland noting that "[only a] fraction of discriminating [message board] posts are being reported ... to the authorities to investigate. Instead, the abuse is just absorbed or ignored" ("Sexuality, Masculinity and Homophobia" 7).

In addition to the negativity presented by fans, the industry of sports journalism also played a role in demonstrating to professional athletes that it was in their best interest to remain closeted. One of the earliest examples is that of British figure skater John Curry, who, immediately after winning an Olympic gold medal in Innsbruck in 1976, was confronted with questions from the media about off-the-record comments he had made regarding his sexuality. Rather than focusing on his impressive victory, the conversation turned to his flamboyant style and the details of his personal life (O'Callaghan). Perhaps the most prominent example remains Billie Jean King, who was outed in 1981 when the *New York Times* reported that she was being sued by her former lover for a share of her assets (Lindsey).[7] Although near the end of her career, King was still active at the time, reaching the semifinals of Wimbledon in 1982 and playing on the doubles circuit through 1990, and estimates suggest that being out cost her nearly $2 million in endorsements (Seibel). Journalists also act irresponsibly in participating in speculation about the sexuality of certain athletes, typically those who are relatively high-profile in their sport. In 1996, national sports columnist Skip Bayless wrote *Hell-Bent* about how the Dallas Cowboys, multiple Super Bowl champions and branded as "America's Team," were coming apart. In that book, Bayless claimed that there were consistent rumors that Cowboys quarterback Troy Aikman was gay, and that those rumors were being propagated by Cowboys head coach Barry Switzer. Although Bayless noted that he himself never claimed that Aikman was gay, many other national columnists responded with concern over the ethics of publishing unsubstantiated rumors about a player's sexuality (Heck).

Complicity of Governing Bodies and the Formal Structure of Sports

While teammates, competitors, fans and journalists are the vast majority of those with whom the athlete will come into contact, it is the athletic governing bodies themselves that ultimately bear responsibility for ensuring that athletes are treated safely and fairly. In this regard, the formal structure of sports organizations represents the greatest failures in dealing with the issues faced by gay athletes. As noted by Hardin et al., "the valorization of sports for providing an 'equal playing field' has been effectively used to dismiss the need for serious discussion of the ways institutional sports reinforce … homophobia" (188). In loudly pronouncing that all that matters is athletic ability, these governing bodies failed to generate positive momentum for gay athletes. That is, in being dismissive of the idea that being gay would have any impact, sports have re-marginalized an already marginalized population. This is because, as argued by Buzinski and Zeigler, "gay people openly playing sports is in many ways subversive," and sports organizations are prone to attempt to minimize conflict (11).

Gay athletes, particularly in team sports, have found themselves at odds with teams and leagues, regardless of whether they were out or closeted. In 1977, Glenn Burke was traded by the Los Angeles Dodgers to the Oakland A's; the 24-year-old outfielder suspected that the trade was because the team knew him to be gay. While not out, Burke made no serious attempts to hide his sexuality, even developing a friendship with Tommy Lasorda, Jr., the openly gay son of Los Angeles Dodgers manager Tommy Lasorda. Within two years of the trade, Burke was out of MLB completely, having been cut by the Oakland A's, who had just hired controversial manager Billy Martin, prone to vulgar outbursts and homophobic language in the clubhouse (Branch "Posthumous Recognition"). While no MLB player was out or known to be gay following Burke's departure, the league only worsened its standing in 1988 when it fired umpire Dave Pallone after nine years of service. Once again, the belief was that the suspicion of being gay had ended an MLB career, with confirmation coming later in the year when Pallone was outed by an article in the *New York Post* (Colker). The situation had still not improved ten years later, when New York Yankees employee Paul Priore sued the team, as well as players Jeff Nelson, Mariano Rivera, and Bob Wickman, for creating a hostile work environment. Priore claimed that New York Yankees players regularly used homophobic slurs towards him because they knew he was gay, that the three named players once tried to sexually assault him with a baseball bat, and that the team fired him when they learned that he was HIV-positive (Lovett).[8]

The issue of homophobia within MLB was thrust into the public view more forcefully in 1999, when *Sports Illustrated* published an interview with Atlanta Braves pitcher John Rocker, in which he disparaged a variety of marginalized groups and made several homophobic remarks. While MLB Commissioner Bud Selig initially appeared to make a strong statement condemning Rocker by suspending him for 73 days, that punishment was reduced to 14 games, which many viewed as insufficient (Rogers). In 2002, Rocker demonstrated that his punishment had been ineffective when, while a member of the Texas Rangers, he made homophobic comments towards fellow diners at a restaurant in Oak Lawn, Texas, a neighborhood well-known for its sizable gay population (Vries). The league demonstrated that it had not made any progress in 2006 when it handed down an undisclosed fine to Chicago White Sox manager Ozzie Guillen and ordered him to undergo sensitivity training for using a homophobic slur to describe Chicago sports reporter Jay Mariotti, yet another punishment considered by many to be far too lenient (ESPN).[9]

The NFL has also suffered from a significant amount of homophobia, not just among players (as discussed previously), but within team and league structure as well. In the prominent instances of homophobic remarks by Jeremy Shockey, Terrell Owens, and Chris Culliver, neither their teams nor the NFL imposed any sanctions other than to encourage half-hearted apologies from the players. Perhaps more importantly, there have been explicit displays of sanctioned homophobia throughout the history of the league. In 2007, just six weeks after winning the Super Bowl as the head coach of the Indianapolis Colts, Tony Dungy attended a ceremony to accept an award from the anti-gay Indiana Family Institute. Despite initially voicing some concerns, and expressing a desire to distance themselves from the event, the team made no further comment on the situation, even when Dungy noted that he was accepting the award on behalf of the Indianapolis Colts (Kusmer and Martin).[10] The Minnesota Vikings also found themselves mired in controversy when, two years removed from his last play in the NFL, former punter Chris Kluwe alleged that he had been dismissed from the team due to his support for same-sex marriage and gay rights. Kluwe stated that his special teams coach Mike Priefer had made homophobic comments regarding his advocacy, and that head coach Leslie Frazier had ordered him to stop speaking about the subject. Only after some public backlash did the Vikings organization agree to investigate, eventually suspending Priefer for three regular-season games and handing down no other punishments (Goessling).

Perhaps the most damning indictment, however, comes for the actions that the league has continually failed to take with regards to how draft prospects are treated at the NFL Combine or individual team workouts. In 2007, when an NFL scout asked closeted offensive lineman Akil Patterson if he was gay, the stunned prospect responded that he was. While Patterson attributed his not being drafted to his lack of preparation and motivation, rather than his sexuality, he wondered how often this question had been asked of other prospects. Given the secrecy surrounding the draft process, it is not surprising that there is no credible data regarding how often teams engage in this line of questioning. However, it was brought to the forefront again in 2013, when both Le'Veon Bell and Nick Kasa were asked if they "liked girls" during their interview sessions. Although the NFL warned teams against these types of questions, no punishments were handed down in 2013, or again in 2016 when Atlanta Falcons assistant coach Marquand Manuel asked cornerback Eli Apple if he "liked girls." Unsurprisingly, given the NFL's lack of action, in March 2018 running back prospect Derrius Guice was asked by an unnamed team representative if he was gay, with the league promising to investigate (Sobel).

With respect to soccer, while the sport experiences a high degree of homophobia, perhaps no organization typifies this more than the English Football Association (FA), which also provides one of the iconic figures in the struggles of gay athletes. In 1981, Justin Fashanu became the first black soccer player in the English First Division to be transferred for a fee of 1,000,000 pounds (equivalent of $1.8 million at the time) and in 1990 he became the first openly gay professional soccer player. While his sexuality was an open secret to many of his teammates and managers, Fashanu only came out when he was paid 70,000 pounds (equivalent of $126,000 at the time) by British tabloid newspaper *The Sun* to tell his story. Although nearing the end of a career marked by turmoil and injury, he played several more years for smaller clubs while openly gay, often finding that while teammates were accommodating, mangers, fans and the FA were not. After coaching in the United States and facing a sexual assault allegation from a 17-year-old player, Fashanu returned to England and hanged himself in an abandoned garage in London in 1998 (Duncan). Despite supporting a campaign to address racism within soccer since 1993, the English FA did not start a similar effort to address homophobia until more than 20 years later. The reason for the long delay was laid at the feet of the individual clubs; the FA pointed to a 2005 survey by the British Broadcasting Corporation (BBC Sport) on opinions about homophobia where all 20 Premier League managers refused to participate as evidence that the clubs were not ready (Williams). While progress was made in 2007 when the FA outlawed homophobic language at all soccer matches, there was a significant setback in 2010 when a proposed anti-homophobia video had to be postponed because the FA was unable to find enough players to participate (Gibson). This seemed to confirm the findings of a 2009 BBC survey, in which 70 percent of fans stated that they had heard homophobic abuse at a soccer match and 64 percent felt that the FA was not doing enough to curb such abuse (BBC Sport). Public relations expert Max Clifford concurred, noting that in late 2009 and early 2010 he had urged several clients playing in the Premier League to remain closeted (Harris and Godwin).

We Can Play: The Rise of Gay Sports Competitions

Given the stark lack of opportunities for openly gay athletes to participate in sports competitions, it is not surprising that some of the earliest efforts to normalize these athletes took the form of self-segregation. As early as 1968, Olympian decathlete Tom Waddell had the idea for a "Gay Olympics" which would feature openly gay athletes competing in a mix of traditional (e.g., soccer, swimming, and diving) and non-traditional (e.g., billiards and bowling) Olympic sports. Notably, the idea did not come to fruition until 1981, when Waddell founded San Francisco Arts and Athletics (SFAA) to begin the planning stages. Almost immediately, Waddell faced numerous obstacles in organizing the competition. In response to concerns about exclusion, the competition explicitly did not require an athlete to be gay, nor were there any qualifying standards, both of which raised questions about the legitimacy of the event as a serious sporting competition for gay athletes. Perhaps more importantly, however, SFAA, Inc. was sued by the United States Olympic Committee (USOC), who sought to prevent the competition from using the word "Olympic" in the name, making the argument that the USOC had exclusive rights to use of the word in connection with athletic competition.[11] The United States Supreme Court ruled in favor of the USOC, and

Waddell was forced to rebrand the event as the "Gay Games" (Markwell and Rowe). The first Gay Games was held in San Francisco in 1982, with the event taking place every four years from that moment. Interestingly, the Gay Games faced competition from the establishment of the Outgames in 2006, when the Gay and Lesbian International Sport Association (GLISA) was formed in response to dissatisfaction with how the Federation of Gay Games was organizing the Montreal 2006 Gay Games (Harvey et al.). Thus, there are currently two separate international sports governing bodies for athletic competitions featuring openly gay athletes, with no plans for the Gay Games and the Outgames to merge, although the latter saw its most recent event in 2017 officially cancelled at the last minute due to financial constraints (Artavia).[12]

In the period between the idea and the actual establishment of the Gay Games, gay athletes formed several organizations for competition in specific sports. One of the first efforts involved the ultra-masculine sport of rodeo, with the first official gay rodeo held in Reno, Nevada in 1976. Despite being given an outlet to perform at a high level while being openly gay, the sport grew slowly, with the establishment of the International Gay Rodeo Association (IGRA) in 1985 spurring more rapid growth that saw 15 to 20 events per year over the next three decades (International Gay Rodeo Association). This same period saw the growth of the Gay Softball World Series, first played with only one division of competition in 1977 after the formation of the North American Gay Amateur Athletic Alliance (NAGAAA). The event grew to three separate divisions by 1991, and in 2017 there were six divisions for men and an entirely separate competition (established in 2007 with the formation of the Amateur Sports Alliance of North America [ASANA]) for women (Seattle Gay News). This mirrors the success of the International Gay Bowling Organization (IGBO), which formed in 1980 and now covers more than 8,000 bowlers across three continents (International Gay Bowling Organization).

While gay sports leagues were finding success, numerous organizations were also working to ensure that openly gay athletes could participate in sports equitably and safely at the high school and college levels. The National Center for Lesbian Rights (formed in 1977), for example, began focusing on sports advocacy in 2001 and six years later helped former Penn State Nittany Lions player Jennifer Harris reach a settlement with Penn State University, women's basketball coach Rene Portland and athletics director Tim Curley.[13] Similar efforts, including the "Changing the Game" initiative (started in 2011) from the Gay Lesbian Straight Education Network (GLSEN, founded in 1990) and the "It Takes a Team" program (started in 1996) at the Women's Sport Foundation (WSF, founded in 1974), focused on educating fellow athletes, coaches and athletic directors in the school environment. Although these efforts are laudable, these organizations remained at arm's length from involvement with professional sports. Indeed, only the Gay and Lesbian Athletics Foundation (GLAF), founded in 1999, explicitly mentioned a focus on increasing the visibility and acceptance of gay athletes in professional sports leagues. Large-scale changes in professional sports would have to wait another decade.

Moving Towards Acceptance?

Can You Play?

The history of athletes coming out is one conditioned by specific expectations about gender, sexuality, and physicality, but is also mediated by "sports capital" (i.e., whether the athlete in question is a superstar). With respect to gender, Buzinski and Zeigler argue that "although a bit simplistic, the biases boil down to this: many female jocks are presumed lesbian unless otherwise proven; male jocks are presumed straight unless there is a public declaration to the contrary" (43). Thus, Zeigler notes that "women coming out are treated differently [because] there is simply a different perceived risk…. Female athletes are also largely not put by our society in the same pantheon as NFL and NBA players—it is unfortunate, but it's also reality" (*Fair Play* 43). Regardless of skill level, the coming out of Brittney Griner and Jason Collins in 2013 were treated radically differently by fans, media, and the sports establishment. Griner came out publicly, to little fanfare, in an interview with SI.com just two days after being selected first in the Women's National Basketball Association (WNBA) draft by the Phoenix Mercury (Moore). Collins, in contrast, came out publicly in a Sports Illustrated story after his 2012–2013 NBA season had ended, and received significant attention from the media, politicians, corporations, and the NBA establishment. While Collins was a free agent at the time, he indicated that he planned to continue his playing career, and he eventually signed with the Brooklyn Nets midway through the 2013–2014 season, after which he retired (Collins). Arguably, Griner received far less attention due to the prevailing assumption that she was gay. Having been a three-time All-American and holding the distinction of being the only NCAA basketball player to score 2,000 points and block 500 shots, Griner had been surrounded by speculation regarding her sexuality even during her high school playing career (Griner). Collins, while often described as a physical defender, team leader, and consummate professional, had a relatively unremarkable NBA career, thus sparking the conversation after coming out that no one would know who he was if he was not gay (Felt).

Even in more unenlightened eras, an athlete's display of supreme ability could be expected to mitigate societal backlash. Bill Tilden, who won three Wimbledon titles and numerous United States Tennis championships in the

1920s, made no secret of his sexuality and was even arrested on morals charges in 1946. Despite this, a 1950 survey of sportswriters named him the greatest tennis player of the half-century (Borges). Similarly, in 1981 when Martina Navratilova, who was at the height of her playing career, came out in an interview with the *New York Daily News*, there were exceptions made. Although she lost as much as $10 million in endorsement contracts, Navratilova was generally supported by the establishment, including competitors and the sport's governing bodies (Tignor). Anderson finds the same phenomenon, noting that "in 2002 … I could find only openly gay athletes who were exceptional athletes among their peers" ("Updating the Outcome" 251).

In addition to gender-based assumptions and the importance of individual skill, the impact of coming out is also predicated on the visibility of the sport in which an athlete participates. Thus, outside of gender stereotypes about women in sport being confirmed when a female athlete comes out, there is also less attention paid because women's sports are, in general, less popular than men's sports (Cooky; Wallace). Arguably, then, the more popular a sport, the more scrutiny coming out will receive. While being openly gay for Amelie Mauresmo (tennis), Sue Bird (basketball), or Abby Wambach (soccer) may have been mitigated by the fact that they participated in stereotypically "lesbian" sports (and did so at a high level), there was presumably less attention paid to Belle Brockhoff (snowboard), Natalie Cook (beach volleyball), and Alexandra Lacrabere (team handball) due to the low visibility of their sport. This would hold true for male athletes as well, with Michael Sam (football), Robbie Rogers (soccer), and Billy Bean (baseball) receiving more attention than J.P. Calderon (volleyball), Kyle Hawkins (lacrosse), and Scott Norton (bowling).

Regardless of "sports capital" or gender and sexuality stereotypes, most organizations appeared to have reached a tipping point in terms of how individual athletes responded to their teammates coming out. By 2006, a *Sports Illustrated* poll of players in the NFL, NHL, MLB and NBA found that the majority would welcome an openly gay teammate (Buzinski, "Moment #29"). This was supported in 2013 when Jason Collins came out, as journalists (sports and otherwise) en masse asked athletes for their opinions regarding gay teammates and opponents, and found widespread support (Zeigler, "187 Pro Athletes' Reactions"). There is reason to believe that this attitude has even spread to the relatively homophobic world of soccer, at least in part. As Zeigler notes, although there were no out players at the 2014 men's World Cup, the 2015 women's World Cup featured at least 17 players or coaches who were openly gay (*Fair Play* 78). In the realm of men's soccer, hope rests in athletes currently undergoing academy training, who are on the verge of signing their first professional contract. Indeed, Magrath et al. found that "as a result of these men belonging to a generation holding inclusive attitudes toward homosexuality, independent of whether they maintain contact with gay men, they are unanimously supportive of gay men coming out on their team" (1). Anderson noted similar results when comparing two cohorts of openly gay male athletes, one of which consisted of those who had come out between 2008–2010 and the other consisting of those who had come out between 2000–2002, finding that the former experienced far less heterosexism in the locker room and far more support from their teammates ("Updating the Outcome" 250). It is important to note, however, that Zeigler found that while most professional athletes say they would be accepting of a gay team-mate, "many of them couch it with a 'as long as he knows how to behave' or 'as long as he doesn't hit on me' disclaimer" (*Fair Play* 65).

Fan Reactions and Social Justice Movements

Given the well-known prevalence of homophobia in soccer, it is instructive to examine how attitudes have changed within that sport, as an example of the progress that has been made. On the heels of the English FA postponing their anti-homophobia campaign in 2010, an online survey of over 3,500 soccer fans found "that, contrary to assumptions … there is evidence of rapidly decreasing homophobia within the culture of [soccer] fandom [and fans] blame agents and clubs for the lack of openness" (Cashmore and Cleland 370). The idea that fans were more concerned with performance on the field of play than with the private lives of athletes was again noted in an analysis of over 3,000 posts across 48 soccer message boards, where Cleland found that "a majority of [fans demonstrated] more inclusivity through the rejection of posts that they [felt had] more pernicious homophobic intent" ("Discussing Homosexuality" 1). This decreased culture of homophobia was highlighted over the next several years by fan reactions to the coming out of Anton Hysen (2011), Robbie Rogers (2013), and Thomas Hitzlsperger (2014). With respect to Hysen's announcement, Cleland found that, contrary to the "homohysteria" surrounding Justin Fashanu's announcement in 1990 virtually no one questioned Hysen's masculinity or ability to play soccer ("Association Football" 1271). Rogers, for his part, after retiring, coming out, and un-retiring, was treated to a normal reaction (i.e., as any other player) from fans upon becoming the first openly gay male athlete to compete in one of the "Big Five" professional sports leagues (Witz). The reaction to Hitzlsperger represents the most comprehensive, and hopeful, analysis, as Cleland et al. found that "just 2% of the 6,106 [message board] comments contained pernicious homophobic intent" (1).

Specific clubs and individual players have also reacted positively in support of the anti-homophobia movement in soccer. Notably, several clubs have made efforts to address homophobia in the stands by providing a mechanism for fans to report such language, with the offenders often banned from those stadia (Fulda). There have been increased instances of public support as well, such as in 2012, when Liverpool FC became the first Premier League club to be involved in an official capacity with an LGBTQ event, with club staff carrying a banner at the Liverpool Pride event (Woodward). The next year, the Stonewall organization in the UK began the Rainbow Laces campaign, urging professional soccer players to wear rainbow laces on their cleats in a show of support. Although not officially sanctioned by the FA, the players' organization, the Professional Footballers Association (PFA) supported the effort to have players on all 92 professional teams participate. While 52 clubs saw players wear the laces, several of the most popular, including Manchester United, Liverpool, and Tottenham refused to join the campaign (Pirks; Wilson).

A significant social justice movement has also emerged in the prototypical masculine sport of hockey, beginning in 2011 with the establishment of You Can Play by Patrick Burke, following the death of his younger brother, openly gay Miami University hockey student manager Brendan Burke. Although a scout for the Philadelphia Flyers, Patrick Burke began the initiative as a personal endeavor with others, including his father, Brian Burke, who was general manager of the Toronto Maple Leafs at the time, looking to champion the rights of gay athletes. While their initial public service announcement featured several high-profile NHL players and was featured during a Boston Bruins-New York Rangers game, it was not until nearly a year later that the NHL officially adopted You Can Play as an organizational standard. However, while the organization has reached out to all major professional sports bodies, only the NHL and MLS have currently committed to joining the cause.

The other large-scale movement related to sports is Athlete Ally,[14] founded by University of Maryland wrestler Hudson Taylor in 2011. Similar to other efforts started by individuals outside of sports governing bodies, Athlete Ally initially focused on developing educational materials and public awareness of the issue of homophobia in sports at all levels. The organization's earliest efforts at providing training to sports bodies culminated in a partnership with the National Collegiate Athletic Association (NCAA) in 2013 to produce an 82-page manual for athletic directors, coaches, and student-athletes on dealing with LGBTQ issues (Branch "N.C.A.A. Advises"). While the NBA had collaborated in 2012 with GLAAD and Athlete Ally to speak to its rookie players, it was in 2013 that a sustained league-wide initiative was first sponsored by a professional sport's governing body (Reese). The NFL Players' Association (NFLPA) was quick to follow in supporting these efforts, largely prodded into action by the advocacy of former NFL linebacker Brendon Ayanbadejo, who would eventually become an ambassador for Athlete Ally (Ayanbadejo).

Governing Body Responses and Initiatives

Over the past decade, major sports governing bodies and individual teams have made significant strides in reaching out to the LGBTQ community. Within domestic professional sports leagues in the United States, it is the NHL which has continually demonstrated the most positive attitudes towards gay athletes. As early as 2005, the NHL acted to prohibit discrimination based on sexual orientation in its collective bargaining agreement (CBA) and this language has remained in place through subsequent CBAs (Mortazavi). The NHL was also the first league to establish an active partnership with You Can Play, with that effort leading to education and outreach at the league's rookie symposium, where incoming players receive information regarding sexual orientation. This has culminated in the development of "Hockey Is for Everyone" month, which in 2018 saw all 31 NHL teams, some for the first time in their history, host an "Inclusion" or "Pride" event (NHL Public Relations). Similarly, MLS established a prohibition against discrimination based on sexual orientation in its 2005 CBA (Major League Soccer).[15] In 2013, it became the second league to develop a program with You Can Play when the players' union and league ownership formalized the partnership at the start of the season, although several teams had already produced public service announcements for the initiative (You Can Play). MLB has made similar progress, adding sexual orientation as a protected class to its CBA in 2011. The league also named former player Billy Bean, who came out publicly in 1999, four years after his career ended, as the "ambassador for inclusion" responsible for providing guidance to teams regarding homophobia, prejudice and discrimination (Almasy). That support has spread to individual teams within MLB, as the majority have joined the It Gets Better Project in filming public service announcements and 26 (out of 30) teams held a Pride Night event in 2017 (Cooper).

Despite having a notable number of openly gay former players, the situation in the NFL and NBA remains decidedly more complicated. Zeigler argues that "the NFL and NBA have engaged [Wade] Davis and [Jason] Collins in arm's-length partnerships" (*Fair Play* 137). As with other leagues, the NFL included a sexual orientation clause in its anti-discrimination language within the 2011 CBA negotiated with the players' union. This was followed by the addition of a discussion on the topic of sexual orientation to the 2013 NFL Rookie Symposium (McManus). However, while the league has had conversations with former NFL running back Wade Davis, they have been at Davis' request as the director of professional sports outreach for You Can Play (Hamilton). That is, the NFL has failed to be particularly proactive regarding homophobia and discrimination within its ranks. Indeed, after some NFL teams filmed public service announcements for It Gets Better, the latter organization removed those videos from the public domain when several players denied having knowingly taken part in the anti-bullying LGBTQ campaign (Abed-Santos). As noted previously, the league has also failed to act on several occasions when potential draftees have been asked questions regarding their sexual orientation. Individual teams have also generally been lacking, as relatively few have sponsored, held, or participated in any "Pride" events. The NBA has found itself in a similar position after instituting a prohibition against discrimination because of sexual orientation in its own 2011 CBA (Garcia). That same year saw the league fine high-profile players Kobe Bryant and Joakim Noah for using gay slurs, but many felt that they had still been slow to act. This was particularly disappointing considering that in 2012 the league had asked Athlete Ally to provide training regarding homophobia and the use of that type of offensive language. Thus, in 2014 the NBA asked former player Jason Collins to speak to the Rookie Transition Program, expanding his role further at the 2015 event (Gleeson). Despite this, when Rajon Rondo used a gay slur against referee Bill Kennedy, who would come out publicly a month later, in December of 2015, the NBA took longer than usual to decide on disciplinary action, with the resulting one-game suspension seen as unsatisfactory by many observers (Windhorst). There was continued skepticism when the league collaborated with the GLSEN during the 2016 season to release a line of Pride month T-shirts, with the move seen as more reflective of marketing concerns rather than true concern for LGBTQ rights (Heitner).

Although the major professional sports leagues in the United States have made marked progress on the issue of homophobia and anti-gay discrimination (albeit some more than others), the most visible sports organizations in the world have been relatively lacking. As mentioned previously, the English Football Association, which is quite possibly the most widely-known and highly-regarded (in terms of competition) organization, has consistently failed to take advantage of numerous grassroots efforts within the sport of soccer. While the Rainbow Laces campaign has received some attention from individual teams and players, the FA has not established an official partnership. Similarly, the efforts of Football v. Homophobia and of the Justin Campaign (named after Justin Fashanu) have slowed down considerably over the past few years given a lack of active support from the FA. This lack of action is mirrored at the international level by soccer's governing body, the Fédération Internationale de Football Association (FIFA), which has faced strong criticism for awarding the next two World Cup competitions to Russia (2018) and Qatar (2022), both of which have a poor record of human rights abuses of the LGBTQ community (Lutz). Despite the addition of human rights language to its organizational statutes and warnings to countries for previous violations, the passage of a "gay rights propaganda" law in Russia lead anti-discrimination group Fare to caution FIFA that the 2018 World Cup had a significant potential for violence against gay fans (Panja). This is notable because the International Olympic Committee (IOC), while criticized for awarding the 2014 Winter Olympics to Russia, saw fit to add sexual orientation to its anti-discrimination language nine months after that event (Hersh). Future Olympic sites, including 2022 Winter Olympics host China, will have to provide assurances that they will protect the rights of gay fans, athletes and staff. As noted by Van Rheenen, this demonstrates that, although there is much progress to be made, sports can provide an avenue for positive change.

The Future of Equality in Sports

Moving forward, professional sports will inevitably face the same concerns that have been present over the past few decades. Individual gay athletes will have to decide their level of comfort with disclosing an intimate part of themselves to their teammates, organizations, and the public, all while knowing that heterosexual athletes are not expected to make those same pronouncements. However, recent evidence indicates that more positive experiences potentially await those who are willing to be out; athletes, teams, and fans appear to be truly embracing the ideal of athletic achievement being paramount (i.e., "can you play?"). Cleland suggests that this is due to "influential media, the rise and success of feminism…, the increasing success and prominence of lesbian, gay, bisexual, and transgender (LGBT) individuals, and the increasing influence of out gay men and lesbians" ("Sexuality, Masculinity and Homophobia" 4). As Mortazavi notes, gay athletes certainly have the full force of the law on their side if any issues arise from their coming out.

Yet, there are far more out individuals in "minor" sports and among female athletes. As noted earlier, the "Big Five" top-tier professional sports leagues in the United States (NFL, NBA, NHL, MLB, and MLS) will not have a single out male athlete during their 2018 competitive seasons. Anderson argues that this is because "the transformative potential of gay athletes in sport is neutralized through … overt homophobia [and] the normalization of homophobic language" ("Openly Gay Athletes" 863). As long as coaches, managers, and sports governing bodies fail to take significant action against this type of behavior, gay athletes may feel the need to remain closeted. Perhaps most importantly, Nylund argues, is the problem that "embedded in this discourse is the assumption that the right, best way for gays and lesbians to live is out" (156). Thus, we wait; not for the next Dave Kopay or the next Martina Navratilova, but the first of the tidal wave of athletes who are active, out and proud.

NOTES

1. This essay follows the terminology preferred by the Gay and Lesbian Alliance Against Defamation (GLAAD).

2. This essay focuses on openly gay, cisgender male and female professional athletes. While there are similar, if not more heightened, issues surrounding participation in professional sports by transgender athletes, the complexity of both topics demands a singular focus.

3. Although he did not name him at the time, in Kopay's autobiography he described former teammate Jerry Smith, who had died of complications from AIDS in 1987, as his first love.

4. It should be noted that Tim Hardaway, more than 10 years removed from his homophobic comments, is now a very active supporter of the LGBTQ community (Bontemps).

5. While Le Saux and Fowler both played for the English national team, in club competition the former was a member of Chelsea Football Club, while the latter played for Liverpool Football Club.

6. In an infamous incident at Dodger Stadium in 2000, a lesbian couple was ejected from the premises when another fan was reportedly offended by their kissing (ABC News).

7. Canadian figure skater Brian Orser was outed in a similar fashion in 1998, when several news outlets discovered that he was being sued by his former lover for a share of his assets. However, Orser fared somewhat better than King, going on to skate professionally through 2007 and then beginning a relatively successful coaching career (Jones).

8. It should be noted that the New York State Court of Appeals declined to hear the case after the lower court ruled against Priore.

9. This incident caused John Rocker to re-emerge, as he publicly supported Guillen and derided the political correctness of sensitivity training.

10. Tony Dungy would, several years later, also claim that he would not have drafted openly gay defensive end Michael Sam because it would have been a distraction for the team (Glenesk).

11. This is even more notable when one considers that there already existed numerous competitions using the word "Olympics," such as Junior Olympics and Special Olympics. The assumption was, then, that the primary reason for the lawsuit in this instance was that the USOC did not wish to be associated with an event featuring openly gay individuals.

12. Currently, these two international gay sports competitions cover over 30 sports and slightly more than 18,000 athletes.

13. Harris had alleged that Portland, who in 1986 famously said that she would not allow lesbians to play basketball for her at Penn State (Fitzpatrick), had dismissed her from the team because she believed that Harris was a lesbian.

14. It should be noted that Athlete Ally, as an organization founded and lead by a cisgender, straight male, has been occasionally criticized by the leadership of other social justice organizations devoted to improving the lives of the LGBTQ community in sports (Petchesky).

15. Although MLS had existed since 1996, due to its establishment within a single-entity owner structure, it was not until *the Fraser v. Major League Soccer* antitrust lawsuit that players were awarded the right to collective bargaining (Mathias).

WORKS CITED

ABC News. "Dodgers Apologize to Lesbian Couple." ABCNews.com. ABC News Internet, 24 August 2000. Web. 12 February 2018.

Abed-Santos, Alexander. "The San Francisco 49ers Still Have a Big Gay Problem." *The Atlantic*. The Atlantic Monthly Group, 1 February 2013. Web. 24 February 2018.

Alfano, Sean. "Ex-NBA Star: 'I Hate Gay People.'" *CBS News*. CBS Interactive, 15 February 2007. Web. 12 February 2018.

Almasy, Steve. "Former Player Billy Bean Named MLBs 'Ambassador of Inclusion.'" CNN.com. Cable News Network, 15 July 2014. Web. 17 February 2018.

Anderson, Eric. "Openly Gay Athletes: Contesting Hegemonic Masculinity in a Homophobic Environment." *Gender and Society* 16.6 (2002): 860–877. Print.

_____. "Masculinities and Sexualities in Sport and Physical Cultures: Three Decades of Evolving Research." *Journal of Homosexuality* 58.5 (2011): 565–578. Print.

_____. "Updating the Outcome: Gay Athletes, Straight Teams, and Coming Out in Educationally Based Sport Teams." *Gender and Society* 25.2 (2011): 250–268. Print.

Anderson, Eric, and Rachael Bullingham. "Openly Lesbian Team Sport Athletes in an Era of Decreasing Homohysteria." *International Review for the Sociology of Sport* 50.6 (2015): 647–660. Print.

Artavia, David. "Meet the Heroes Who Saved the World Outgames." TheAdvocate.com. The Advocate, 14 June 2017. Web. 8 March 2018.

Ayanbadejo, Brendon. "End Homophobia in Professional Sports." *USA Today*. USA Today, 6 February 2013. Web. 25 February 2018.

BBC Sport. "Football 'Failing on Homophobia.'" *BBC Sport*. BBC, 12 August 2009. Web. 23 January 2018.

Bird, Sharon R. "Welcome to the Men's Club: Homosociality and the Maintenance of Hegemonic Masculinity." *Gender and Society* 10.2 (1996): 120–132. Print.

Bontemps, Tim. "A Hall of Fame Crossover: Tim Hardaway Goes from Gay Rights Pariah to Advocate." *Washington Post*. Washington Post, 17 February 2017. Web. 18 February 2017.

Borges, Ron. "Tilden Brought Theatrics to Tennis." ESPN.com. 3 February 2018. Web. 3 February 2018.

Branch, John. "N.C.A.A. Advises on Sexual Orientation Issues." *New York Times*. New York Times, 4 March 2013. Web. 12 January 2018.

_____. "Posthumous Recognition: M.L.B. to Recognize Glenn Burke as Baseball's Gay Pioneer." *New York Times*. New York Times, 14 July 2014. Web. 22 February 2018.

Buzinski, Jim. "Moment #29: Majority of Pro Athletes Say They Would Welcome a Gay Teammate." Outsports.com. VOX Media, 4 September 2011. Web. 3 February 2018.

_____. "Owens, Garcia and Gay." Outsports.com. VOX Media, 12 August 2004. Web. 15 February 2018.

Buzinski, Jim, and Cyd Zeigler. *The Outsports Revolution: Truth and Myth in the World of Gay Sports*. New York: Alyson Books, 2007. Print.

Cashmore, Ellis, and Jamie Cleland. "Fans, Homophobia and Masculinities in Association Football: Evidence of a More Inclusive Environment." *The British Journal of Sociology* 63.2 (2012): 370–387. Print.

Chaudhary, Vivek. "Gay Taunts Led to Le Saux Outburst." *Irish Times*. Irish Times, 3 March 1999. Web. 12 February 2018.

Cleland, Jamie. "Association Football and the Representation of Homosexuality by the Print Media: A Case Study of Anton Hysen." *Journal of Homosexuality* 61.9 (2014): 1269–1287. Print.

_____. "Discussing Homosexuality on Association Football Fan Message Boards: A Changing Cultural Context." *International Review for the Sociology of Sport* (2013): 1–16. Sage Journals. Web. 25 February 2018.

_____. "Sexuality, Masculinity and Homophobia in Association Football: An Empirical Overview of a Changing Cultural Context." *International Review for the Sociology of Sport* (2016): 1–13. Sage Journals. Web. 25 February 2018.

Cleland, Jamie, Rory Magrath, and Edward Kian. "The Internet as a Site of Decreasing Cultural Homophobia in Association Football: An Online Response by Fans to the Coming Out of Thomas Hitzlsperger." *Men and Masculinities* 19.1 (2016): 1–21. Print.

Colker, David. "Secret Behind the Mask: A Former Umpire Discusses One of His Life's Tough Calls: Being Gay and in Pro Baseball." *Los Angeles Times*. Los Angeles Times, 22 June 1990. Web. 22 February 2018.

Collins, Jason. "Parting Shot: Jason Collins Announces NBA Retirement in His Own Words." SI.com. Time Inc, 19 November 2014. Web. 3 February 2018.

Collins, Rebecca L. "Content Analysis of Gender Roles in Media: Where Are We Now and Where Should We Go?" *Sex Roles* 64.3–4 (2011): 290–298. Print.

Connell, R.W., and James W. Messerschmidt. "Hegemonic Masculinity: Rethinking the Concept." *Gender and Society* 19.6 (2005): 829–859. Print.

Cooky, Cheryl. "Despite Soaring Popularity, Women's Sports Got More Coverage a Generation Ago." *FAIR.org.* 19 June 2015. Web. 3 February 2018.

Cooper, Mariah. "Yankees One of Four MLB Teams to Never Have Held a Pride Night." *Washington Blade.* Brown, Naff, Pitts Omnimedia, 4 October 2017. Web. 17 February 2018.

Cox, Barbara, and Shona Thompson. "Facing the Bogey: Women, Football and Sexuality." *Football Studies* 4.2 (2001): 7–24. Print.

Demetriou, Demetrakis Z. "Connell's Concept of Hegemonic Masculinity: A Critique." *Theory and Society* 30.3 (2001): 337–361. Print.

Denison, E., and A. Kitchen. *Out on the Fields: The First International Study on Homophobia in Sport.* Out on the Fields, Web. 25 April 2018.

Duncan, Amy. "John Fashanu Breaks Down After Turning His Back on Gay Brother Justin Who Killed Himself Over Rape Claims." *Metro.* 5 October 2017. Web. 27 January 2018.

Elling, Agnes, and Jan Janssens. "Sexuality as a Structural Principle in Sport Participation." *International Review for the Sociology of Sport* 44.1 (2009): 71–86. Print.

ESPN. "Guillen Fined, Ordered to Take Sensitivity Training for Slur." ESPN.com. 23 June 2006. Web. 23 February 2018.

Felt, Hunter. "Jason Collins, First Openly Gay Player, Retires: Our Indifference Is His Triumph." *Guardian.* Guardian News and Media Limited, 20 November 2014. Web. 3 February 2018.

Fitzpatrick, Frank. "PSU Fines Women's Basketball coach: School Probe Finds Portland to Blame in Sex-bias Case." *Philadelphia Inquirer.* Philadelphia Media Network, 19 April 2006. Web. 3 February 2018.

Fulda, Owen. "Leicester Ban Three Supporters for Homophobic Chanting at Brighton Game." *Daily Express.* Express Newspapers, 19 September 2017. Web. 28 January 2018.

Garcia, Michelle. "NBA Will Protect Gay Players." TheAdvocate.com. The Advocate, 9 December 2011. Web. 21 February 2018.

Gibson, Owen. "Gay Rights Groups Attack FA Delay Over Anti-homophobia Film." *Guardian.* Guardian News and Media Limited, 8 February 2010. Web. 26 January 2018.

GLAAD. *GLAAD Media Reference Guide.* Tenth Edition. Print.

Gleeson, Scott. "Rookie Transition Program Elicits 'Straight Allies' in the NBA to Root Out Homophobia." *USA Today.* USA Today, 19 August 2015. Web. 21 February 2018.

Glenesk, Matthew. "Tony Dungy Says He Wouldn't Have Drafted Michael Sam." *Indianapolis Star.* IndyStar.com, 21 July 2014. Web. 5 February 2018.

Goessling, Ben. "Mike Priefer: 'Learned Hard Lesson.'" ESPN.com. 24 July 2014. Web. 5 February 2018.

Griner, Brittney. *In My Skin: My Life On and Off the Basketball Court.* New York: It Books, 2014. Print.

Hamilton, Xavier. "Gay Former NFL Player Wade Davis Works to End Homophobia in Pro Sports." Vibe.com. Billboard, 9 March 2018. Web. 9 March 2018.

Hardin, Marie, Kathleen M. Kuehn, Hillary Jones, Jason Genovese, and Murali Balaji. "'Have You Got Game?' Hegemonic Masculinity and Neo-Homophobia in U.S. Newspaper Sports Columns." *Communication, Culture and Critique* 2 (2009): 182–200. Print.

Harris, Nick, and Hugh Godwin. "Two Top Gay Footballers Stay in Closet: Max Clifford Says Football 'Steeped in Homophobia' as FA Reveals Premier League Stars Are Reluctant to Speak Up for Gay Rights." *Independent.* 20 December 2009. Web. 23 January 2018.

Harvey, Jean, John Horne, Parissa Safai, Simon Darnell, and Sebastien Courchesne-O'Neill. *Sport and Social Movements: From the Local to the Global.* London: Bloomsbury Press, 2013. Print.

Heck, Jordan. "Skip Bayless 'Dumbfounded' Troy Aikman Got Upset over Gay Claim." *Sporting News.* Sporting News Media, 23 November 2016. Web. 17 February 2018.

Heitner, Darren. "All 30 NBA Teams Release LGBT Pride Month T-Shirts." Forbes.com. Forbes Media, 7 June 2016. Web. 21 February 2018.

Hersh, Philip. "IOC Moves to Support Gay Rights in Olympics." *Chicago Tribune.* 8 December 2014. Web. 21 February 2018.

International Gay Bowling Organization. "What is IGBO?" *IGBO.org.* 1 February 2018. Web. 1 February 2018.

International Gay Rodeo Association. "About the Archives: Who, What, Why, and When." *GayRodeoHistory.org.* 25 November 2017. Web. 8 March 2018.

Jones, Abigail. "The Frozen Closet." *Newsweek.* Newsweek, 30 January 2014. Web. 17 February 2018.

Kopay, David, and Perry Deane Young. *The David Kopay Story: An Extraordinary Self-Revelation.* New York: Plume Publishing, 1988. Print.

Kusmer, Ken, and Deanna Martin. "Dungy's Gay Marriage Comments Draw Support, Criticism." ESPN.com. 22 March 2007. Web. 5 February 2018.

Lindsey, Robert. "Billie Jean King Is Sued for Assets Over Alleged Lesbian Relationship." *New York Times.* New York Times, 30 April 1981. Web. 12 February 2018.

Lovett, Kenneth. "Ex-Worker's Suit Versus Yankees Strikes Out." *New York Post.* NYP Holdings, 23 December 2003. Web. 22 February 2018.

Lutz, Tom. "Russia and Qatar World Cups Are 'Insane' Due to Homophobia, Says Robbie Rogers." *Guardian.* Guardian News and Media Limited, 20 January 2015. Web. 19 February 2018.

Magrath, Rory, Eric Anderson, and Steven Roberts. "On the Door-Step of Equality: Attitudes toward Gay Athletes Among Academy-Level Footballers." *International Review for the Sociology of Sport* (2013): 1–18. *Sage Journals.* Web. 12 February 2018.

Major League Soccer. "Collective Bargaining Agreement between Major League Soccer and Major League Soccer Players Union, December 1, 2004-January 31, 2010." Web. 23 February 2018.

Markwell, Kevin, and David Rowe. "The International Gay Games: Subverting Homophobia or Selling Out?" *International Sports Studies* 25.1 (2014): 5–20. Print.

Mathias, Edward. "Big League Perestroika? The Implications of Fraser v Major League Soccer." *University of Pennsylvania Law Review* 148.1 (1999): 203–237. Print.

McManus, Jane. "Rookies to Hear about Sexuality." ESPN.com. 19 June 2013. Web. 24 February 2018.

Moore, Elliott. "Brittney Griner Publicly Comes Out as Gay in Interview with Sports Illustrated." *GLAAD.org* 18 April 2013. Web. 3 February 2018.

Mortazavi, Sayed Masoud. "Elimination of the Locker Room Closet: Analysis of Current Laws and Professional Sports Leagues' Policies Toward Gay Athletes." Journal of Civil Rights and Economic Development 28.4 (2016): 479–511. Print.

NHL Public Relations. "Hockey Is for Everyone Month Begins: NHL, NHLPA Campaign Celebrates Diversity, Inclusion Throughout February." NHL.com. 1 February 2018. Web. 17 February 2018.

Nylund, David. "When in Rome: Heterosexism, Homophobia, and Sports Talk Radio." *Journal of Sport and Social Issues* 28.2 (2004): 136–168. Print.

O'Callaghan, Eoin. "Adam Rippon, John Curry and Figure Skating's Complex History with Gay Athletes." *Guardian.* Guardian News and Media Limited, 17 February 2018. Web. 17 February 2018.

Panja, Tariq. "Ahead of World Cup, Fans Are Warned About Homophobia and Racism in Russia." *New York Times.* New York Times, 28 November 2017. Web. 21 February 2018.

Petchesky, Barry. "How One Gay Athlete's Coming Out Led to an Activists' War." Deadspin. com. Gizmodo Media Group, 20 May 2014. Web. 21 May 2014.

Pirks, Natalie. "Rainbow Laces: Campaign Hindered by Naive Communication." *BBC Sport.* BBC, 19 September 2013. Web. 28 February 2018.

Pringle, Richard. "Masculinities, Sport, and Power: A Critical Comparison of Gramscian and Foucauldian Inspired Theoretical Tools." *Journal of Sport and Social Issues* 29.3 (2005): 256–278. Print.

Pugmire, Lance. "Emile Griffith Dies at 75; Champion Boxer Struggled with His Sexuality." *Los Angeles Times.* Los Angeles Times, 23 July 2013. Web. 12 February 2018.

Reese, Phil. "Teaching Acceptance to the Pros." *Washington Blade.* Brown, Naff, Pitts Omnimedia, 28 August 2013. Web. 12 January 2018.

Rogers, Phil. "Arbitrator's Ruling Rocks Selig's Power: Braves Closer John Rocker Can Return to Camp Thursday and to the Atlanta Roster by April 18." *Chicago Tribune*. 2 March 2000. Web. 22 February 2018.

Rubin, Adam, and Dave Goldiner. "Mets Star: I'm Straight: Relaxed Piazza Quashes Rumors That He's Coming Out." *New York Daily News*. NYDailyNews.com, 22 May 2002. Web. 12 February 2018.

Seattle Gay News. "Seattle to Host Largest Gay Softball World Series this August." *Seattle Gay News*. 1 February 2008. Web. 8 March 2018.

Seibel, Deborah Starr. "Billie Jean King Recalls Women's Rights Struggle of Her Time." *New York Post*. NYP Holdings, 31 August 2013. Web. 12 February 2018.

Sobel, Ariel. "Why do NFL Teams Keep Asking Prospects if They're Gay?" TheAdvocate.com. The Advocate, 9 March 2018. Web. 9 March 2018.

Strauss, Chris. "Niners CB Culliver Says Gay Players Wouldn't Be Welcomed." *USA Today*. USA Today, 30 January 2013. Web. 12 February 2018.

Tignor, Steve. "Martina's Moment." Tennis.com. 29 April 2013. Web. 3 February 2018.

Vacchiano, Ralph. "Shockey Makes a Stern Apology for Gay Slurs on Radio." *New York Daily News*. NYDailyNews.com, 27 September 2002. Web. 12 February 2018.

Van Rheenen, Derek. "A Skunk at the Garden Party: The Sochi Olympics, State-sponsored Homophobia and Prospects for Human Rights through Mega Sporting Events." *Journal of Sport and Tourism* 19.2 (2014): 127–144. Print.

Vries, Lloyd. "Rocker Rocks the Boat Again." *CBS News*. CBS Interactive, 6 August 2002. Web. 23 February 2018.

Wallace, Kelly. "The Real March Madness: When Will Women's Teams Get Equal Buzz?" CNN.com. Cable News Network, 14 March 2016. Web. 3 February 2018.

West, Candace, and Don H. Zimmerman. "Doing Gender." *Gender and Society* 1.2 (1987): 125–151. Print.

Williams, Matt. "Is Homophobia in Football Still a Taboo?" *BBC Sport*. BBC, 10 November 2005. Web. 27 January 2018.

Wilson, Jeremy. "Footballers Urged to Tackle Homophobia in Game by Wearing Rainbow Laces in Their Boots." *Telegraph*. Telegraph Media Group, 16 September 2013. Web. 28 February 2018.

Windhorst, Brian. "Referee Bill Kennedy, Following Slur by Rajon Rondo, Announces He's Gay." ESPN.com. 15 December 2015. Web. 19 February 2018.

Witz, Billy. "Milestone for Gay Athletes as Rogers Plays for Galaxy." *New York Times*. New York Times, 27 May 2013. Web. 3 March 2018.

Woodward, Robert. "Liverpool to Be First Premier League Club Represented at Official LGBT Event." *Guardian*. Guardian News and Media Limited, 10 July 2012. Web. 28 February 2018.

You Can Play. "Major League Soccer and MLS Players Union Announce You Can Play Partnership." *YouCanPlayProject.org*. You Can Play, 12 June 2013. Web. 17 February 2018.

Zeigler, Cyd. "187 Pro Athletes' Reactions to Jason Collins." Outsports.com. VOX Media, 6 May 2013. Web. 3 February 2018.

_____. *Fair Play: How LGBT Athletes Are Claiming Their Rightful Place in Sports*. New York: Akashic Books, 2016. Print.

Behind the 8-Ball

The Status of Gender Inequality and Discrimination in Sport

Meghan E. Fox *and*
Francisco A. Villarruel

Femininity and its perceived stereotypes have contributed substantially to how females are viewed both domestically, as well as in the international community. In this essay, however, the focus of discussion will be on females in the United States. Women in the United States have faced ongoing adversity on multiple fronts, pushed toward some roles and away from others based merely on their gender and peoples' preconceived notions about what that means. Consequently, female athletes have long been hampered by these prejudices. Dating back to the start of the 20th century when sports began to emerge as a popular part of American culture, access to sports was denied to females because they were viewed as "too competitive, too strenuous, and too unfeminine" for their involvement (Pieper 50). Gender norms and societal values held steadfast to these thoughts for the first half of the century. Through the 1950s, athletics were seen as a strictly masculine activity, with words such as "amazon" or "muscle moll" being used to frame thoughts of females' participation in sport as undesirable (Pieper 50).

Societal ideas started to be reframed with the passing of Title IX and the Equal Rights Amendment (ERA) in 1972. These enactments by Congress offered regulatory relief towards gender inequality, particularly in secondary and post-secondary settings, and provided greater access to females in the field of education, and by extension, athletics. Despite the successes of Title IX, there is still plenty of room for positive change. There has been improvement regarding female's involvement in athletics, however there are still many stereotypes that persist. Under-recognition of female's talent, systemic causes of inequalities in comparison to men's athletics, and gender stereotyping are prominent faults in female's athletics rules and policy making. When compared to male student-athletes—especially in post-secondary programs— female student-athletes incur a similar incidence rate of sports-related injuries, and devote as many hours in training, but are more successful academically than their male counterparts (Reinbrecht 261). Research has also shown that women with sports backgrounds identify their experiences as an influential factor in their professional success (Schachter 46). In this regard, should equality in sports and opportunity for females not be of significant and immediate importance, being directly related to high levels of academic success and career achievement? Title IX is a viable solution, but there are many complex challenges that come with it and need redress. Future studies on the successes and limitations of Title IX will aid in determining the future direction for female's athletics. On a larger scale, athletics needs to transition from a commercial model to a participation model in order to allow further growth in opportunity for females and males alike. With additional research and adjustment to the model of athletics, the path to building a sports world with less stereotyping and more equity is possible but will require earnest input and effort from many different parties.

Stereotypes, Prejudices and the Female Identity

Prejudices and biases are and have been long-standing institutions rooted in the heart of society in the United States, with sports receiving no exemption. It is common knowledge that females historically have been underserved in terms of opportunity in sports and fair treatment as athletes. Attempts to gain more equality in sport, such as the inception of the Title IX ruling in 1972, have helped make strides toward equal treatment of female athletes, but have not been a universal fix. Societal stereotypes about females and systematic problems are still prevalent within sports today. Cultural biases in sports are nurtured by the idea of industry gender imprinting, which is defined as perpetuating what is acceptable and valued with respect to masculinity and femininity in society (Micelotta et al. 94). Research has supported that such gender imprinting is pervasive and has negatively affected females in all aspects of the male-dominated sports industry through three basic "liabilities": (1) identity, (2) conformity, and (3) differentiation (Micelotta et al. 94).

The female identity has been hampered by gender stereotyping and social norms within the sports world. It can be contended that there is an implied second-class status for women's teams. Female athletes generally receive inferior equipment, differential funding and facilities that are not always of the same quality, and reduced frequency and prevalence of mainstream media coverage as compared to their male counterparts (Hastie). At secondary and collegiate levels, segregation of male and female sports goes as far as to render differences in the naming of men's and women's teams. Men's teams are generally named after the school itself, whereas the name of women's teams typically include references to gender, such as "Lady." For example, a high school with a Viking as a mascot will name the men's team the "Vikings," whereas the women's team is referred to as the "Lady Vikings." This second-class status and treatment coincides with the postulation that females have athletically inferior bodies. With these athletically inferior bodies they are viewed as unable to keep up with the athletic rigors required by various sports—or, in other words, compete at the same level as the superior male athlete.

The game of tennis has long been at the center of the debate of femininity, athleticism, and equality (Schultz 16). In 1881 following a long-standing pattern of women as losing competitors, Major Wingfield, the inventor of Lawn Tennis, was determined to identify the cause of such predictable gender inferiority. Following a match with a female competitor and noting their distinctively differing sports dress, he suggested they each weigh their apparel. The female player's outfit weighed almost 11 pounds to Wingfield's donning of just over five pounds. He declared the socially accepted and gender accepted differences in sports garment as rationale for unfavorable disadvantage for women players and recommended a new standard in lawn tennis attire (Schultz 15). This led *Godey's Lady Book and Magazine* to publish an article in 1887 which included a guide to what a lady tennis player should wear. The article listed multiple elements, including a loose-fitting Norfolk shirt, serge drawers which were to be worn to the knee, and a loose-fitting skirt worn below knee length. These are all notable in that they assured modesty, but also allowed for better comfort (Schultz 15–16). We start to see here, that even in the early years of organized sport in the United States, modesty was a major factor in guiding the development of women's attire. Women were allowed to play the sport, but the primary concern was assuring modesty. This attitude implies that women were allowed to play because men decided to let them, not because it was their right.

Another example of a uniform discrepancy was depicted in the movie *A League of Their Own* (1992) which was based on a true story from 1943. In the movie, females who were allowed to play baseball had to wear skirts during competition (*A League of Their Own*). This uniform requirement was solely for the spectators' pleasure rather than performance enhancement, as skirts were not protective of flesh or privacy. Though change has occurred to create a more even playing field since these examples, differences in standards across sports still exist today.

Tennis has been at the center of conflict between sports and femininity over the course of sports history. In 1973, Billie Jean King faced off against Bobby Riggs in a match that later became known as "the Battle of the Sexes." With the match taking place a short time after the creation of Title IX, it became a catalyst for the movement demanding female's equality in sports, especially when King beat Riggs in straight sets (Paule-Koba 712). While King was not involved in the creation of Title IX, she took it up as a banner, and frequently fought against its critics in the public eye. King also founded and assisted in developing many platforms for the expansion of women's sports. She created a magazine, *womenSports*, which showcased female athletes when other magazines would not. She also founded the Women's Sports Foundation, which advocates for female athletes and for Title IX, and created both World Team Tennis and the Women's Tennis Association (WTA) (Paule-Koba 713). More recently, tennis has experienced dispute regarding sponsorship. In 1995, the WTA was reluctant to accept sponsorship from Tampax, a product designed to enable women to remain physically active. This provides further evidence of the stigmatism affiliated with femininity. At that time, Ann Worcester, the WTA's chief executive officer, voiced her concerns and related rationale: "We think that at a critical time when we're trying to increase the popularity of the Tour, we did not believe Tampax sponsorship would be in our best interest. Seventy-five percent of the insiders and experts we polled felt this would have a long-term negative impact" (Schultz 47). Schultz summarized it this way: "From the beginning, the makers of commercial tampons struck advertising gold by featuring sport and athletic women, but because the tampon's primary selling point is that it conceals the social taboo of menstruation, real women athletes and their respective organizations often recoiled from the association" (48). Martina Navratilova, a tennis standout, expressed her disappointment that the WTA would shun such a product that has been key in making women's physical activity in sports possible (Schultz 48).

Throughout the modern sports world in the United States, discrepancies in rules and standards for males and females exist in all competition levels from youth to professional. Among these discrepancies, we again find tennis, in the professional ranks, males play five sets while females only play three. These disparities riddle other sports as well. In official competition, female basketball players use a smaller sized ball than males. In the game of volleyball, nets are lower in female's competitions. Female golfers play from closer tee boxes, which lead to shorter courses. In lacrosse, females are equipped with far less protective equipment and prohibited from the same amount of physical contact as male lacrosse players ("Rules"). Similarly, in ice hockey, females are not allowed to engage in body checking while males are allowed and encouraged as this is considered an important component in their game tactics ("IIHF Rules"; Terlep). They have changed the rules of the sport to make it less physical, baselessly citing physicality concerns as the reason for the differences. This is the antithesis of sports like rugby and soccer, which are very popular internationally, and have no differences in rules despite being very physical in nature. Co-ed sports also give females certain advantages during play that make the game "easier" (McDonagh and Pappano A17). With varying playing standards, such as the aforementioned, sport causes more segregation based on sex than equality in opportunity. Each of these differences undermines female athleticism, doting them inferior. Their athletic ability in endurance and strength are considered subpar to that of their male counterparts, which is highlighted by the differences in rules (McDonagh and Pappano A.17). Historically, females have been viewed as frail and fragile when compared to males; and thus, not well made for the rigors of sport. This is perhaps the reason sports programs have largely been male dominated, shaped by masculine behaviors and practices within the industry (Micelotta et al. 99).

The female stereotype has interfused the very culture of sports, permeating all levels of competition. Certain sports have been deemed socially appropriate and readily accepted for female's participation, while others have been regarded as too harsh and unladylike. Sports, such as discus and shot put, require great muscular strength to optimally perform. The muscular physique does not fit with the petite, slim image that is the poster child of the perfect woman's body (Pieper 35). The stigma associated with having "big muscles" deters sport participation for young female athletes who are concerned with body image above all else. Studies have shown that roughly 90 percent of women are unhappy with their body image and have tried dieting to improve it. Additionally, it is estimated that 60 percent of college-age women do not think they have "the ideal body type" ("11 Facts About Body Image"). These are staggering statistics when examined through any lens, but especially when considering the mental toll and added pressure this places on an athlete while they are concurrently readying themselves for sports competition.

Under-Recognition of Female Sports

Soccer and the United States
Women's National Team

Female athletes frequently face under-recognition for their athletic displays when compared to their male counterparts. Title IX has attempted to reduce females' barriers to sport and increase access, however these efforts only address an aspect of female inequity, not the cause of prejudices. In addition to the differences previously noted, there are many other challenges, including equivalent pay, recognition, spectatorship, and professional future in sport. Recognized as one of the most successful national teams in the most popular sport around the world, the United States Women's National Soccer Team (USWNT) has not been immune to the effects of gender discrimination. Winning three World Cups and four Olympic gold medals, their success has been unequaled in the United States, and they have far outshone the accomplishments of the Men's National Team (USMNT). However, they have always received less pay and inferior treatment when compared to the USMNT, both historically and present day. Carli Lloyd, current captain of the women's team, stated this about the U.S. Soccer Federation (the organization that runs both the men's and women's teams): "We feel like we're treated like second-class citizens because they don't care as much about us as they do the men" (O'Donnell).

A year apart, in 2014 and 2015, the U.S. men's and women's teams both competed in their respective World Cup. While the USMNT was eliminated in the first round of knockout play for the second consecutive cup, the USWNT team took home first place, after losing in the final match in the previous cup. Germany was victorious on the men's side, and was awarded $35 million by FIFA, while the USWNT was awarded only $2 million by FIFA. This delta of $33 million is unsurprising when the annual pay distribution for each team is examined. In 2014–2015, the salaries of the top player for the men's and women's team were compared by CBS News and upon a breakdown by game the female player received three times less pay. Hope Solo was paid $366,000 after playing in 23 games, while Tim Howard was paid $398,495 for playing in a mere eight games. In addition to pay differences, there exist other discrepancies in standards of treatment based on gender. For example, when traveling to a match the women's team often flies coach, while the men's team flies first class (O'Donnell). Additionally, the women's team typically has to compete on turf, which is known to pose prominent injury risks, while the men enjoy competition on natural grass. This disparity is far reaching, even requiring sod be laid down for a men's game, irrespective of cost, if they play at a stadium with turf (Dockterman). Such disparate treatment is remarkable considering performance-based outcomes. The USMNT recently failed to qualify for the 2018 World Cup, which many purport was an embarrassing moment in U.S. soccer history. By comparison, the USWNT will head into the 2019 World Cup heavily favored to win. Historically, the women have never finished worse than third place in the seven World Cups played since 1991. The men, on the other hand, have competed since 1930 when they finished in third place, which remains their best finish ever ("FIFA World Cup Archive"). With these obvious disparities at the most elite level, a trickle down and expansion effect would be expected across all sporting levels.

Impact of Sports Media

Media coverage is a dynamic medium for information relay, recognition, and entertainment, and plays a significant role in spectator intrigue and engagement during any sporting competition or event. With sports imbedded as a dominant force in American society, sports media coverage has garnered exponential influence over millions of people. It therefore comes as no surprise that the media have played a role in the lackluster viewership of women's sports. The coverage of women's sports programming over the past three decades has been starkly less than that devoted to men's programming. Differences are found both in the number of women in sports media broadcasting, and in the lack of airtime dedicated to women's sport-related programming. Ironically, while female's participation in sports in the United States has increased, coverage of such programs has declined over recent years (Walker and Melton 82). This decline in television coverage is occurring despite the fact there are some women's sports teams earning favorable ratings. The USWNT recently set ratings records for soccer in the United States, with 23 million viewers for the 2015 World Cup Final. These are higher ratings than any men's soccer game in U.S. history, and are numbers comparable to a World Series game in baseball ("Women's World Cup Final").

It has been purported that sports viewership depends on making a connection between spectators and the stories behind the athletes. Lower ratings of women's sports programs are associated with the premise that the athletes', coaches', and teams' stories remain untold. In an interview, ESPN journalist Kate Fagan explained: "In women's sports, because of lack of exposure, the casual fan knows nothing about either team. The casual fan knows very little background information about the players, teams, and coaches, because the media doesn't spend as much time telling stories about women's sports, as they do with the men's sports" (Walker and Melton 86). Patterns of funding and appropriation of resources in sports suggest an affinity for high-level masculine programs, such as American football, that are manifested by fierce competition and demonstration of power. Even male sports programs that do not comparably embody the same masculine characteristics receive only nominal funding and airtime, a challenge also confronted by women's sports programs. In 2013, women's programs received a lackluster 0.4 percent of commercial sponsorships and 5 percent of sports television airtime (Micelotta et al. 100). With the obvious disparity in coverage and adverse effects on female athletic programs, sports media continues to use its limited coverage of female athletes to highlight physical appearances, storylines about femininity, or heterosexuality (Walker and Melton 83). This has limited the popularity of female athletes, and consequently caused unfavorable effects on female's athletics as a whole.

The lack of exposure has also caused a difference in sponsorship opportunity for men's and women's athletics. The Women's National Basketball Association (WNBA) pioneered the use of sponsor patches appearing on professional jerseys in the United States (Sandomir). While commonplace in foreign countries, American professional teams were hesitant to commit to advertising on jerseys. In 2017, the NBA followed this precedent and began using sponsor patches as a way of boosting revenue (Kutz). Because of the high exposure the jerseys receive, some men's teams are charging as much as $20 million per season for a small shoulder patch. Comparably, the WNBA has larger advertisements on their jerseys, but due to limited revenues and exposure they typically charge around $1 million per sponsorship (Sandomir). These differences are also evident when comparing money for television sponsorship. ESPN pays the WNBA $12 million annually to broadcast games, while in contrast, ESPN and Turner Sports are currently in the midst of a nine-year, $24 billion broadcasting partnership with the NBA (Lefton and Ourand; Rubin). The financial gap in sponsorship money is not limited to basketball and soccer. In golf, both the men's (PGA) and women's (LPGA) professional golf associations host a major championship, and title sponsors pay for the purse, which is the money split by the players depending on where they finish. In 2017, the men's purse was set at $10.5 million, while the women's was only set at $3.5 million ("2017 PGA Championship"; "2017 KPMG Women's PGA Championship"). These continued disparities in fund allotment across sports are noticeable evidence that discrimination exists and remains prevalent, even in these times of hyperawareness.

Title IX

History of Title IX

The U.S. government has put forth efforts to reduce females' barriers to sport. One major effort was the establishment and passage of Title IX. Originally, there had been five different bills introduced to Congress proposing to end sex discrimination in education. While there was agreement that such discrimination should end, agreement could not be reached on how to do it (Vest and Masterson 60). In 1972, the United States Congress passed Title IX as part of the Educational Amendments to the 1964 Civil Rights Act (CRA). Since its inception, Title IX has been a leap forward in equality for females in work, sport, and education. This legal provision has a twofold primary purpose: (1) prevent federal funding being issued to academic institutions engaged in discriminatory actions that precluded educational opportunities based on sex, and (2) provide individual mechanisms for redress (Lanser

180). Title IX requires that all institutions of higher education provide student access to sport participation on a gender-neutral basis ("Requirements under Title IX"). When Title IX was first passed in 1972, only 15 percent of college athletes were women. Fast forward to the turn of the century, and that number had risen to 42 percent (Anderson et al. 225). However, debate remains whether the goals established under this legislation have been achieved or if it has instead delivered unintended, undesirable results. The National Collegiate Athletic Association (NCAA) attempted to derail Title IX policies from their inception. In 1974, the NCAA asked the Department of Health, Education, and Welfare to lobby for an exclusion of athletics from the new law. The NCAA also supported the proposed Tower Amendment, which would have exempted men's football and basketball from Title IX coverage. Justly so, this proposed change was challenged in court for its constitutionality and lost (Bryjak 62).

Designed to assess equality of treatment and compliance to Title IX, the Equity in Athletics Disclosure Act (EADA) requires approximately 700 institutions in NCAA Divisions I, II, and III to report their compliance to the law. For intercollegiate athletics, Title IX applies to three fundamental areas: (1) financial assistance to athletes, (2) treatment, benefits, and opportunities for intercollegiate athletics, (3) equal opportunity. There is a three-prong test that has been established to measure compliance to this legislation:

> 1. Substantial Proportionality—this part of the test is satisfied when participation opportunities for men and women are "substantially proportionate" to their respective undergraduate enrollments.
> 2. History and Continuing Practice—This part of the test is satisfied when an institution has a history and continuing practice of program expansion that is responsive to the developing interests and abilities of the underrepresented sex (typically female).
> 3. Effectively Accommodating Interests and Abilities—This part of the test is satisfied when an institution is meeting the interests and abilities of its female students even where there are disproportionately fewer females than males participating in sports [Anderson et al. 228].

While compliance is measured based on these three tests, noncompliance is determined based on failure in all three. Title IX holds that "no person in the United States shall, on the basis of sex, be excluded from participation in, be denied the benefits of, or be subjected to discrimination under any education program or activity receiving Federal financial assistance" ("Title IX, Education Amendments of 1972"). Since most schools receive Federal financial assistance, scholastic and collegiate sports fall under Title IX. However, the law also applies to access to higher education, athletics, career education, education for pregnant and parenting students, employment, learning environment, math and science, sexual harassment, standardized testing, and technology (Forry 725).

The final regulations for Title IX were made available in 1975 and required all schools to be compliant by 1978 (Stevenson 488). Since its enactment, there have been some significant historical milestones related to Title IX. In 1974, the aforementioned Tower Amendment was proposed to exempt revenue-producing sports, such as football, when determining compliance. This amendment was, however, voted down by the U.S. Senate. In 1984, the U.S. Supreme Court ruled in *Grove City v. Bell* that Title IX does not apply to athletic departments since they do not receive Federal funding. This ruling temporarily cancelled Title IX coverage of intercollegiate sports. In 1988, Congress passed the Civil Rights Restoration Act of 1987 in response to the 1984 Supreme Court decision. This clarified that Title IX applies to all activities and programs in K-12 schools and higher education institutions. In 1992, the Supreme Court ruling for *Franklin v. Gwinnett County Public Schools* found that prevailing Title IX plaintiffs could receive monetary damages. In a Federal Appeals Court case, *Cohen v. Brown University*, it was ruled that the university's argument of women being less interested in sports did not justify discrimination in women's sports. A decade later in 2006, the Department of Education's Office of Civil Rights asserted that requirements for compliance testing could be met using electronic surveys to determine female students interest in playing sports (Schachter 49). However, in 2010, the U.S. Department of Education withdrew the policy. Women's groups long criticized the survey because non-response could be considered as a lack of interest, negatively affecting women's opportunities (Brady 01C). This reversal was applauded as a victory by both the NCAA and women's sports groups, while being viewed as a disappointing setback by men's sports advocacy groups. According to a statement by then-vice president Joe Biden, "We have a long way to go still, and we want to take away every barrier that exists. Forty years from now if we still need Title IX, we will have failed" (Sander). Biden was further quoted as stating Title IX will "allow women to realize their potential—so this nation can realize its potential" (Jones 8; Paulson 3).

Title IX: Assessing Its Current State

The effect of Title IX on sport continues to be controversial, therefore it is the section of the law that is most frequently in the public spotlight causing discussion (Forry 725). The positive effects of Title IX cannot be understated, with the evidence of many success stories. In the years following Title IX, the numbers of females participating in sports skyrocketed. Specifically, at the high school level, a significant surge in sport program involvement has been recognized. Pre-legislation, 300,000 female student-athletes competed in high school sports in the United States. Comparatively, 40 years after Title IX's enactment, increased access led to nearly 3.2 million female competitors, reflecting a 1,000 percent increase in participation (Lanser 181–182). Two years after the enactment of Title IX, there were still vast differences in numbers of athletic scholarships given by schools. At that time, 50,000 men received scholarships nationwide, while the number was actually less than 50 for women ("Title IX: 25 Years"). Today, it is estimated that over 200,000 women participate in college sports compared to 30,000 before the legislation was passed, with many of these receiving financial aid from their school in return for their participation (Lanser 181–182). Additionally, there has been an increase in the number of women's teams per school at the college level. The average number of women's sports teams has risen from 2.5 per school in 1970 pre-legislation, to an average of 8.73 teams in 2012 (Bower and Hums 214). It is maintained that the skills females learn by participating in athletics teach them to face fears, confront limitations, and perform in public. These opportunities continue to grow as access to athletics for females continue to increase.

These opportunities are considered a pathway that will have effects not only for today, but for a lifetime. It has been maintained "[t]here are blessings that come from women being able to play sports and then contribute to society because they got that educational scholarship." Inasmuch, "80 percent of women executives point to their sports experiences as an influence" in their career success (Schachter 46). The NCAA currently sponsors 88 championships in 29 sports for both men and women's college teams. Although Title IX was enacted in 1972 and put into force in 1978, the first women's championship competition was not until 1980, the NCAA National Rifle Championship. Additionally, a women's team did not receive a first place in a NCAA championship until 1981 when Pfeiffer University, a Division II school, took the first spot in field hockey (Kennedy 34). According to the National Coalition for Women and Girls in Education, despite the significant strides that have been made by Title IX, high school females receive about 1.1 million fewer opportunities than high school males to play sports. While sports have been recognized as a natural comfort zone for males, they are considered a bridge to opportunities for females. When females play on old fields or gyms that are in disrepair while males enjoy the most state of the art facilities, inequity becomes the argument. This is not considered a radical feminist view, but rather a perspective that maintains that sports are good for females and Title IX was designed to address some of these disparities (Conniff).

The U.S. Department of Education agrees that Title IX has had a positive impact. One of the biggest changes is that there has been a substantive increase in the number of women who decided to attend college. With this, other positive results include

1. women completing four-year degrees increased from 18 percent to now being equivocal to men.
2. women receiving medical and dental degrees significantly increased.
3. the proportion of women receiving law degrees increased from 7 percent to 43 percent.
4. the proportion of women earning doctoral degrees increased from 25 to 44 percent.
5. female participation in school athletics has increased 400 percent (Anderson and Bourassa).

While there remain critics, others maintain Title IX provides athletic opportunities for females in sports. It is argued that female's sports tend to represent the purest form of athletics and academics and have kept alive the ideology of the scholar-athlete (Conniff).

Critiques of Title IX

There are critics that argue that Title IX helps some, while it ignores the needs of others. In one study of high school students, sports participation was viewed as an activity that served the privileged. They maintained that students of married, wealthy, educated parents were more likely to play sports. Therefore, while Title IX provided additional access for females, it did so more exclusively for the protection of the top tier of the income distribution (Stevenson 502). It has also been contended that males need sports more than females. Sports have "provided men with psychological separation from the perceived feminization of society while also providing dramatic symbolic proof of the natural superiority of men over women" (Messner 200). Our culture has applauded males for participation in sports and provided resources to support this endeavor. Researchers maintain that males need sports as a socialization forum, while females can find other avenues to achieve the like (Rhoads 90). Additionally, it has been argued that it has created unintended outcomes of segregation by sex and reinforced ideas that males and females should not play together (National Coalition).

In Congressional testimony, Nancy Hogshead-Makar, former swimming collegiate athlete at Duke University and Olympic champion and now professor of law at Florida Coastal School of Law, indicated that there are a few previously discredited arguments against Title IX that have reappeared in recent times:

1. That Title IX is a quota law.
2. That these quotas force schools to cut men's teams.
3. That women's opportunities are inflated—that is, they do not

desire opportunities in sports because of a purported lack of interest in athletics.

Hogshead-Makar contends that all these claims are factually unsupportable. She further maintained that Title IX provides protections for both men and women sports and ensures that educational decisions are not based on stereotypes about males and females. In agreement, another study evaluated the impact of Title IX on men's sports and concluded that institutions are more likely to add female teams rather than reduce or eliminate men's programs (Anderson and Cheslock 310). Conversely, Rhoads contends that the effect of Title IX on athletic departments has resulted in 21,000 spots for male athletes cut from sports programs and 359 male teams eliminated (88). However, it should be acknowledged that some of these numbers are skewed. The elimination of sports programs has mainly occurred at the NCAA Division I level and is due to the university's money allocation choices (Cook 1–2). The dilemma for athletic directors is that they are under pressure to increase revenue. The easiest way for them to accomplish this is through successful football and basketball programs. However, while there is a push to do this, there remains the responsibility to proactively increase the number of females in sports to comply with Title IX. Sometimes these two objectives come into conflict with one another (Kennedy 35). College football has long been noted as a producer of commercial benefits. The first football television contract was signed by the NCAA for just over $1 million in the 1950s and by 1993, Division I-A football programs alone amassed approximately $6 million per school (Reinbrecht 251). From a commercial stance, the motive of some universities who purposely put a greater amount of money into sports that produce the greatest amount of revenue (i.e., football), while marginalizing and eliminating those who are not producing as much revenue, is understandable (Cook 1–2). However, this unfairly creates criticism of Title IX which, in and of itself, is not to blame.

While there are those who see Title IX as a continuous journey, others believe the policies have arrived at the final destination. One research study, involving high school and collegiate athletic directors' perspective on Title IX, concluded that Title IX has made no changes in the number of female athletes in recent years. Therefore, they believe that Title IX has accomplished its original purpose and female participation in sports has now been stabilized (Vest and Masterson 61). It is maintained "[as] with affirmative action, the law's opponents argue that the job is done—women have reached equality and no longer need special attention. This argument resonates with girls of the post–Title IX generation, who feel pangs of guilt when Title IX is blamed for the elimination of minor men's sports" (Conniff). These advocates for females in sports suggest that societal discrimination has played a role in female's interest in sports. As they purport, "Women aren't less interested in sports. Society conditions them" (Rhoads 93). It is argued that cheerleading and competitive dance should be recognized as a sport under tracking purposes for Title IX. Since female's interest is high in these areas, it should be given the competitive sports status it deserves ("A Title IX Ruling").

Title IX has changed the landscape of athletics. It has prompted more comparable budgeting and participation numbers between males and females, as well as provided opportunities for females that previously were not in existence (Vest and Masterson 60). While it has led to unfavorable outcomes, such as men's sports teams being reduced or eliminated to bring about athletic parity, this may be the price to be paid for gender equity. In a CBS poll of 1,000 adults, a substantive 77 percent supported gender parity in collegiate sports (Bryjak 63). This stands as an indicator that societal paradigms are beginning to shift, and the playing field is leveling for females in athletics and academics.

Impact on Professionals

One aspect of Title IX that has shown surprising results is, statistically, it has hindered women seeking professional careers in athletics, whether in coaching or administration. This has led to much debate. While there has been a 185 percent increase in coaching positions since the enactment of Title IX, 98 percent of these new positions have been filled by men. This demonstrates a shift from 90 percent of women's teams being coached by women prior to Title IX to only 40 percent afterward. In male dominated sports, the prevalence of women in administrative and coaching positions has been even more disparate. For example, as of 2007 only 6 of the 120 Division I Football Bowl Subdivision (FBS) schools had a female serving as their athletic director. A nominal 3 percent of collegiate men's teams had female coaches, with no women serving as either head or assistant coach for any men's baseball, basketball, football, or hockey team (Lanser 182–183). The percentages of females coaching men's teams are marginally higher at the Division II and Division III levels, at 7 percent and 8 percent, respectively (Women's Sports Foundation 21). Societally, it tends to be acceptable for men to coach women's sports, but not vice versa. Therein lies the double standard of sports in America today. In a recent study, men reported that Title IX had led to discriminatory hiring practices, yet female coaches still trail in numbers to their male counterparts (Bower and Hums 226). The hangover effect of men having a historical advantage of access to participate in athletics and gaining valuable experience in working in athletic programs, coupled with unconscious biases, continues to perpetuate the idea that women are simply unqualified or uninterested to assume such coaching responsibilities. This can be considered a carryover from inaccurate characterizations that remain evident today and extend into the business world (Lanser 183).

A 2016 survey of college coaches showed some reasoning as to why Title IX has been less helpful in professional ranks. Over 2,200 coaches of women's teams from all levels of the NCAA responded to the survey about sex-related hiring practices and equality. Two-thirds of participants surveyed thought it was easier for men to get top-level jobs in women's sports, and three-fourths thought men had an easier time negotiating salary increases (Women's Sports Foundation 2–3). The most concerning result of the survey was the coaches' perception of institutional support. Female coaches reported feeling more concern than male coaches about approaching anyone in an administrative role about issues regarding Title IX. One-third of all survey responders reported that they avoided bringing up Title IX issues because it could "risk losing their job" (Women's Sports Foundation 3, 29). This divide in how coaches view job security is concerning, and shows that Title IX is a complex issue that requires a vast amount of oversight. To help combat the concerns of coaches, and help prevent future issues, some athletic programs have started performing audits within their athletic departments. The goal of these audits is to ensure Title IX mandates are being followed, especially in regard to coach compensation and equal access to funding for both men's and women's teams. In the limited data, this has shown positive results (Women's Sports Foundation 58).

Women who are attempting to make careers in athletics have had a tough time breaking into the field. Based on the characteristics of the male-dominated sports industry, professional career paths in the field are generally assumed to require masculine traits. This often leads to discriminatory hiring practices that favor male candidates (Micelotta et al. 100). Women tend to be found in areas such as compliance and academic support, whereas areas like event management, coaching, and administration are dominated by men (Whalen 2). The lack of women in athletics has led to a monopolizing affect in the industry. Women have struggled to network because of the shortage of diversity, which has in turn caused more women to feel isolated and leave the profession. It has been purported that young women better envision themselves in roles of authority when they have female leaders as role models. There is supporting research that contends that the lack of female leaders contributes to the negative stereotypes of women in sports (Lanser 185). Women have also stated that "knowing sports trivia and recent statistics is important when conversing with male colleagues" (Whalen 5). Many men look at sports trivia and knowledge as a test to see if women really "know sports." Knowledge of such trivial information has led to disparate treatment, with the associated prejudices difficult to remove.

Women who work in athletic administration positions have revealed that the leading challenges of these roles are conflict of family and work, as well as gender discrimination (Machida-Kosuga et al. 23). These issues can lead to job burnout, which further the isolation felt by women. Thus, a problematic cycle in athletics has been inadvertently created. With the shortage of women in the field, others feel discouraged from seeking athletic employment (Whalen 5). One positive, perhaps, is the fact that professional sports leagues have been more progressive than colleges. A number of NBA and NFL teams employ women as coaches, and the leagues employ women as officials (Whalen 16). There is hope that this could pave the way for college and high school athletics, and eventually numbers may begin to even out.

Implications for Females' Futures

Acosta and Carpenter revealed their lack of confidence in Title IX achieving its ideal aims as they remarked "implementation of the federal anti-sex discrimination legislation known as Title IX is akin to an aggravating trip that seems to take forever to arrive at its destination" (22). They further indicated that the timeframe in which the law has had to make an impact and create the desired change can now be measured in terms of nine generations of students. However, these researchers contend that the desired end-result of Title IX is yet to be fully realized. Indicators of success under this law would include the following outcomes.

1. Title IX requirements are viewed as the normal paradigm rather than things to be circumvented or feared.

2. The institutional role of athletics relates to the mission of the college or university in demonstrable ways.

3. The value of the athletic experience is determined not by the fan base but by the experience of the individual athlete.

4. College presidents have higher salaries than athletic directors or coaches.

5. Coaching compensation relates to the job being done, not to the sex of the athletes being coached, the sex of the coach, or the sport being coached.

6. Supporters of athletics teams focus on program-wide loyalty rather than to a particular sport.

7. Negative pressures on life-balance issues have been eliminated.

8. Self-delusional notions that big-time football programs contribute financially to an institution are understood to be false and thus no longer motivate bad administrative decisions.

9. Women coaches of men's teams are accepted and supported for their coaching skills, without regard to their sex.

10. Women athletic directors are not an endangered species.

11. Decisions about hiring and firing coaches and administrative staff are made by school leaders rather than fans and alumni [Acosta and Carpenter 23].

To parity and achieve these kinds of results, there are four notable barriers Acosta and Carpenter contend need to be mitigated for greater distributive equity: (1) compensation, (2) time, (3) respect, and (4) will (23). For example, a challenge remains for colleges to ensure equal compensation is given to sports teams, regardless of gender, and to solve equity-based funding issues. Some schools search for creative solutions to allow both men and women teams to be equally funded, while others reduce or eliminate funding in some programs to comply with the legislation. The latter fuels the debate about unintended consequences of Title IX.

Efforts to improve the language and correct the issues involved with Title IX have been constant. There are different means of studying the effects of Title IX, but research has shown the following tests to be successful in helping instill good practices in sport. Research has shown these three tests to be successful at determining if non-discriminatory practices in athletics are in place.

1. A test of quantitative sameness in the sense of equal numbers, numbers proportional to overall numbers of participants. This test is applied to participation rates and scholarships.

2. A test of equivalence in effect in the sense of whether women and men are similarly able to play their sport. This test is applied to factors that differ by sports, such as equipment, transportation costs, or crowd management costs.

3. A test of full and effective accommodation in the sense of whether sports are offered at kinds and levels of opportunity needed to provide opportunities that suit the interests of the existing or anticipated student body. This test is applied to sport selection and competition levels, but does not require integration of sports or selection of exactly the same sports for men and women [Frances 86].

It has been shown that females who participate in sports reap tangible present and future benefits. Those females who participate in high school sports have been found to be 20 percent more likely to persist to graduation and continue on to higher levels of education. Multiple personal and educational benefits have been realized by female students' athletic participation. Such outcomes include teamwork, discipline, focus on excellence in undertakings, and skills honed while playing competitive sports (Reinbrecht 251). All of these positive traits have the opportunity to be built upon with the expansion and enhancement of Title IX. In addition to advances in education, there have been increases in the workplace. Females are starting to work full-time in positions that have been traditionally thought of as male-dominated occupations. These growths have been shown to be tied to increases in high school sports participation for females (Cook 1–2). In addition, multiple studies have maintained that women in leadership positions at Fortune 500 companies and in sports leadership positions, such as athletic director or coach, frequently outperformed their competition (Lanser 184–185). Such successes in business should not be ignored.

Recent trends have also shown a rise in public support for women's rights, and an interest in their physical welfare (Schultz 128). This is a significant societal shift in how women are viewed. One of the first examples of this, post-legislation, comes from the June 1978 edition of *Time*. This edition included a feature article titled "Comes the Revolution," which focused on women in sports and their symbolism during this time of athletic metamorphosis. The article credited the fitness craze, feminist movement, and legislative mandates with the evolution of women in sports. They also noted that these created new ideals of beauty from more feminine to masculine regarded traits, such as playing competitively and aggressively for themselves as individuals. A second and follow up cover story was published in 1982 which outlined the progress made, but left question to societal acceptance: "You've come a long way, sister. The sports for which you were once only a cheerleader now serve as your after-work recreation and, thanks to Title IX, part of your school-age daughter's curriculum. Spurred by feminism's promise of physical, domestic, and economic freedom, you have done what few generations of women have dared or chose to do. You have made muscles—a body of them—and it shows. And you look great" (Schultz 124–125).

These trends could be beneficial in evening out the playing field in athletics, both as participants and administrators. To help encourage the expansion of women's roles in athletics, there are many strategies that can be put in place to assist the women in these roles. Research shows that challenging job assignments, frequent feedback about development, and supportive behavior from colleagues and peers can lead to enhanced success in administrative jobs for women (Machida-Kosuga et al. 6–7). Another way to expand the number of women in leadership roles in the future is to teach the idea of leader self-efficacy, which is found to be prevalent among women in administrative positions (Machida-Kosuga et al. 21). Based on social cognitive theory, leader self-efficacy should reflect leaders' acquisition of core competencies needed to lead effectively while also providing the impetus for action they need to persevere in developing themselves and maintaining ambitious career goals. Female athletic administrators' leader self-efficacy is positively related to their ascendance to higher levels of leadership status (Machida-Kosuga et al. 21). If women in athletic administration roles can be bolstered by support around them instead of pushed out by male colleagues, we could start to see job growth in that area for women. Although this is a sound strategy for growth, it could take many years for anything to come to fruition. More initiative on the part of hiring committees and recruiting firms, along with potential changes to Title IX language, will be needed to instill real change. Based on the presented evidence, conditions are more equal today than at any point in history. These ideas and trends are reason enough to be optimistic about the future of women in athletics.

Conclusion

Females in sports, both those who participate and those that work professionally, still face discrimination on a daily basis from many fronts. They statistically are paid less, receive less recognition for their work, are given fewer media opportunities, and athletes have fewer options to play professionally. The fight for equality for females in sport is of paramount importance, as research has shown participation in sports can increase future success in careers for females (Schachter 46). Participating in athletics can help teach females to lead, be members of a team, and the importance of dedication. The enactment of Title IX in 1972 was a necessary step. The legislation helped females to begin to earn some of the same rights as males in education and athletics, though some critics still maintain that its policies are segregating in nature. While Title IX has anecdotally amplified some of the differences between males and females, the positive impact it has had on female's sports is unparalleled. Before the establishment of Title IX, very few women's athletic teams offered any financial aid for athletes. Since its enactment, collegiate sport participation amongst females is up over 600 percent, and many of those athletes are able to receive full or partial scholarships (National Coalition). According to the NCAA and its requirements for regulatory compliance, Title IX mandates equal treatment for male and female student-athletes in the following areas.

a. The provision of equipment and supplies
b. Scheduling of games and practice time
c. Travel and per diem allowance
d. Opportunity to receive coaching and academic tutoring
e. Assignment and compensation of coaches and tutors
f. Provision of locker rooms, practice, and competitive facilities
g. Provision of medical and training facilities and services
h. Provision of housing and dining facilities and services

  i. Publicity
  j. Recruitment ["Women, Gender Equity, and Title IX"].

These are progressive mandates. However, they need to be built upon as inequality remains. Hopefully with the increasing levels of access, and continued work and collaboration on Title IX, increasing levels of equity will follow. The continued fight against discrimination and injustice in sport is an issue that begins at youth levels and render ramifications for a lifetime. With Title IX policies in place, while there is still much room to grow, the future of females in sports has never been brighter.

WORKS CITED

Acosta, R. Vivian, and Linda Carpenter. "Are We There Yet? Thirty-seven Years Later, Title IX Hasn't Fixed It All." *Academe* 95.4 (2009): 22–24. *Academic Search Premier*. Web. 27 December 2017.

Anderson, Deborah, and John Cheslock. "Institutional Strategies to Achieve Gender Equity in Intercollegiate Athletics: Does Title IX Harm Male Athletes?" *American Economic Review* 94.2 (May 2004): 307–311. *Business Source Premier*. Web. 27 December 2017.

Anderson, Deborah, et al. "Gender Equity in Intercollegiate Athletics: Determinants of Title IX Compliance." *Journal of Higher Education* 77.2 (March/April 2006): 225–250. *Academic Search Premier*. Web. 28 December 2017.

Anderson, Tim, and Cheryl Bourassa. *Point: The Importance of Title IX Legislation*, 2016. *Points of View Reference Center*. Web. 29 December 2017.

Bower, Glenna, and Mary Hums. "The Impact of Title IX on Career Opportunities in Intercollegiate Athletic Administration." *Journal of Intercollegiate Sport* 6.2 (Dec. 2013): 213–230. *EBSCO*. Web. 28 December 2017.

Brady, Erik. "Title IX Model Survey Policy to be Rescinded." *USA Today*. USA Today, 20 April 2010. Web. 29 December 2017.

Bryjak, George. "The Ongoing Controversy Over Title IX." *USA Today*. USA Today, July 2000). Web 29 December 2017.

Conniff, Ruth. "Title IX: Political Football." *The Nation* 276.11 (2003). *Academic Search Premier*. Web. 27 December 2017.

Cook, Sarah. "Title IX Is 40 Years Old: Why Aren't We There Yet?" *Women in Higher Education* (2012): 1–2. *Wiley Online Library*. Web. 28 December 2017.

Dockterman, Eliana. "U.S. Women's Soccer Team Refuses to Play on Turf." *TIME*, Time, 8 December 2015. Web. 11 March 2018.

"11 Facts About Body Image." *DoSomething.org*. Web. 27 December 2017.

"FIFA World Cup Archive." *FIFA*. FIFA. Web. 27 December 2017.

Forry, Joan. "Out of Play: Critical Essays on Gender and Sport/Equal Play: Title IX and Social Change/Playing with the Boys: Why Separate Is Not Equal in Sports." *Journal of Women in Culture & Society* 34.3 (2009): 722–727. Web. 27 December 2017.

Francis, Leslie. "Title IX: An Incomplete Effort to Achieve Equality in Sports." *Journal of the Philosophy of Sport* 43.1 (March 2016): 83–89. Web. 28 December 2017.

Hastie, Emma. "Despite Progress Made Under Title IX, Gender Inequality Persists in High School Sports." *The Buffalo News*. Buffalo News, 9 November 2017. Web. 11 March 2017.

Hogshead-Makar, Nancy. "Title IX: Building on 30 Years of Progress." *FDCH Congressional Testimony. Points of View Reference Center*, 27 June 2002. Web. 29 December 2017.

"IIHF Rules." *International Ice Hockey Federation*. IIHF, Web. 11 March 2018.

Jones, Joyce. "Obama Administration Touts Title IX Policy Change." *Diverse Issues in Higher Education* 27.7 (May 2010): 8. *Academic Search Premier*. Web. 29 December 2017.

Kutz, Steven. "19 NBA Teams Have Now Sold Ad Space on Their Jerseys." *Market Watch*. Market Watch, 13 November 2017. Web. 14 March 2018.

Lanser, David. "Title IX and How to Rectify Sexism Entrenched in NCAA Leadership." *Wisconsin Journal of Law, Gender & Society* 31.2 (Fall 2016): 179–203. Web. 27 December 2017.

A League of Their Own. Dir. Penny Marshall. Perf. Tom Hanks, Rosie O'Donnell. Columbia, 1992.

Lefton, Terry, and John Ourand. "ESPN Signs Six-Year Extension with WNBA That Is Worth $12M Per Year." *Street & Smith's Sports Business Daily.* American City Business Journals, 28 March 2013. Web. 14 March 2018.

Machida-Kosuga, Moe, John Schaubroeck, and Deborah Feltz. "Leader Self-Efficacy of Women Intercollegiate Athletic Administrators: A Look at Barriers and Developmental Anecdotes." *Journal of Intercollegiate Sport* 9.2 (December 2016): 157–178. Web. 27 December 2017.

Messner, Michael. "Sports and Male Domination: The Female Athlete as Contested Ideological Terrain." *Sociology of Sport Journal* 5.3 (1988): 197–211. Web. 28 December 2017.

McDonagh, Eileen, and Laura Pappano. "Playing with the Boys: Why Is Gender Segregation in Sports Normal? Males and Females Should Play Together." *The Sun* 6 February 2008: A17. ProQuest. Web. 27 December 2017.

Micelotta, Evelyn, Marvin Washington, and Iva Docekalova. "Industry Gender Imprinting and New Venture Creation: The Liabilities of Women's Leagues in the Sports Industry." *Entrepreneurship: Theory & Practice* 42.1 (January 2018): 94–128. EBSCO. Web. 27 December 2017.

National Coalition for Women and Girls in Education. *Title IX at 40: Working to Ensure Gender Equity in Education.* Washington, D.C., 2012. Web. 27 December 2017.

"NCAA Playing Rules." *National Collegiate Athletic Association.* Web. 28 December 2017.

O'Donnell, Norah. "Match of their Lives." *60 Minutes.* CBS Interactive, 20 November 2016. Web. 30 December 2017.

Paule-Koba, Amanda. "Pressure Is a Privilege: Billie Jean King, Title IX, and Gender Equity." *Reviews in American History* 40.4 (2012): 711–715. ProjectMUSE. Web. 28 December 2017.

Paulson, Amanda. "College Sports: White House tweaks Title IX rules." *Christian Science Monitor.* Christian Science Monitor, 20 April 2010. Web. 29 December 2017.

Pieper, Lindsay. *Sex Testing: Gender Policing in Women's Sports.* Champaign: University of Illinois Press, 2006. Print.

Reinbrecht, Elizabeth. "Northwestern University and Title IX: One Step Forward for Football Players, Two Steps Back for Female Student Athletes." *University of Toledo Law Review* 47.1 (2015): 243–277. EBSCO. Web. 29 December 2017.

"Requirements Under Title IX of the Education Amendments of 1972." *US Department of Education Office for Civil* Rights. Web. 28 December 2017.

Rhoads, Steven. "Sports, Sex, and Title IX." *Public Interest* 154 (Winter 2004): 86–98. Academic Search Premier. Web. 29 December 2017.

Rubin, Jason. "Just Admit the NBA Deal Is Screwing You, ESPN." *Huffington Post.* Huffington Post, 29 March 2017. Web. 14 March 2017.

"Rules: Keeping the Game Fair." *US Lacrosse.* US Lacrosse, Web. 11 March 2018.

Sander, Libby. "Education Department Nixes Bush-Era Policy on Title IX Compliance." *Chronicle of Higher Education* 56.33 (20 Apr. 2010). Academic Search Premier. Web. 28 December 2017.

Sandomir, Richard. "In W.N.B.A., Jersey Sponsorship Could Set New Standard." *New York Times.* New York Times, 31 May 2009. Web. 14 March 2018.

Schachter, Ron. "Title IX Turns 35." *University Business* 10.3 (2007): 44–50. Web. 29 December 2017.

Schultz, Jaime. *Qualifying Times: Points of Change in U.S. Women's Sport.* Champaign: University of Illinois Press, 2014. EBSCO. E-book

Stevenson, Betsey. "Title IX and the Evolution of High School Sports." *Contemporary Economic Policy* 25.4 (October 2007): 486–505. Web. 29 December 2017.

Terlep, Sharon. "(Technically) No Checking in Women's Hockey." *Wall Street Journal.* Dow Jones & Company, 10 Feb. 2014. Web. 11 March 2018.

"Title IX, Education Amendments of 1972." *Dol.gov.* Web. 27 December 2017.

"A Title IX Ruling That Won't Draw Cheers." *Chronicle of Higher Education* 56.41 (2010). *Academic Search Premier*. Web. 29 December 2017.

"Title IX: 25 Years of Progress." *Ed.gov.* 9 July 1997. Web. 28 December 2017.

"2017 KPMG Women's PGA Championship Purse, Winner's Share, Prize Money Payout." *The Golf News Net*. Golf News Net, 28 June 2017. Web. 14 March 2018.

"2017 PGA Championship Prize Money, Purse, and Exemptions." *Professional Golf Association*. The PGA of America/Turner Sports Interactive, 13 August 2017. Web. 14 March 2018.

Vest, Becky, and Gerald Masterson. "Title IX and Its Effect on Sports Programs in High School and Collegiate Athletics." *Coach & Athletic Director* 77.5 (2007): 60–62. Web. 28 December 2017.

Walker, Nefertiti A., and E. Nicole Melton. "Creating Opportunities for Social Change in Women's Sport through Academic and Industry Collaborations: An Interview with Kate Fagan." *Journal of Intercollegiate Sport* 8.1 (June 2015): 82–95. *EBSCO*. Web. 28 December 2017.

Whalen, Kelsey. "Discrimination Against Women in the Sport Industry." Honor's thesis, Eastern Kentucky University, 2017. Web. 30 December 2017.

"Women, Gender Equity, and Title IX." *NCAA*. Web. 29 December 2017.

Women's Sports Foundation. *Beyond X's and O's: Gender Bias and Coaches of Women's College Sports*. 2016. PDF file.

"Women's World Cup Final Is Most-Watched Soccer Match in U.S. History." *US Soccer*. US Soccer, 8 July 2015. Web. 30 December 2017.

Sportswomen in Wheelchairs

Doubly Discriminated Against but Duly Impressive

LINDA K. FULLER

According to Hodges et al., "media popular culture have ... frequently used stereotypes" to depict people with disabilities. They wrote that their representations could be summarized as "vulnerable and pitiable: portrayals of disabled people as childlike dependents who need help and charity from others; 'Supercrip'—inspirational stories of determination and personal courage to overcome 'adversity'; Portrayals of disabled people as less than human (e.g., 'freak shows,' 'exotic'); Characters primarily defined by their disability rather than other aspects of their identity; [and] Disabled people presented as unable to participate fully in everyday life" (Hodges et al. 173). This is to say that stereotypes of disability, which typically have no bearing on reality and instead present uni-dimensional images, tend to fall into categories of pitiable, weird or freakish, frightening, fun(ny) and/or the butt of jokes, asexual, tragically burdensome or victimized, and, at the other extreme, inspirationally super-human ("supercrip"), or as the ultimate noble hero/ heroine joyously overcoming all odds. The (bio)medical model of disability is mainly concerned with correcting or curing, assuming that interventions are necessary for a "normal" existence; well-meaning, it nevertheless perpetuates a negative notion about disabilities. Not unlike charity, legitimacy, social, or moral models, many people see a spectrum of issues rather than considering the individual him/herself. Relative to wheelchairs, this essay's approach is to look at the *person* in them, not at the apparatus itself.

International Paralympic Games

The International Paralympic Games (IPGs) have followed the regular Olympic Games since 1960. Described by Ian Brittain as "the second largest multi-sport festival on the planet" (1), the Paralympic Games were introduced in 1948 in London for post-war injured servicemen as an outgrowth of the Stoke Mandeville Hospital for veterans with spinal cord injuries. The first International Games for the Disabled were held in the UK in 1952, and then the Paralympic Games began in 1960, in Rome. Women have been included from the start.

Table 1 shows the year and location for each of the Summer and Winter events. It also includes the number of National Paralympic Committees (NPCs), and numbers and percentages of female Paralympians.

Table 1. Female Paralympians' Participation, 1960–2016

Year	Place	NPCs	# of women	% of women
1960	Rome, ITA	17	44	32.5
1964	Tokyo, JAP	19	72	30
1968	Tel Aviv, ISR	28	199	25
1972	Heidelberg, GER	41	270	25
1976	Ornskoldsvik, SWE	16	37	19
1976	Toronto, CAN	40	274	21
1980	Geilo, NOR	18	70	23
1980	Arnheim, NED	42	426	26
1984	Innsbruck, AUT	21	94	22
1984	Stoke Mandeville, UK, and New York, U.S.	54	535	25.5
1988	Innsbruck, AUT	22	77	20
1988	Seoul, KOR	60	679	22
1992	Tignes-Albertville, FRA	24	77	21
1992	Barcelona & Madrid, ESP	83	700	23
1994	Lillehammer, NOR	31	90	19
1996	Atlanta, USA	104	790	24
1998	Nagano, JAP	31	122	22
2000	Sydney, AUS	122	990	25.5
2002	Salt Lake City, USA	36	87	21
2004	Athens, GRE	135	1165	25.5
2006	Torino, ITA	38	99	21
2008	Beijing, CHI	146	1383	34.5
2010	Vancouver, CAN	44	121	24
2012	London	164	1523	34.5
2014	Sochi, RUS	174	129	23
2016	Rio de Janeiro, BRA	159	1671	38.6

"Sport, and particularly the Olympics," Katie Ellis has noted, "is a site of popular culture where feelings of national pride are elicited and performed" (133). However, this has not been the case for the Paralympics where athletes are characterized as individuals overcoming adversary rather than representatives of a nation. A wheelchair athlete explains, "It is as if people cannot identify with a disabled person. I mean, when Sweden wins a gold medal in archery or ice hockey or football or pentathlon or something—then it is 'we' who won the gold medal. If it is a disabled person who wins a gold medal—then it is 'they'" (Wickman 157). Despite having the "double whammy" discriminations of gender and disability, sportswomen in wheelchairs nevertheless have an increasingly impressive sports record that continues to grow. They are, literally, on a role. Beginning with a brief description of women's wheelchair sports, this essay includes a review of the literature on wheelchair sportswomen, a theoretical background based on Gendered Critical Discourse Analysis (GCDA), and a description of their sports. Citing many case studies, it concludes that female para-athletes' biggest problem is winning over perceptions of them not as "supercrips" but instead as "regular" people who just happen to participate in, and excel at, various sports—in their wheelchairs.

Women's Wheelchair Sports

Sometimes referred to as adaptive or para-sports, wheelchair sports are played by men and women with disabilities in a range from amateur to elite. In the Paralympics, multisport events vary only in that they are made up of athletes with various physical and/or sensory impairments (e.g., muscle power, passive range of movement, limb deficiency, leg length difference, short stature, hypertonia, ataxia, athetosis, vision impairment, and levels of intellectual impairment). For women in wheelchairs, those sports include archery, athletics, badminton, basketball, biathlon, curling, cycling, equestrianism, fencing, para-triathlon, powerlifting, rowing, rugby, shooting, skiing, softball, and tennis.[1]

There are a number of organizations for the "disabled"/"variously abled" in sport. All of these organizations are heavily invested in helping their constituents, even if media reportage about them remains lacking. Organizations such as the American Athletic Association for the Deaf, National Foundation of Wheelchair Tennis, National Handicapped Sports, National Wheelchair Athletic Association, Special Olympics International, U.S. Association for Blind Athletics, Wheelchair Sports, USA, and others are pivotal to encouraging and supporting various athletes. Here are some examples of wheelchair competitions won by Paralympian women from around the world that best explain the range of sport that can be accomplished in wheelchairs.

- **Archery**, an initial Paralympic sport in Rome in 1960, was won by Margaret Maughan (GBR), paralyzed from the waist down and treated at Stoke Mandeville Hospital. Gizem Girismen (TUR) has held the world champion title for the women's individual recurve W1/W2 since winning the gold medal at the Beijing Paralympics in 2008.

- For **para-athletics**, Omara Durand of Cuba is considered the fastest female Paralympian, having earned triple gold medals at the 2016 Rio Paralympics and setting a world record in the T12 100-meter race of 11.40 seconds, despite being visually impaired. Honorable Chantal Petitclerc, a Canadian wheelchair racer and Senator, has earned total of 14 medals since the Paralympics in Atlanta in 1996. Terezinha Guilhermina (BRA), winner of both the 100-meter and 200-meter races in the T11 class at the 2012 London Paralympics, is totally blind.

- **Para-biathlon**, introduced at the 1988 Innsbruck Paralympics, has featured blind Nordic skier Verena Bentele (GER) who won the "Laureus World Sportsperson of the Year with a Disability" award in 2011. Visually impaired Oksana Shyshkova (UKR) holds the national sports title of Master of Sport in para-athletics.

- Canada has dominated wheelchair **curling**, which is open to female athletes with physical disability in the lower part of the body. Ina Forrest and Sonja Gaudet took the gold medal at the Paralympics in Vancouver in 2010 and in Sochi in 2014.

- Two notable English **para-cyclists** include five-time gold medalist Dame Sarah Storey, who is also a Paralympic swimmer, and Baroness Tanni Grey-Thompson.

- Wheelchair users with poor trunk balance and/or impairment of all four limbs in **equestrianism** include Sophie Christiansen (GBR). She was born prematurely with cerebral palsy and took up horse riding as a form of physiotherapy at a local Riding for the Disabled Association (RDA). She earned eight gold medals in three successive Paralympic Games between 2008 and 2016. Saysunee Jana, whose first name in Thai means "lightning," has won Women's Epee Individual B in **fencing** three times despite her paralysis. After having both legs amputated below the knee and both arms from the forearms, Beatrice "Bebe" Vio (ITA) used special prosthetics to hold her foil such that she fences from her shoulder, winning the gold medal in Foil B at the 2016 Rio Paralympics.

- The **para-triathlon**, which debuted at the 2016 Paralympics in Brazil, consists of a sprint race of 750-meter swimming, 20-kilometer cycling, and 5-kilometer running, and included several different wheelchair categories. Three notable American participants have included Megan Fisher, Beth Price, and Melissa Stockwell.

- In **para-powerlifting**, Lucy Ejike (NIG), a victim of polio, has taken medals in five Paralympic Games, setting a record at the 2016 Rio Paralympics with a powerlift of 142 kilograms.
- Working under **Adaptive Rowing** classifications, Pam Relph (GBR) was the first double gold medalist (in London in 2012 and Rio in 2016). Birgit Skarstein (NOR) also qualified for cross-country skiing in Sochi in 2014.
- Wheelchair pistol and rifle are part of **para-shooting**. The first American woman winner is McKenna Dahl, born with amyoplasia arthrogryposis in her left hand and both feet, such that her muscles were formed improperly, at the Paralympics in Rio in 2016.
- Since the Paralympics in 1976 in Örnsköldsvik, **para-skiing** has been part of the program. Helen Ripa (SWE) swam at the 1992 Paralympics in Barcelona but then took up cross-country skiing and winning a gold medal at the Sochi Paralympics in 2014. Sit/ski sports are for athletes with various leg impairments and varying degrees of torso control.
- Wheelchair **rugby** is a mixed-gender sport. Canada's number one, Miranda Biletski has stated, "The international stage for wheelchair rugby wheelchair is very much accepting of female athletes…. My teammates definitely do not hold back with the hits when we train and practice. I think sport and fitness are important for everyone regardless of its type of physical limitations. That is something that is really evident with rugby, a sport filled with a lot of really amazing athletes [who] lead normal productive lives. They don't expect any handouts or special treatment" ("Big Read").
- Natalia Partyka (POL), consistently been ranked number one in the world in **table tennis**, was born without a right hand and forearm
- Esther Vergeer (NED), the best-known Paralympic **wheelchair tennis** champion stated, "My parents brought me up to be a good goal-setter. I know what I want to achieve and I know what I have to do for it. Of course it's hard to say if I would have this same spirit, the same abilities and the same talent if I was an able-bodied girl, but there is a part of me that is a fighter." She has won over 470 matches.

There are numerous other examples of women who participate in sports in their wheelchairs. For example, Sarah Bunting has mentioned some of the wheelchair tennis players in her book: Jiske Griffioen, born with Spina Bifida, has joined fellow Dutch wheelchair tennis icon Esther Vergeer by also winning the Australian Open, the French Open, Singers Master, and Paralympics in 2008 and in 2012; Dana Mathewson, paralyzed by the rare neurological disease Transverse Myelitis, is on the wheelchair tennis team at the University of Arizona; and Jordanne Whiley, who has won four Grand Slams, is considered the UK's most successful wheelchair tennis player of all time.

And then there is *Push Girls*, an American reality television show featuring four women in wheelchairs and the obstacles they faced. Depicted as "normal" Los Angelenos, albeit in wheelchairs, their stories not only helped explain how para- and quadriplegics managed their lives, but also showed real people dealing with physical and psychological challenges (Angelo; McKay). On a broader scale, it allowed a general audience to witness the complexities of their life stories.

Literature Review on Sportswomen in Wheelchairs

That notion of invisibility permeates much of the personal experiences described by Paralympians (DePauw). Brittain wrote, "while sports opportunities for persons with disabilities continue to emerge in many international communities, athletes with disabilities and disability-specific sports largely remain segregated and invisible from the mainstream sports environment" (56). Probably no group represents discrimination and/or exclusion in sport better than women Paralympians. Encouragingly, Darcy, Frawley, and Adair have declared that "each successive Paralympic Games has made contribution to this growth: introducing new sports, encouraging more countries to attend, increased scope of broadcasting, record ticket sales, and alternative media channels to promote the event and its athletes" (1).

Most research on "disabled" female athletes deal with the Paralympics. For wheelchair sportswomen, most information comes from their respective groups, whether baseball, basketball, rugby, tennis, or other sports. Purdue and Howe discuss a paradox, inviting us to "See the sport, not the disability." Take the case of Hannah Cockroft, born in Halifax, West Yorkshire, in 1992 with cerebral palsy, and later experiencing brain complications. She eventually competed in wheelchair basketball, wheelchair racing, seated discus, swimming, and wheelchair rugby and was trained by Dr. Ian Thompson, husband of Lady Tanni Grey-Thompson, the UK's beloved wheelchair racer and later track athlete. Also known as "Hurricane Hannah," at the Paralympics in Rio in 2016, Cockroft won three gold medals in Women's 100 meters, 400 meters (setting a world record of 58.78 seconds), and the 800 meters T34 Finals. Working with the Leeds City Council Sports Development and involved in a degree course in Media and Journalism at Coventry, she helped launch 17 Sports Management Limited, a sports management company that represents disabled athletes.

Quinn and Yoshida take what they call the Paralympic Paradox even further. Looking at the duel social roles that Paralympians assume, they consider that, "in the first role, the Paralympic athlete engages in elite sport performance by striving to achieve, despite a physical difference. This role is constructed primarily for the non-disabled audience. The second role is that of link or mediator between sport, athletic achievement and physical difference. This socially constructed role targets the community of people with a disability" (103). Marie Hardin, over the years. has probably written the most about women in wheelchairs. Early on, she brought to our attention how the disabled have historically been excluded from sport in terms of media attention and advertising. Arguing about their exclusion "in the realms of sport— where they fail to meet standards of the 'ideal sporting body'—and in advertising, where they also fail to meet an ideal-body standard" ("Marketing" 108), she calls for us to recognize the "able-bodied ideal" that is inherent in capitalist hegemony.

In her doctoral dissertation, Kim Wickman applied feminist poststructural thinking to identify how female and male wheelchair racers construct and perform their identities, comparing their responses to how they are represented in the Swedish sports media. What she found was that the subject of "disabled sportswomen" was usually concealed and neutralized in the discourse of able-ism, even if the athletes themselves felt empowered "being able" to perform as sportspersons.

Using "auto drive" technique for qualitative data collections, Hargreaves and Hardin used input from 10 women wheelchair athletes to reveal three themes: (a) the participants were consumers of both mainstream and disability print media; (b) they were tired of the media stereotypes; and (c) they believed that the media is partially responsible for the lack of coverage of women and individuals with disabilities in sports media as a whole.

Theoretical Approach: Gendered Critical Discourse Analysis (GCDA)

Dialogue determines how values are communicated. Messages between sender(s) and receiver(s) become critical to the process of interpretation. Analyzing language, then, becomes important to understand how much of the more-than-$60-billion industry of sport is described in masculine terms—patriarchal, war-like, sexist, even violent (Fuller, *Female Olympians*). Critical Discourse Analysis, which is concerned with social prowess, dominance, and inequality, includes the following notions:

1. Discourse is shaped and constrained by social structures (e.g., class, gender, age) and by culture.

2. Discourses shape and constrain our individual identities, relationships, and knowledge/belief systems.
3. Discursive language and practices are constrained by societal rules and conventions.

My own developing theory of Gendered Critical Discourse Analysis (GCDA) accepts norms between men and women and recognizes ongoing rhetorical, economic, and socio-political power plays between the sexes. As such, this theory can have implications for other-abled athletes in terms of racial, religious, and human rights discrimination. Whether dealing with the rhetoric of hetero-normativity or hegemony, public or policy-related discourse, sport is truly a common language.

LeClair sensitizes the reader to the language of disability by discussing how, with the 2006 passage of Article 30 at the UN Conference on the Rights of Persons with Disabilities, "the historical framing of disability as a social welfare issue, charity-based and medically defined, was replaced by a rights-based approach to support inclusion" (4). Confronting the issue of disability as the opposite of ableism, she points out, "Disability has been associated with religious or spiritual punishment and images of evil, so irrational fears led to active policies of discrimination, abuse and even extermination" (10). Do not label disabled athletes' performances as "inspirational"—their least favorite word (Cottingham et al.; Schpigel). My reference for females has been "grit and glam" (Fuller, "Grit and Glam").

Both the Olympic Games and the Paralympic Games continue to grow. With that evolution comes with individual athletes who are at last getting their well-deserved attention. Hodges et al. have noticed how, after the London Paralympics in 2012, the Paralympics in particular have had a "noticeable impact" on how disability sport is discussed. Realize this above all. Wheelchair athletes just want to be known as sportspeople, their sport simply adaptive.

Conclusions

If sport is a microcosm of the sociocultural world in which gendered power relations and discriminatory practices take place, "other" outside of the mainstream too often becomes suspicious, and by default excluded. Part of the issue is discursive, so we need to get rid of terms like "cripples" and instead use neutral language such as "athlete with a disability" rather than "disabled athlete." As Elisabet Apelmo reminds us, "weak" is the opposite of "we"—all part of why we need to encourage disabled women to develop strategies to resist stereotypes that marginalize and consider them as "other" (8).

Further, if the standard of sport is an able-bodied male, sportswomen in wheelchairs can help turn that paradigm on its head. After all, why should any "disabled" people face any form of discrimination? Why should *different* indicate deviant when it really is a positive frame? Just as sport is a signifier of our changing, dynamic culture, and language is a means to deciphering much of its significance, we have much to learn from our sisters in wheelchairs, especially those who happen to be athletes.

Battling the dual constraints of gender equity and acceptance of "ableism" in terms of media/body terms, sportswomen in wheelchairs deserve our attention, as well as our applause. Let the Games begin.

NOTE

1. Para-badminton is scheduled to debut at the Paralympics in Tokyo in 2020. Wheelchair basketball, contested since 1960 for men and 1968 for women, has been won by Canada three times, Germany three times, and the United States four times. Although wheelchair softball began in Minneapolis in 1976 under the auspices of the National Wheelchair Softball Association (NWSA), the sport to date is not included in the Paralympics.

WORKS CITED

Apelmo, Elisabet. *Sport and the Female Disabled Body*. New York: Routledge, 2017. Print.
Angelo, Megan. "They're Pretty, Normal and in Wheelchairs." *New York Times*, New York Times, 1 June 2012. Web. 1 May 2018.
"Big Read: Women in Wheelchair Rugby." *Paralympic Movement*. International Olympic Committee, Web. 31 January 2016.
Brittain, Ian. *The Paralympic Games Explained*. New York: Routledge, 2016. Print.
Bunting, Sarah. *More than Tennis: The First 25 Years of Wheelchair Tennis*. London: Premium Press, 2001. Print.
Cottingham, Michael, Joshua R. Pate, and Brian Gearity. "Examining 'Inspiration': Perspectives of Stakeholders Attending a Power Wheelchair Soccer Tournament." *Canadian Journal of Disability Studies* 4.1 (2015): 59–89. Print.
Darcy, Simon, Stephen Frawley, and Daryl Adair, ed. *Managing the Paralympics*. Basingstoke: Palgrave Macmillan, 2017. Print.
DePauw, Karen P. "The (In)visibility of DisAbility: Cultural Contexts and 'Sorting Bodies.'" *Quest* 49.4 (2012): 416–430. Print.
Ellis, Katie. *Disability and Popular Culture: Focusing Passion, Creating Community and Expressing Defiance*. New York: Routledge, 2016. Print.
Fuller, Linda K. *Female Olympians: Tracing a Mediated Socio-cultural/political-economic Timeline*. Basingstoke: Palgrave Macmillan, 2016. Print.
_____. "Grit and Glam: Female Paralympians' Reframing and Revisioning of 'Disability' in 2012 London." International Association for Media and Communication Research. Hyderabad, India, 2014. Address.
Hardin, Marie. "Marketing the Acceptably Athletic Image: Wheelchair Athletes, Sport-related Advertising and Capitalist Hegemony." *Disability Studies Quarterly* 23.1 (2003): 108–125. Print.
Hargreaves, Jean Ann, and Brent Hardin. "Women Wheelchair Athletes: Competing against Media Stereotypes." *Disability Studies Quarterly* 29.2 (Spring 2009): n. pag. *Disability Studies Quarterly*. Web. 1 May 2018.
Hodges, Caroline E., Daniel Jackson, and Richard Scullion. "Voices from the Armchair: The Meanings Afforded to the Paralympics by UK Television Audiences." *Reframing Disability?: Media (Dis)Empowerment and Voice in the 2012 Paralympics*. Ed. Daniel Jackson, Caroline E. M. Hodges, Mike Molesworth, and Richard Scullion. New York: Routledge, 2015. Print.

LeClair, Jill M., ed. *Disability in the Global Sport Arena: A Sporting Chance*. New York: Routledge, 2012. Print.

McKay, Hollie. "'Push Girls' Reality Stars Seek to Dispel the 'Sloppy Wheelchair Stereotype.'" *Fox News Entertainment*. Fox News Network, 3 June 2013. Web. 1 May 2018.

Purdue, David E.J., and P. David Howe. "See the Sport, Not the Disability: Exploring the Paralympic Paradox." *Qualitative Research in Sport, Exercise and Health* 4.2 (2012): 189–205. Print.

Quinn, Nancy, and Karen Yoshida. "More than Sport." *Canadian Journal of Disability Studies* 5.4 (2016): 103–117. Print.

Schpigel, Ben. "Paralympic Athletes' Least Favorite Word: Inspiration." *New York Times*. New York Times, 17 September 2016. Web. 1 May 2018.

Wickman, Kim. "Bending Mainstream Definitions of Sport, Gender and Ability: Representations of Wheelchair Races." Diss. Umea University, Sweden. 2008. Print.

Discrimination or Oversight?

Making Disability Visible in the Sport Management Classroom

JOSHUA R. PATE *and* ROBIN HARDIN

Disability is the largest minority group in the world with more than 1 billion people who identify as having a disability of some type, representing 15 percent of the global population (World Health Organization/World Bank 7). Excluding people from society merely because of their disability status, whether an actual or socially constructed stigma, has reinforced a medical model approach to disability rather than the social model.

This essay aims to explore how disability has been invisible within sport and how sport management educators can combat this oversight by infusing disability within curriculum. After a brief overview and background of the medical and social models of viewing disability, it will examine how sport has influenced the way disability is both viewed and accepted across the United States as well as the United Kingdom, and how that becomes a potential warning sign of how disability is often missing within sport management curriculum in higher education. Allowing disability to become invisible within sport management education can be connected to the lack of media coverage provided toward disability sport, and the inspirational/pity tone such coverage takes when traditional media include disability in sport conversations.

The essay concludes by suggesting that true inclusion—or infusion—of disability within higher education sport management curriculum should be the goal of academic institutions seeking to fully and appropriately prepare future professionals for the sport industry.

Medical Model Versus Social Model

While there are multiple lenses through which to view disability, two distinct models have traditionally explained how society views disability: the medical model and the social model. The medical model views disability through the lens of rehabilitation and correction of a problem that places responsibility on people with impairments to adapt (Thomas 18). Disability is a medical condition, according to this model, that needs to be fixed to bring the individual back to "normal." This view continues to be a discriminatory lens because people continue to view disability as something that may be cured, rehabilitated, or corrected so the individual can return to a normal state. One way the medical model view is exposed is when someone uses outdated and inappropriate language (e.g., handicap) when speaking about people with disabilities. Language preferences for people with disabilities vary depending upon the geographic location, as people in North America often prefer person-first language which emphasizes the person over the label (e.g., person with a disability) but people in the United Kingdom often avoid elements of person-first language (e.g., disabled person) to be more direct in communicating. Put simply, it may be impossible to understand everyone's preference to language related to disability (Pate and Hardin 366). A more tangible example of the medical model lens in sport settings is when a press box at an older football stadium has no elevator and is only accessible by stairs, or when a video board is not captioned for the Deaf community. These examples emphasize disability as the problem that needs correcting rather than society not adapting to become more inclusive.

The social model, on the contrary, views disability as a socially-constructed issue due to society's lack of adjusting (Oliver, "The Social" 1024). The social model "disconnects our conceptualization of disability from illness and pain so as to ensure that no judgement about the lives of people with disabilities is distorted by uncritical assumptions about their suffering" (Silvers, Wasserman, and Mahowald 76). Examining the previous examples through the social model, the football press box is viewed as inaccessible because the facility has not been updated, so perhaps media members are placed in an alternative location to enhance access for all. Regarding the video board example, the social model approach would ensure that the video board is captioned or that attendees have access to alternative methods of receiving captioned messages (e.g., renting a handheld device). The social model approach places responsibility on society for adjusting rather than the individual with a disability. It should be noted that the disability community has been critical of the social model in that it may not connect with the experiences or potential pain that come with impairment (Oliver, "Defining" 11–12), thus revealing that no model is without flaw or all-encompassing of viewing or explaining disability experiences. Shakespeare also contends the social model neglects impairment as part of people's lived experiences and assumes oppression (199–201). Shakespeare, however, suggests the strengths of the social model include its use for political unity and self-esteem (198). Still, Oliver, who introduced the social model, argued some 30 years later that it should either be replaced or re-invigorated ("The Social" 1026). Yet, others suggest the social model is the most relevant way to view disability despite the need for continuing evolvement of the model (Levitt 593).

It is important to note these two distinct models because discrimination has historically been present in sport through the medical model lens. For the purposes of this essay, we define disability sport as sport activities for people with disabilities at the competitive and recreational levels. Those sport activities are widely available for people with physical and intellectual disabilities. Only in recent decades has disability sport received greater acceptance and attention at the most elite level of competition, but recreational programming remains relatively ignored or viewed with pity and charity. An evolution of acceptance of disability sport can be credited to international disability sport movements developed in different regions of the world.

Sport's Influence on Viewing Disability

The overall lack of social inclusion for elite sport for people with disabilities within the North American culture can be traced directly back to a general feeling of pity toward disability, and therefore disability overall, given the institutionalization of people with disabilities up until the 1960s and early 1970s (Braddock and Parish 40). Across North America, primarily in the United States, disability sport has been invisible while distinctly operating beneath the public sphere through local programming and leagues (e.g., challenger league baseball), Paralympic Sport Clubs, Special Olympic regional networks, and national teams at the most elite level. These teams, tournaments, games, and opportunities often go unnoticed by the public and yet offer a new world of career opportunities for the sport management graduate in the areas of administration, communication, event management, facility management, governance, marketing, and programming.

While this essay focuses mostly on the physical nature of disability, it is important to note the historical context of intellectual disabilities and sport within the United States and around the world. People with intellectual disabilities were given an international sport stage in the United States when the first International Special Olympics were held in 1968 at Soldier Field in Chicago. Visions of a major sporting event for people with intellectual disabilities were first created by Eunice Kennedy Shriver in 1962 when she began a summer camp for youth with intellectual disabilities at her Washington, D.C., home. Rather than institutionalizing people with intellectual disabilities, the goal of Shriver's camp was to explore the athletic and physical potential of those individuals. In 1967, the Chicago Park District proposed a plan to Shriver and the Kennedy Foundation for a track meet modeled after the Olympics, and Shriver challenged the organizers to expand the event to a global scale. One year later, in July 1968, the Kennedy Foundation and Chicago Park District held the first Special Olympics with approximately 1,000 athletes from the United States and Canada and 200 events that included broad jump, high jump, sprints, softball throw, swimming, water polo, and floor hockey ("A Revolution").

Special Olympics has grown to become the largest public health organization for people with intellectual disabilities in the world, serving nearly five million athletes in 172 countries ("What We Do"). The World Summer Games are now held every four years, as are the World Winter Games. Additionally, Special Olympics supports regional competitions across the world in Asia, Canada, and Europe. The 2015 World Summer Games in Los Angeles hosted 6,500 athletes from 165 countries competing in 25 sports ("Los Angeles 2015"). As seen in the evolution of the Special Olympics, sport for people with intellectual disabilities is an opportunity for sport management graduates to pursue employment and for the sport management student to learn about in the classroom regarding marketing, event management, and governance.

Competition and opportunities for people with physical disabilities in sport evolved on an international stage through the Paralympic Games and the efforts of Dr. Ludwig Guttmann. Guttmann, in 1948, organized an archery competition among rehabilitation patients at Stoke Mandeville hospital during the same day as the opening ceremony for the Olympic Games. Sixteen injured solders competed in those first-ever Stoke Mandeville Games, which evolved to incorporate other athletes from neighboring countries in the years to follow (Brittain 10). The evolution of the competition among people with physical disabilities culminated in 1960 when the first recognized Paralympic Games took place in Rome shortly following the conclusion of the Olympic Games.

When London hosted the 2012 Summer Games, the Paralympics were declared as a single moment that will transform the way disability and disability sport will be seen. The touted successes of those 2012 Paralympic Games were due to the elite level of international disability sport competition returning to its original birthplace and celebrating the progress toward disability inclusion made throughout Europe since Guttmann's 1948 archery competition.

Including Disability in Sport Management Education

The multiple ways in which disability and disability sport have been included within the fabric of society are best captured by DePauw's three stages that define how disability is viewed in sport: Invisibility of Disability, Visibility of Disability, and (In)Visibility of DisAbility (424–425). These three stages are imperative for sport industry leaders to recognize when tasked with offering an inclusive sport experience. Disability has been and continues to be ignored in many sport communities as well as society's dialogue of sport. When it is included, it is often addressed in an improper and patronizing way. Thus, the one place where future sport management professionals can be educated about the historical oversight of an entire demographic in sport is indeed the sport management classroom. The remainder of this essay will offer insight on how disability sport has been traditionally viewed through DePauw's first two stages, and how intentional inclusion of disability in sport management curriculum and classroom design can move the industry toward the third stage.

Invisibility of Disability

DePauw's first stage is Invisibility of Disability, which describes when "people have not been included nor even considered as possible participants in sport" (424). Barriers for people with disabilities to participate in sport can be a lack of organized sport programs, lack of informal early experiences in sport, lack of access to coaches and training programs, lack of accessible facilities, and limiting psychological and sociological factors (DePauw and Gavron 13–14). These barriers prevent people with disabilities from participating in sport, and yet benefits to sport participation for people with disabilities are among the most critical for this population's social success: physical well-being, social inclusion, enhanced employment prospects, and enhanced self-esteem (Misener and Darcy 2).

Disability has been invisible to the sport world because of limited programming for participants at a variety of levels. A lack of understanding on how to include people with disabilities in sport begins at the elementary school level where classes of typically-developing students often omit opportunities for children with disabilities to participate or offer little adapted physical activity for all students to learn. Lee et al. found that 62.4 percent of elementary schools in the United States had students with long-term disabilities, and 58.9 percent of those schools had students with long-term disabilities who participated in required physical education (450). Most of those schools (77.2 percent) had students participate in the typical physical education class, but 31.3 percent had students separated into an adapted physical education course (Lee et al. 450). Perhaps a bigger barrier for the holistic education of society on disability inclusion is that primary and secondary schools need to enhance their inclusion of disability sport and/or adapted sport into regular programming for all students (Davis 54). Teaching disability sport in general curriculum promotes inclusion while developing a more comprehensive and holistic educational curriculum. Avoiding the inclusion of such programming, then, reinforces the invisibility of disability sport to youth. Similarly, not including disability sport within the college sport management classroom—future professionals within the industry—is negligent because it omits career opportunities in segments that are targeted toward a minority population.

The potential for reverse inclusion—where able-bodied students participate in adapted sport activities—is often overlooked. There does not have to be a separation of able-bodied students and students with disabilities. Adapted sports are just that—adapted. It does not mean a person has to have disabilities to participate in those sports. A physical education class can include disability sports that will allow participation by everyone and create an inclusive environment. This will be a positive step in demonstrating that disability does not mean inability to participate in sports or recreational activities. Including this option in elementary school physical education classes will be a step in increasing awareness in regard to disability sport as students will learn at young age about an alternative form of sport compared to their own knowledge and experiences. It will also enhance those who choose to pursue a sport management degree and a career in the sport industry. They will have a much better understanding of adapted and disability sport than people who have not participated.

Disability sport is often minimized or overlooked in society's attention of sport overall, as has been the case in media coverage of disability sport. Media often tell society what to think about (McCombs and Shaw 184) and how to think about it (Goffman 21). Thus, a lack of media coverage of disability sport is considered a reflection on society's view of the issue. The 2012 Paralympic Games in London were widely considered to be the most successful international disability sport event that shaped the ways people view disability. The host country experienced unprecedented television coverage as British public television network Channel 4 aired 400 hours of live footage, which reportedly reached 69 percent of the UK's population (Lazarus). The blanket coverage earned the network five nominations at the Sport Industry Awards 2013 for sport brand of the year, best use of public relations, best integrated sports marketing campaign, sports website of the year, and best television commercial (Degun). Television's counterparts in the print media covered the Paralympic Games with special printed sections in their newspapers and online sections of newspaper websites.

Great Britain earned the second-most overall medals and third-most gold medals in the 2012 Paralympics. In contrast, the United States finished fourth in the overall medal count and sixth in gold medals and American viewers saw minuscule amounts of media coverage of the event. NBC aired 5.5 hours of tape-delayed television coverage on its cable channel, NBC Sports Network: four one-hour highlight shows during competition, and a 1.5-hour highlight show one week following the conclusion of the Paralympic Games (Dumlao). Paralympic coverage did not appear to be a priority of U.S. print and online media, appearing minimally among the nation's most popular newspapers and their websites—and it was widely criticized by supporters of the Paralympic movement (Associated Press).

A lack of North American media attention toward the disability sport movement continued past the 2012 Paralympic Games despite the event's transformative reputation. The 2014 Sochi Winter Paralympic Games were broadcast in the United States a mere 52 hours on television compared to 1,539 hours of televised coverage for the Olympic Games (Kay; United States Olympic Committee), and the 2016 Rio Summer Paralympic Games had 70 hours of television coverage compared to 6,755 hours for the Rio Olympics (Lancaster; "How to"). NBC was contracted to broadcast 94 hours of televised coverage for the 2018 PyeongChang Winter Paralympic Games and 2,400 hours of televised coverage for the Olympics ("NBC Olympics"; OlympicTalk).

Other countries have indeed given greater media attention to the Paralympic Games, in particular Channel 4 in the United Kingdom following those transformative 2012 Paralympics. Channel 4's Paralympic air time for the Paralympics that followed were: 150 hours in 2014 and 700 hours in 2016 (Anderson; "Channel 4").

The uniqueness and perhaps irony of the absent attention in the United States is the amount of resources NBC and other networks spend on coverage of other sports. NBC, Fox, and ESPN spend $6 billion annually on rights to broadcast National Football League games; Fox, NBC, SBS, and Bell spend $4.8 billion annually for FIFA World Cup rights; BT Sports and Sky Sports spend $2.6 billion on English Premier League rights while TNT and ESPN also spend $2.6 billion on National Basketball Association rights ("Sportscaster"). NBC paid $1.33 billion for rights to the 2016 Rio Olympics, and $870 million for the 2014 and 2018 Winter Olympics in Sochi and PyeongChang, respectively ("Sportscaster"). A lack of spending toward Paralympic sport specifically reinforces the notion that sport for people with disabilities is not a product media deem worthy of the general public's attention, which establishes the invisibility of disability. McCombs and Shaw's agenda setting theory for mass media argues that media set the public's agenda by telling us what to think about (177). In the present example, media have the opportunity to tell us whether or not to think about disability, disability sport, and elite athletes who are competing at the highest level of disability sport. Ignoring or diminishing such an agenda relays that it is not important enough to think about for the public.

Oversight of sport for people with disabilities through media representation creates a system of omission and discrimination where a segment of the population is ignored. Sport for able-bodied athletes, from recreational to elite levels, is established as "normal" and anything else lives on the margins.

It could be argued that media set this agenda—that disability sport is not worthy of coverage because it is not important enough to our society. This type of discrimination certainly exists. However, financial gain is typically part of the engine that drives media decision-making to account for advertising, ratings, and contracted content. Sports programming rights fees provide evidence of finances dictating decisions, as the NFL ($39.6 billion), NBA ($24 billion), MLB ($12.4 billion), and Premier League ($7 billion) rank as the top four largest sports television broadcasting rights deals that all top the billion-dollar mark ("Top 10"). The NFL, NBA, and MLB contracts each span nine years. Therefore, the simplistic answer that media tell society what to think about in disability sport, then, is flipped upside down; consumers decide what is important information and entertainment, and media provide it. It is the consumer who drives ratings, choosing whether or not to watch or follow an event such as the Paralympic Games. And it is the consumer who ultimately decides whether to watch Paralympic sport, Special Olympics, or an X Games adapted event (e.g., Monoskier X). However, if the consumer is uneducated on the existence of disability sport at an elite, competitive level, how or why would he or she pursue it?

While lack of traditional media coverage has perpetuated the invisibility of disability in sport, and therefore a baseline understanding of it from sport management students, social media have become a platform of advocacy for the disability community overall. Society's oversight of disability sport leads to group polarization, and Sunstein suggests that group polarization has assisted in social justice movements such as that of disability rights through social media (86). Thus, traditional forms of media have perpetuated the invisibility of disability sport while social media have provided a platform for those injustices to be mended by giving visibility to the minority group. In this case, the minority group may be disability sport or even athletes with disabilities. For example, U.S. athletes at the 2012 Paralympic Games in London received little media coverage in their home country and therefore used Twitter as means of self-representation, sharing public knowledge such as results and outcomes as well as sharing behind-the-scenes information such as team camaraderie conversations and photographs (Pate, Hardin, and Ruihley 157).

The decision to ignore disability sport through traditional media reflects societal biases and prejudices of how the public normalizes able-bodied sport and marginalizes disability sport. If a person chooses not to consume disability sport, they likely will not choose to participate or become educated on disability sport in their daily decision-making and likely have not been exposed to disability sport in the past. Mere exposure to disability sport tends to enlighten one's choice to consume it, participate in it, or become an advocate for disability and disability sport (McKay, Block, and Park 332). Without exposure or education in formalized settings (e.g., the sport management classroom), disability is invisible within sport.

Visibility of Disability

Visibility of disability is when "disability is still visible and considered 'less than' or not equal to able-bodied ability" (DePauw 424). Referencing back to the aforementioned Paralympic media coverage example, Goffman's framing analysis takes media coverage a step further by explaining media tell the public what to think about as well as how to think about it (21). The frame, as Goffman explained and countless other researchers have examined, presents a window into the world of a specific issue or event. Media's frame, then, becomes a mere glimpse of what the bigger issue may be, and therefore sends a message of what is and what is not important for society to know—as well as how society should know it. For Paralympic media coverage, when the event is covered on television, the way it is covered is a mere frame through which to view the Paralympics and disability sport. As is often the case, disability sport is presented through the lens of being an inspirational story, particularly through feature stories on athletes and their overcoming adversity to compete in sport.

Media professionals have the ultimate input on the content that is selected, emphasized, and eventually presented to the public. This is also interpreted by the audience as what happened and what was relevant (Gitlin 42). It is through this understanding that media consumers start to comprehend a frame as a snapshot of an occurrence through the lens of the presenter, in this case the media professional (Mirabito, Huffman, and Hardin 64). The compilation of these frames has a significant impact on the consumer's formation of a reality and a conceptualization of a subject based on this process (Chong and Druckman 102).

Goffman maintained that people actively classify, organize, and interpret life experiences to make sense of them (21). These interpretations, or frames, influence the perceptions of the events or the presentation of information.

Gitlin defined frames as the "persistent selection emphasis, and exclusion" of information (7). Framing is conceptualized differently but there is general agreement that framing "means the perspective a person applies to define" a person, event, or issue (Takeshita 23). A frame is a "central organizing idea or story line that provides" meaning to events or people (Gamson and Modigliana 3) as well as placing information in context so that certain aspects of the event, person, or issue receive more attention (Pan and Kosicki 57). Frames "call attention to some aspects of reality while obscuring other elements" which can have different effects on media consumers (Entman 55). Entman summarized framing as involving the selection and highlighting of certain aspects of an event, issue, or person, and the exclusion of other information (53).

This all relates to the classroom because students are entering academia with preconceived notions of disability and adapted sport and athletes with disabilities based on their media consumption and the way disability sport is presented to them (Ghanem 156). There are other things that influence the perception of disability sport. Relationships with family and friends with disabilities, participation in adaptive sports, or even having a disability will influence the interpretation of the news stories about disability sport and athletes with disabilities. Media do and will continue to influence perception. Those perceptions will also depend on the personal characteristics and experiences of the media consumer (Severin and Tankard 249).

The discussion of media influence triggers the question of how disability sport and athletes with disabilities have been presented to media consumers and students in higher education. The traditional media model presented has been referred to as the supercrip image (Hardin and Hardin, "The 'Supercrip'"). This entails the news story focusing on the disability of the athlete rather than the athletic achievement of the participant (i.e., medical model). So, when disability sport does receive media coverage, it is often inspirational in nature, highlights pity or sorrow, and attempts to instigate feel-good emotions (Cottingham, Pate, and Gearity 78).

A case study by Cottingham et al. of a power wheelchair soccer tournament included interviews with spectators at the event. The spectators found the athletes inspirational and believed inspiration was an appropriate way to describe the athletes at the event (Cottingham et al. 70). Athletes with disabilities, though, do not want to be seen as inspirational but instead want to be seen as athletes (Hargreaves and Hardin). The athletes do not see themselves as inspirational, but know others see them that way (Cottingham et al. 70).

The supercrip label describes a person with a disability who overcomes external expectations (Hardin and Hardin, "The 'Supercrip'"). It is as though the person with a disability overcomes overwhelming odds to become an athlete and compete in disability sport in a superhero-like story (Goggin and Newell, "Fame"). These athletes are often competing at a high level of athleticism, but their disability is the focus and not the athletic accomplishments. The supercrip frame in many instances garners more attention than the athlete or the competition (Cottingham et al. 78). This idea of the supercrip may evolve because the athletes are doing things the general public cannot comprehend or never expected from someone with a disability. The athletes, though, are simply making adaptions to compete in sport. They are not heroic in their actions nor do they want to be perceived as heroic. These athletes want to be recognized for their athletic accomplishments not their disability for being heroic in some sense (Cottingham et al. 78–79; Hargreaves and Hardin).

The sport management classroom is the initial setting where this awareness can be enhanced if professors include disability sport within their course content. This does not mean to simply have a class dedicated to disability sport or adaptive recreation, as Shapiro et al. contend (105). These topics should be intertwined within the curriculum just as any other topic would be and infused into the curriculum.

(In)Visibility of DisAbility

DePauw's third stage is (In)Visibility of DisAbility, when "athletes with disabilities are visible in sport as athletes or a time when an athlete's disability is no longer visible" (425). The third stage is the ideal world for true inclusion of disability in sport, portraying disability as a characteristic of the athlete similar to race, ethnicity, gender, or eye color. Disability is not ignored, undermined, or over-celebrated; it is acknowledged and equally included. Even within the titling of the stage, "in" is placed in parentheses as a double meaning that disability is included (in) and therefore becomes invisible. Furthermore, the "a" in "DisAbility" is capitalized to emphasize ability over the lack of (real or perceived) ability. Simply put, ability is emphasized and included in sport regardless of the level.

This stage does not ignore disability in the world of sport that often emphasizes physical prowess and superiority. It does not overemphasize and patronize routine accomplishments of people with disabilities in sport. Instead, viewing disability in sport through this third stage ensures disability is included in the offering of sport just as any other demographic category would be. Full inclusion gives voice for people with disabilities in sport settings. Misener and Darcy stated: "In a sporting context, for example, the goal is to provide people with disability choice to participate in sport in the way that they want to, with whom they want to participate, and in the way they wish to participate" (4). Misener and Darcy point to the Inclusion Spectrum as a method for identifying varying ways of integrating people with disabilities in sport.

— Fully integrated: People of all abilities participate without adaptation or modification, such as a community fun run;
— Modified integrated: People with disabilities participate with some modification to rules, equipment, or area with mixed context of ability, such as using a ramp delivery system in bowling;
— Parallel: People with disabilities participate in the same activity but access it in their own way, such as integrating a disability version of sport within the able-bodied version;
— Adapted: People without disabilities participate in activities designed specifically for people with disabilities with parity reached through common adaptation, such as wheelchair basketball for people of all abilities;
— Discrete: People with disabilities participate in activities with similarly abled peers, such as goalball [4].

It is imperative for sport and recreational professionals operating a community's unorganized play and recreational opportunities to also be mindful of the Inclusion Spectrum. Suggested methods of including people with disabilities may be useful in regular communication with community physical education instructors, recreation professionals at private organizations and childcare facilities, and the college student studying sport management.

The aforementioned items in the Inclusion Spectrum will not magically appear in sport or recreational programming. Sport management professionals must carefully consider the items and then plan appropriately for the inclusion. The concept of fully-integrated programming or educational settings can be ensuring that a community fun run is held on a smooth surface that will allow for the use of wheelchairs as well as provide a safe route for individuals who may have other mobility constraints. Community recreational leagues or college intramural competitions can include adapted sport opportunities or sports designed specifically for people with disabilities (i.e., goalball). This does not mean that there needs to be wholesale changes to programming at the community recreation center. There should certainly be community feedback and a gauging of interest of this type of programming. It may be prudent to have activities for people with disabilities at one location in the community to maximize resources and bring the disability sport community together for networking and establishing a sense of community before striving for integration. Nevertheless, these discussions should first be occurring in the sport management classroom so future professionals are prepared to enter a more diverse workplace.

There can be the inclusion of adapted physical education courses in the curriculum, and students can develop a deeper understanding of adapted sport. The class does not have to be required, but students who want to pursue a career in adapted sport can be encouraged to take the class with both able-bodied students and with students with disabilities. Furthermore, faculty should be encouraged to collaborate with campus recreation programs to seek guidance on adapted sport and recreation opportunities that already exist on campus and incorporate those into both participation and management exercises for students. Conversely, if adapted sport and recreation opportunities are nonexistent on campus, perhaps there is no greater educational lesson for the sport management student than to identify gaps in service at their own campus setting while working to fill those gaps through programming design and implementation of disability sport opportunities. A specific disability sport class is not required but an awareness of disability sport should appear throughout the curriculum (Shapiro et al. 107). It is important to include assignments that relate to disability sport into the curriculum, as well. A potential assignment would be a needs assessment of an adapted sport program at a community recreational center. This can also be accomplished by ensuring volunteer opportunities are available for students at organizations that provide recreational and sport programming for people with disabilities. Relationships should be developed with those organizations so volunteer opportunities can be cultivated which could potentially lead to more internship opportunities for students. Other recommendations include the introduction of disability sport through actual participation in those sports. It is in these learning situations where disability becomes part of the fabric of sport during the students' most critical educational moments.

Conclusion and Recommendations

The misconceptions surrounding disability sport can be overcome in the sport management classroom. Pitts and Shapiro explored disability content covered in introduction sport management courses and found the Americans with Disabilities Act, Paralympic sport, Special Olympics, and facility accessibility were the top topics addressed and only topics addressed in more than 30 percent of classes (38). The authors acknowledge, however, that a low response rate (58 faculty) may have skewed results as faculty already offering disability sport content may have been more inclined to respond whereas faculty not offering disability sport content may have avoided responding (Pitts and Shapiro 42).

Omission of disability sport from the classroom may be simple oversight but can be countered with proactive educators who approach inclusivity of disability in a similar manner they do for gender, race, and international sport—and the sport management classroom is a prime location given it is a relatively young field and in a constant state of improvement (Pitts 46). Where disability differs from other demographical topics often covered in sport sociology courses is that disability may be studied through the sociological lens, but also through more management-centric courses that require the student to problem-solve and plan. Disability inclusion education is needed in the basic sport management courses and understanding how best to include disability-related issues within sport management curriculum may be a top challenge for educators and faculty.

The World Health Organization/World Bank provided recommendations for inclusion of people with disabilities, each of which can be applied to the sport setting and used within the sport management classroom.

> 1. Enable access to all mainstream systems and services (e.g., courses in facilities, programming)
> 2. Invest in specific programs and services for people with disabilities (e.g., courses in sociology, programming)
> 3. Adopt a national disability strategy and plan of action (e.g., courses in management, planning, and evaluation)
> 4. Involve people with disabilities (e.g., courses in sociology, programming, management)
> 5. Improve human resource capacity (e.g., courses in human resources)
> 6. Provide adequate funding and improve affordability (e.g., courses in management, finance)
> 7. Increase public awareness and understanding (e.g., courses in sociology, communication)
> 8. Improve disability data collection (e.g., courses in research)
> 9. Strengthen and support research on disability (e.g., courses in research).

Dedicating separate courses to focus on disability in sport may enhance education, but specialty courses reinforce segregation—that disability sport is different from other sport (Shapiro et al. 105). Shapiro et al. suggest the infusion model is a more inclusive and practical approach to incorporating disability sport into sport management curriculum because of its "systematic approach to integrate knowledge and understanding of disability and disability issues throughout curriculum" (106).

Level One of the infusion model is a single, isolated exposure unrelated to other courses to establish initial awareness of disability issues, in this case, within sport management. For an individual course, the faculty member may include a lecture on a disability-related topic, invite a guest speaker to share research on a disability issue, or require a single assignment for reflection and demonstration of knowledge on disability in sport (Shapiro et al. 107).

Level Two is multiple experiences within a course or across multiple courses where students acquire knowledge from repeated exposure. Faculty may cover disability within a course across multiple lectures or may require multiple, extended activities in class that engage the student in a deeper manner than just an isolated learning moment (Shapiro et al. 107–108).

Level Three is infusion, where "disability topics and issues are interwoven throughout curricula, becoming an integral and natural component of each course" (Shapiro et al. 111). Reaching Level Three infusion is the optimal goal of including disability within sport management curriculum. Examples of infusion are highly engaging experiences that shape attitudes such as experiential learning opportunities that place students in real-life, hands-on learning environments. A student, for example, may complete an internship with a Paralympic Sport Club or complete practicum work at a community recreation center that focuses much of its programming on disability sport and serving people with disabilities. A less rigorous and formal experience may be regular wheelchair sport recreational opportunities for all students on campus as part of the routine activities expected during the overall college student experience. Infusion of disability in the sport management classroom highlights DePauw's (In)Visibility of DisAbility stage, incorporating disability into the fabric of a program's curriculum (425). This inclusion can break down negative preconceived stereotypes of disability that students may bring into academic programs, all while reshaping future sport management professionals' attitudes into minds that are searching for ways to always include disability into their work.

While infusion at Level Three is optimal, we contend that sport management education must first make a concerted effort to achieve Level Two of the infusion model where disability in the sport management classroom is more than merely a lecture or guest speaker—which is the present state of sport management's inclusion of disability. Faculty should first work to include disability in multiple facets of class and curriculum. Just as faculty often refer to the same examples within the classroom and too often refer to examples from major elite sport such as baseball, basketball, football, hockey, and soccer, the initial challenge should be for faculty to engage students in cases and discussion that include disability sport settings and challenges. An in-class example of ethical decision-making and doping is cyclist Lance Armstrong, but perhaps a more challenge and expansive example could be the Russian Paralympic athletes that were banned from 2016 competition in Rio for widespread doping allegations. Or perhaps a complex case that students may take on in a sport governance class is the classification systems within elite disability sport.

Moving disability sport from a singular topic covered in one class or just once per semester toward multiple examples and assignment-related activity should be the first achievable goal by faculty. Only when that is mastered can sport management programs strive for infusion of disability throughout the curriculum and throughout the college student experience. Infusion of disability sport within core courses of sport management curriculum requires buy-in from faculty and commitment from department chairs. Once supported, some suggestions of infusion within core sport management courses are as follows:

— **Communication/Media:** An ongoing examination of language use toward athletes with disabilities and how media coverage of disability sport can compare and contrast with other portrayals and communication of segments of sport.

— **Ethics:** Infusion within a sport ethics course may include critical analysis of how prosthetic limbs are used in disability sport and athletes are portrayed as "bionic" athletes in addition to general sport issues such as doping and cheating within the elite levels of disability sport.

— **Event Management:** An event management course should consistently analyze accessibility of events at entrances, parking, and seating, in addition to accommodations that should, are, and are not provided for volunteers, attendees, and participants with disabilities.

— **Facility Management:** Infusion may include topics related to the Americans with Disabilities Act of 1990 (ADA) in regard to parking accessibility and seating accessibility. Those courses should also include topics related to providing access to participating in sports at the facility. This would entail discussions on how to design a facility that will have accessible locker rooms, pools that will have ramps rather than wall stairs, including adapted sport equipment in budget requests, as well as having space available for adapted sport programming.

— **Governance:** Infusion in sport governance courses include analysis and inclusion of governing bodies that oversee and manage adapted sport. Topics would include what activities are available and what resources are required to provide the participation opportunities. Examples can be used at high school, intercollegiate, club, elite amateur, federations, and professional levels.

— **Intercollegiate Athletics:** Infusion within an intercollegiate athletics course may explore challenges to including disability sport under the NCAA governance structure, explore how universities are providing disability sport as recreation, club, and varsity options, and analyze how conferences such as the Eastern College Athletic Conference (ECAC) can and have implemented policies for contesting disability sport championships at the college level.

— **Law:** Aside from the ADA compliance and understanding, sport law courses may examine case law related to disability sport and challenge students to analyze alternative outcomes.

— **Marketing and Promotions:** A marketing and promotions course could explore patterns of advertising and promotion of disability sport and develop a marketing plan for mainstreamed disability sports such as wheelchair basketball and alpine skiing.

— **Programming:** A sports programming class should include topics related to providing opportunities for athletes with disabilities, both physical and intellectual. Examples and assignments within this course may include the elite level of sport but also community recreation, outdoor recreation, and campus recreation.

— **Sociology:** In addition to examining how the social and medical models weave throughout sport, a sociology course may explore the portrayal of disability through inspiration and supercrip, and barriers to inclusion in disability sport.

Developing a consistent and expected inclusion of disability within the sport management classroom is not only a step forward for sport management programs across the country, but it is a holistic educational approach to preparing students to enter into the industry. Sport management educators would be remiss to overlook service to an entire demographic or ignore how segments of the industry (e.g., communication, events, facilities, etc.) affect the experience of an entire demographic. Thus, it becomes paramount for the sport management educator to strive to make disability part of the fabric of learning while moving toward full infusion of disability within sport management curriculum. Creating this infusion of disability sport into the curriculum is something that takes planning and discussion among faculty. It should not merely be an edict that every class have some sort of disability sport discussion in it. That would be somewhat patronizing and could potentially provide inconsistent discussion of disability sport. Faculty should work to determine how they want to infuse disability sport into the curriculum, develop a strategic plan for the inclusion of the topic, and then evaluate the process. This would ensure consistent messaging, inclusion of a wide variety of topics, and optimal student exposure to disability sport. Faculty should also consider measuring student attitudes and awareness once they enter the major in regard to disability sport and then measure them again prior to graduation to determine if the curriculum infusion is beneficial to the students.

WORKS CITED

Anderson, Gary. "Channel 4 Reveals Sochi 2014 Line-up for 150 Hours of Coverage." *Inside the Games*, Dunsar Media Company, 3 February 2014. Web. 15 January 2018.

Associated Press. "Full TV Coverage for Paralympics, Just Not in US." *ESPN*. ESPN, 23 August 2012. Web. 15 January 2018.

Braddock, David L., and Susan L. Parish. "An Institutional History of Disability." *Handbook of Disability Studies*. Ed. Gary L. Albrecht, Katherine D. Seelman, and Michael Bury. New York: Sage, 2001. 11–68. Print.

Brittain, Ian. *The Paralympic Games Explained*. New York: Routledge, 2010. Print.

"Channel 4 Unveils Rio Paralympics Team." *Channel 4*. Channel 4 Television Corporation, 14 July 2016. Web. 30 January 2018.

Chong, Dennis, and James N. Druckman. "A Theory of Framing and Opinion Formation in Competitive Elite Environments." *Journal of Communication* 57 (2007): 99–118. Print.

Cottingham, Michael, Joshua R. Pate, and Brian Gearity. "Examining 'Inspiration': Perspectives of Stakeholders Attending a Power Wheelchair Soccer Tournament." *Canadian Journal of Disability Studies* 4.1 (2015): 59–89. Print.

Davis, Ronald W. "Adapted Sport." *Adapted Physical Education and Sport*. Ed. Joseph P. Winnick, and David L. Poretta. Champaign, IL: Human Kinetics, 2017. 41–58.

Degun, Tom. "Channel 4's London 2012 Paralympic Coverage Shortlisted for Sport Industry Awards. *Inside the Games*. Dunsar Media Company, 18 February 2013. Web. 30 January 2018.

DePauw, Karen P. "The (In)Visibility of DisAbility: Cultural Contexts and 'Sporting Bodies.'" *The Thirty-First Amy Morris Homans Lecture*, 1997. PDF file.

DePauw, Karen P., and Susan J. Gavron. *Disability and Sport*. Champaign, IL: Human Kinetics, 2005. Print.

DePauw, Karen P., and Grace Goc Karp. "Preparing Teachers for Inclusion: The Role of Higher Education." *Journal of Physical Education, Recreation, and Dance* 65 (1994): 51–53. Print.

Dumlao, Ros. "U.S. Paralympics Finally Get TV Coverage on American Soil." *Denver Post*. Digital First Media, 14 August 2012. Web. 1 January 2018.

Entman, Robert M. "Framing: Toward Clarification of a Fractured Paradigm. *Journal of Communications* 43.4 (1993): 51–58. Print.

Gamson, William A., and Andre Modigliana. "Media Discourse and Public Opinion on Nuclear Power: A Constructionist Approach." *American Journal of Sociology* 95.1 (1989): 1–37. Print.

Ghanem, Salma. "Filling the Tapestry: The Second Level of Agenda Setting." *Communication and Democracy: Exploring the Intellectual Frontiers in Agenda-Setting Theory*. Ed. Maxwell McCombs, Donald L. Shaw, and David Weaver. Mahwah, NJ: Lawrence Erlbaum Associates, 1997. 3–14. Print.

Gitlin, Todd. *The Whole World Is Watching: The Mass Media in the Making and Unmaking of the New Left*. Berkley: University of California Press, 1980. Print.

Gliedman, John, and William Roth. *The Unexpected Minority: Handicapped Children in America*. New York: Harcourt Brace Jovanovich, 1980. Print.

Goffman, Erving. *Frame Analysis: An Essay on the Organization of Experience*. Cambridge: Harvard University Press, 1974. Print.

Goggin, Gerard, and Christopher Newell. "Frame and Disability: Christopher Reeve, Super Crips, and Infamous Celebrity." *M/C Journal: A Journal of Media and Culture* 7.5 (2010): 1–6. Print.

Hardin, Marie, and Brent Hardin. "The 'Supercrip' in Sport Media: Wheelchair Athletes Discuss Hegemony's Disabled Hero." *Sociology of Sport Online* 7 (2004). Web. 30 January 2018.

Hardin, Brent, and Marie Hardin. "Distorted Pictures: Images of Disability in Physical Education Textbooks." *Adapted Physical Activity Quarterly* 21.4 (2004): 399–413. Print.

Hargreaves, Jean Ann, and Brent Hardin. "Women Wheelchair Athletes: Competing Against Media Stereotypes." *Disability Studies Quarterly* 29 (2009). Web. 15 January 2018.

"How to Watch the 2016 Rio Olympic Games." *NBC Olympics*. NBCUniversal, 2 February 2016. Web. 30 January 2018.

Kay, Alex. "NBC Olympics Schedule 2014: Full Viewing Guide for Sochi Games." *Bleacher Report*. Bleacher Report. 7 February 2014. Web. 15 January 2018.

Lancaster, Marc. "Rio Paralympics 2016 TV Schedule: Where to Watch the Games." *Sporting News*. Sporting News Media, 6 September 2016. Web. 15 January 2018.

Lazarus, Susanna. "Channel 4 to Broadcast 2014 and 2016 Paralympic Games." *RadioTimes*. Immediate Media Company. 8 February 2013. Web. 15 January 2018.

Lee, Sarah M., et al. "Physical Education and Physical Activity: Results from the School Health Policies and Programs Study 2006." *Journal of School Health* 77.8 (2007): 435–463. Print.

Levitt, Jonathan M. "Exploring How the Social Model of Disability can be Re-invigorated: In Response to Mike Oliver." *Disability & Society* 32.4 (2017): 589–594. Print.

"Los Angeles 2015." *Special Olympics*. Special Olympics, Web. 30 January 2018.

McCombs, Maxwell E., and Donald L. Shaw. "The Agenda-Setting Function of Mass Media." *Public Opinion Quarterly* 36.2 (1972): 176–187. Print.

McKay, Cathy, Martin E. Block, and Jung Yeon Park. "The Impact of Paralympic School Day on Student Attitudes Toward Inclusion in Physical Education." *Adapted Physical Activity Quarterly* 32.4 (2015): 331–348. Print.

Mirabito, Timothy, Landon Huffman, and Robin Hardin. "The Chosen One: The Denver Post's Coverage of Tim Tebow." *Journal of Contemporary Athletics* 7.2 (2013): 51–68. Print.

Misener, Laura, and Simon Darcy. "Managing Disability Sport: From Athletes with Disabilities to Inclusive Organisational Perspectives." *Sport Management Review* 17 (2014): 1–7. Print.

"NBC Olympics to Present Unprecedented 94 Hours of Paralympic Television Coverage in March." *Team USA*. United States Olympic Committee. 29 January 2018. Web. 30 January 2018.

Oliver, Michael. "Defining Impairment and Disability: Issues at Stake." *Disability and Equality Law*. Ed. Elizabeth F. Emens, and Michael A. Stein. New York: Routledge, 2013. 3–18. Print.

_____. "The Social Model of Disability: Thirty Years On." *Disability & Society* 28.7 (2013): 1024–1026. Print.

OlympicTalk. "Breakdown of NBC Olympics Record 2,400 Hours of PyeongChang Programming." *NBC Sports*. NBCUniversal. 28 November 2017. Web. 30 January 2018.

Pan, Zhongdang, and Gerald M. Kosicki. "Framing Analysis: An Approach to News Discourse." *Political Communication* 10.1 (1993): 55–75. Print.

Pate, Joshua R., and Robin L. Hardin. "Best Practices for Media Coverage of Athletes with Disabilities: A Person-First Language Approach." *Routledge Handbook of Sport Communication*. Ed. Paul M. Pedersen. New York: Routledge, 2013. 359–368. Print.

Pate, Joshua R., Robin L. Hardin, and Brody J. Ruihley. "Speak for Yourself: Analysing How US Athletes Used Self-Presentation on Twitter During the 2012 London Paralympic Games." *International Journal of Sport Management and Marketing* 15.3/4 (2014): 141–162. Print.

Pitts, Brenda G. "Examining the Sport Management Literature: Content Analysis of the *International Journal of Sport Management*." *International Journal of Sport Management* 17.2 (2016): 1–21. Print.

Pitts, Brenda G., and Deborah R. Shapiro. "People with Disabilities and Sport: An Exploration of Topic Inclusion in Sport Management." *Journal of Hospitality, Leisure, Sport & Tourism Education* 21 (2017): 33–45.

"A Revolution Begins." *Special Olympics*. Special Olympics, Web. 30 January 2018.

Severin, Werner J., and James W. Tankard. *Communication Theories: Origins, Methods, and Uses in the Mass Media*. New York: Longman, 1979. Print.

Shakespeare, Tom. "The Social Model of Disability." *The Disability Studies Reader*. Ed. Lennard J. Davis. New York: Routledge, 2017. 195–203. Print.

Shapiro, Deborah R., et al. "Infusing Disability Sport into the Sport Management Curriculum. *Choregia: Sport Management International Journal* 8.1 (2012): 101–118. Print.

Silvers, Anita, David T. Wasserman, and Mary Briody Mahowald. *Disability, Difference, Discrimination: Perspectives on Justice in Bioethics and Public Policy*. New York: Rowman & Littlefield Publishers, 1998. Print.

Sportscaster. "Largest Sports League TV Contracts Worldwide as of September 2016 (in Billion U.S. Dollars Per Year)." *Statista—The Statistics Portal*. Web. 15 January 2018.

Sunstein, Cass R. *#Republic: Divided Democracy in the Age of Social Media*. Princeton: Princeton University Press, 2017. Print.

Takeshita, Toshio. "Exploring the Media's Role in Defining Reality: From Issue Agenda-Setting to Attribute Agenda-Setting." *Communication and Democracy: Exploring the Intellectual Frontiers in Agenda-Setting Theory*. Ed. Maxwell McCombs, Donald L. Shaw, and David Weaver. Champaign, IL: Lawrence Erlbaum Associates, 1997. 15–28. Print.

Thomas, Nigel Brian. "An Examination of the Disability Sport and Mainstreaming in Seven Sports." Diss. Loughborough University, 2004. Print.

"Top 10 Biggest TV Rights Deals in Sports (Currently Active)." *Totalsportek2*. 19 January 2017. Web. 14 March 2018.

United States Olympic Committee. "Television Schedule Set for Sochi 2014 Paralympic Winter Games." *U.S. Paralympics*. United States Olympic Committee. 19 February 2014. Web. 15 January 2018.

"What We Do." *Special Olympics*. Special Olympics. Web. 30 January 2018.

World Health Organization/World Bank. *World Report on Disability*. 2011. PDF file.

As American as Football, Basketball and Oppression Pie

An Analysis of the Evolution of Racial Policing in American Team Sports

LaToya T. Brackett

One of the most infamous pastimes in the United States is watching organized sports. It has been said that apple pie and baseball are synonymous with being an American. Although there is room for debate, these two things have defined America and being an American. Yet the juxtaposition of race in this story is most often lost, and if not lost, contested, rejected and considered not a part of being American. This pastime of sports is one of the best documentations of what it means to be an American. As sports altered in racial makeup over the history of the United States, so too did other social structures. The integration of certain sports, like the historic period in baseball when Jackie Robinson broke the color barrier, is one such documentation. Robinson has since been praised by the American public even retiring his jersey number—#42. It is a great statement about America to embrace such a great player as Jackie Robinson, with no regards to his race as it is seen today. As a great Negro baseball player, back then, he was not as easily accepted as American public memory recalls today. Muhammad Ali died in 2016 and was praised so heavily as the Greatest. Yet when he first called himself the Greatest, Americans rejected him, and rejected the notion of a black man being the greatest at anything a white man could do. Both men were protesters to the system of American sports, and thus the American traditions at that time. They pierced through the hegemony of American professional sports, by questioning where they fit within sports and within the society that created and perpetuates the traditions of professional American sports.

Today the protest is once again alive, but this time in football. Colin Kaepernick has lit a fire in the American fabric surrounding the American flag, with particular emphasis on the tradition of saluting the flag as the Star Spangled Banner plays before each and every game. Yet his fire, just as Ali's fire, has been misinterpreted as an individual fight, and as a separate fight from what is most often accepted as American. Both Ali and Kaepernick protested because of a consistent and conditioned plight of blacks to be guaranteed their rights as Americans. Being both black and American their plight affects everyone. And that is America's pie. You can add flavors to it, make it fancier or more unique, alter the outside, and spice up the inside, but at the end of the day, the basic ingredients that create that American pie will always reside in the original recipe. Thus, race and the role of the institutionalization of American racism is still present in American sports.

This essay will examine the white gaze that privileges itself as the American gaze on the protests by black athletes and analyze how the once overt white gaze is now subtler but still present today. By understanding the gaze, and three of the major components to rejecting black athletes in both the NBA and NFL, one is better able to follow the evolution of racial policing within these two team sports. This essay will demonstrate how and why a constitutional right to protest became a signal to the white dominant audience to make Colin Kaepernick public enemy number one. Colin Kaepernick in August 2016, as a San Francisco 49ers quarterback, chose to protest the National Anthem in order to demonstrate his outrage of the continual violence against black bodies in the United States. In his gaze, the American flag, and its associated freedoms, protection, and equality did not extend to everyone, particularly the black community of which he too is defined and could have easily been one of the victims if not for his own privileges in life. For him his individual privilege did not outweigh the collective oppression, and the desire to be the *American* the flag alludes to. Kaepernick after a year of protest never faltered in his stance and consequently never received a football contract making him unemployed in the 2017 NFL season. Despite his rejection he continued to demonstrate his outrage by giving monetarily to groups that do the hands-on work in communities hit hardest by the U.S. systems of oppression. As he continued his work in silence, many football players continued "his" protest on the field by kneeling or locking arms, or even placing a hand on the shoulder of a teammate who chose to kneel. These continued demonstrations during the 2017 season has once again awakened the racist insides of the American sporting tradition, reminding us that the American sports fabric has not truly changed. Because the ingredients have always remained the same, despite the mixing of additional components throughout time. With every integration, firsts, and inspirational stories comes the greater understanding that sports were for whites only and are still defined by whites only sports experiences. It is this white gaze that influences the sports industry on all levels. This gaze is more recognized as the oppressive means by which American athletes, particularly black and other marginalized athletes, continually must mitigate in hopes to be successful under the rules of America. As opportunities allow black athletes to be definitional in sport culture, they are tasked with straddling double standards, and maintaining strength as rules alter without their identities incorporated, but with a white gaze. They debate whether to contest the gaze in their own way or reside in the way the gaze defines them. Black athletic protest has continued and has been reimagined but what they protest remains the same—institutionalized racism implemented through the white gaze.

The White Gaze

The white gaze is the major concept to be utilized in understanding the double standards placed upon black NFL and NBA players in the 21st century. In this particular analysis, it will be defined as the requirements, desires, understanding, and traditions of the American white dominant society placed upon the world of organized sports. This white dominant society made up, and continues to make up, the fan base and the consumers of this American pastime. History provides a foundational understanding of the ways in which the fan base and consumer base remained white. Without a racially integrated society, sports culture could only have been defined by the gaze of whites. Despite continual integration within American society and sports, professional sports have remained for whites only. The National Football League (NFL) and the National Basketball Association (NBA) are two team sports leagues that are examples of this juxtaposition.

The white gaze consists of traditional components that establish the hegemonic way in which professional sports are played, watched, and managed. When someone breaks with what has been established as "the way," it disrupts society. Due to only understanding the way in which the dominant identity created the tradition, there is only one way to respond—rejection. Muhammad Ali was heavily rejected, and he was even stripped of his titles and his eligibility to fight. Today Colin Kaepernick has been rejected as well, and with a less obvious rejection as Ali, but still with the inability for him to play for a team. Kaepernick has filed an official suit against the NFL for colluding to blackball him and to keep any team from signing him despite his abilities (Belson). The rejection occurs from individual whites and from the organizations, such as the NFL and NBA, that are predominantly owned and managed by whites as well. Why wouldn't Ali want to fight for his country? Why wouldn't Kaepernick want to stand during the National Anthem? Don't they know they should feel blessed to have the opportunities they have because they are American? These are the types of approaches by individual voices attacking these men, and by the voices of those that fully understand and engage in the traditions of American sports. The traditions that align with their own personal and collective identity as white Americans. It is a white gaze.

On the other hand, as the late Dr. W.E.B. DuBois stipulated in the early 20th century, blacks have a double consciousness. "One ever feels his two-ness—an American, a Negro; two souls, two thoughts, two unreconciled strivings; two warring ideals in one dark body, whose dogged strength alone keeps it from being torn asunder" (DuBois 2). In relation to U.S. sporting tradition and hegemonic requirements, blacks have the required capability to be both black and American as it is defined by dominant society, thus they know how to be accepted by the white gaze. However, at times, one's blackness and Americanness may collide creating a black American who shares their own frustration with an American identity and the American system that does not integrate fully the "darker brother," as Langston Hughes spoke to in his poem, "I, Too." African Americans as a collective identity were raised within American dominant society under a white gaze and only accepted when they fit within that gaze. They must understand that they are required to defer to white authority, must desire to live the way whites desire to live, must be cognizant of the way in which whites understand society for themselves and for African Americans, and must be willing to conform to the traditions of whites only. This is the way that African Americans are able to be considered American too. Yet this way is no way to live and is a second-class citizenship. Many blacks, since their first encounters with white Americans, have objected to this. In consideration of the white gaze's focus on the black body, African Americans will be identified using the term black throughout the remainder of this essay.

By definition, to protest is to state disapproval of or objection to something. Muhammad Ali disapproved of the U.S. presence in Vietnam. He also objected to being required to fight for a country he saw as not willing to fight for him. Colin Kaepernick disapproved of the consistent lack of responsible responses to the continued killings of black people by police. He objected to the notion that the U.S. flag and the Star Spangled Banner represented *all* Americans. In their protests they too received disapproval because they were breaking the traditions of sports, and the objection, or a major objection related to their usage of their identity as pro athletes. They used this identity in order to be heard. White dominant society prescribed that they not be heard, but particularly that they should not be heard sharing a dissenting opinion. This prescription occurs even on the less obvious protests within sports, beginning with integrating sports to maintaining black cultural identities despite the white gaze demanding they do not.

The Black Athlete in White Controlled Sports

It can be convenient to look at the integrated images of the players in professional sports today and forget the struggles that allowed for such numerical integration. The struggle is mostly remembered by those that did the struggling, those that protested the segregated industry of professional sports, those that were mostly the oppressed. Briefly it should be recalled some of the most recognized moments integrating professional sports. The most infamous is Jackie Robinson who is hailed as integrating professional Baseball when he joined the Brooklyn Dodgers in 1947. Offered the position by Branch Rickey, Robinson joined America's favorite sport at the time, baseball, which he had to play the American way. He was under the white gaze and Branch Rickey, having known the system that he was integrating, required Robinson to be the "ballplayer with guts enough not to fight back." Components about Jackie Robinson's life prior to his sports career express a man who was the type to fight back. He was a lieutenant in the Army, but he did not appreciate the segregation that reminded him and other black men that the United States needed their bodies to fight but did not respect their humanity to give them the same rights. As the morale officer of his battalion, he altered the protocols of the post exchange at Fort Riley—he fought for his men to have more seats in the segregated snack space (Robinson and Duckett 14). This was a small victory with little push back. It was when he refused to sit at the back of the bus on the Army post that he would earn a Court Marshall and eventually an honorable discharge in 1944. In his autobiography, Robinson states, "I had no intention of being intimidated into moving to the back to the bus" (Robinson and Duckett 19). Unfortunately, the fight he once had for civil rights would not be recognized but rather hidden. Robinson, the American baseball player, became a symbol for the correct way to integrate. Robinson's lack of obvious protest as a baseball player created an ease for the white gaze but it created tension for some black Americans who wondered if he was a supporter of the civil rights fight. Robinson fought to do what he enjoyed, playing baseball professionally. Each time he stood up at bat, he fought the crowd's racism by excelling in his play. "Jackie Robinson had to watch every *p* and *q*, had to dot every *i* and cross every *t*, because he was the first and couldn't afford to be perceived as flashy or arrogant or 'some kind of hot dog.' Because Robinson had gone through all that, [players like Willie Mays] had the luxury of being lavishly creative" (Rhoden 150). His success was playing baseball exceptionally and for the white gaze. He was a pioneer that would lead the way for diverse players, and their diverse personal styles during play and outside of it.

In juxtaposition to the well-versed story of baseball integration, it should always be recognized that the first black man to integrate professional baseball, was actually Moses Fleetwood Walker in 1884. At the time the segregation of the sport was not based on an official rule, but rather it was based on tradition. Integrating less than two decades after the U.S. Civil War, Walker's lack of support aligned with Robinson's, but extended beyond by pushing him out of the league in 1889. Walker, unlike Robinson, was not an exceptional player and this hindered his ability to break the barrier and remain a major league player (Hill). He is often forgotten and overshadowed with the well supported story of baseball integration made successful by the great Jackie Robinson.

In 1908, Jack Johnson was the first back heavyweight boxing champion. He traveled to Australia to gain the title. The most memorable moment of Johnson's career was his fight with the "Great White Hope" Jim Jeffries in 1910 in which he defeated Jeffries in contradiction to the desire of the white dominant society. "When he entered the ring to fight Jeffries, the band began playing 'All Coons Look Alike to Me' ... [a]fter the fight, riots broke out throughout the United States; eight Blacks were killed by roving gangs of whites" (Rhoden 95). This white reaction to being defeated by a black athlete was to ensure that blacks would not be encouraged by the victory to protest the legal segregation that was in place in the United States. William Rhoden states a contextual understanding for why success in sports was more than just an individual win for the fighter or player, but due to a disconnect "from the American dream ... sports often seemed the only venue where the battle for self-respect could be vigorously waged" for blacks (Rhoden 14). It was, in theory, egalitarian. Johnson would later be in legal turmoil for charges of kidnapping that were established without cause. He fled the country for a while and would return to serve some of his prison time. He died in 1946 in a car accident (Rhoden). Jack Johnson led the way for the many great black fighters, including Mohammad Ali. He would be a reference for the way in which violence would characterize future black athletes.

In 1936 Jesse Owens won three gold medals at the Berlin Olympic Summer Games. The Nazi party ruled Germany at the time and established publicly the pro–Aryan policies by selecting Aryans only for German representation in the Olympics. This created a divide within the United States between those that believed in protesting the Olympics and those that believed participating and defeating the Germans would be a better choice. Jesse Owens was a successful track competitor, who had his own experiences with racism in America beginning with his childhood in the deep segregated south. David Wiggins states that Owens strove for a steady career in a vocational field, and like other black athletes at the time, he attended a vocational high school where he also blossomed as a track star. His track highlights offered him the opportunity to attend the Ohio State University where he would be courted to join a large delegation of black athletes to represent the United States in the 1936 Olympics. The National Association for the Advancement of Colored People (NAACP) was one of the intellectually driven organizations that originally pressed for a boycott of the Olympics. Owens originally supported the boycott, but would be convinced to attend, to defeat the opposition. No matter the desire to boycott or compete both sides were contending with the idea that the United States desired to defeat Germany despite the United States' own lack of recognition of their own racist system (Dyreson). Americans, and even black Americans, had issue with Owens representing the United States. Black Americans wondered about how he could go abroad to represent a country that would not agree, in written form, that the United States was committing crimes in the name of similar justifications the Germans were utilizing. Despite the goal of the games to prove Aryan superiority, Owens showed Germany and any anti–Semitics across the globe that a black man could defeat a white man (Tomlinson). As integrators of professional sports, this was a most basic form of protest for black Americans. In 1968 track stars Tommie Smith and John Carlos raised their fists as they ascended the winners' platforms at the Mexico City Olympics adding direct visual protest to their win. Their protest was rejected, and they were stripped of their medals.

The racial integration of two team sports, basketball and football are not as engrained within American memory as other sports. In 1950 three black Americans were drafted into the NBA: Chuck Cooper for the Boston Celtics, Earl Lloyd for the Washington Capitols (now defunct), and Nat Clifton for the New York Knicks (Rhoden). The NFL has an interesting story of integration, in which some blacks played during the early years of the leagues under what would be considered club sports. As the sport became a more defined industry, blacks were banned from participating. In 1946, four men would officially integrate the NFL: Kenny Washington and Woody Strode signed with the Los Angeles Rams while Marion Motley and Bill Willis signed with the Cleveland Browns (Rhoden; Stewart and Anderson). This occurred a year before Jackie Robinson integrated the MLB. Despite the integration of the NBA and NFL being less present in public memory, it is here where the best examples reside of how the white gaze on sports is still heavily influential in assuring black players understand their role in the game. The NFL and NBA are leagues where the individuality of players is most policed. Individuality does not fit with the way in which sports are supposed to be played based on traditions, understanding, requirements, and desires of the white majority who established the organizations and continue, with majority numbers, to manage them. The white gaze.

According to the Institute for Diversity and Ethics in Sport, both the

NBA and NFL are owned primarily by whites. The NFL only has two owners of color, both of Asian descent as of 2016 (Lapchick and Marfatia 8). The NBA's majority and controlling ownership was 91.4 percent white in 2016, 2.9 percent African American and a total of 5.7 percent people of color (Lapchick and Balasundaram 27). The NBA players were 74.4 percent African American and 19.1 percent white in 2016. For the NFL there were 69.7 percent African American players and 27.4 percent white players the same year. In 1990 the NFL had 39 percent white players and the NBA in 1990–91 season was composed of 28 percent white players. The player representation has diversified over the years, and the NBA ownership has also increased its diversity, but the NFL's ownership diversity increase resides mainly in the category of gender not race.

Select Racial Demographics
of the NFL and NBA in 2016 and 2007 Seasons

	White Players	African American Players	White CEOs/ Presidents	African American CEOs/ Presidents	White Head Coaches	African American Head Coaches
NFL 2016	27.4%	69.7%	97.1%	0.0%	81.3% *26	15.6% *5
NFL 2007	31%	66%	100%	0.0%	81.0% *26	19% *6
NBA 2016	19.1%	74.4%	93.1% *54	6.9% *4	70.0% *21	20.0% *6
NBA 2007	20.7%	75.0%	76.7% *23	23.3% *7	60.0% *18	40.0% *12

*Denotes number in individual persons

Data from "The 2017 Racial and Gender Report Card: National Football League" and "The 2017 Racial and Gender Report Card: National Basketball Association."

Racial Equality Versus Racial Equity
in the NBA and NFL

Despite the two leagues being represented by a majority of black players, the management and ownership remains a majority white. The definition of the term equality relates directly to equal opportunities and rights. Blacks are the majority of the players in the NFL and NBA, which aligns with the definition of equality, because equal opportunities are indeed plentiful as players and are more accessible in management. When defining equity, it is most important to understand the requirement of being fair and impartial— an egalitarian management. This is not the experience of black players in the NBA and NFL. They may have equal access to being drafted, but their experiences within the leagues are not held to the same standards as white players. Focusing on blacks in the athletic component of the leagues, the following direct examples of inequitable management will reveal the less direct racism experienced by black players in professional sports. These instances of inequitable management have evolved into a more subtle and passive aggressive form. These acts, along with others that suppress opportunities for players of color, are racist due to the institutional power and authority that supports disadvantaging players of color while consistently supporting white players with similar situations. The definition of racism being utilized for this article, and the contextualization of the white gaze, is presented by Sensoy and DiAngelo. They write: "In the United States and Canada, racism refers to White racial and cultural prejudice and discrimination, supported by institutional power and authority, used to the advantage of Whites and the disadvantage of peoples of Color. Racism encompasses economic, political, social, and institutional actions and beliefs that perpetuate an unequal distribution of privileges, resources and power between White people and peoples of Color" (Sensoy and DiAngelo 228). As Jackie Robinson approached the plate, he was called the N-word time and time again, a very easily identifiable act of racism. The Sensoy and DiAngelo definition reveals the institutionalization of racism and how even if racist words are not clearly used, race may still be a foundational reason someone is being treated poorly. If the managing system is one that was defined by the majority and consistently run by the majority, then it is doing so under the majority's definitions which creates, in the United States, a white gaze. Such a lens would perpetuate the privileging of whites and the disadvantaging of peoples of color. The major ways in which these racist acts within sports occur is in response to a black player's (1) association with violence, (2) personal dress, and (3) the way in which he stylizes their way of play.

Violence

The black athlete has continually become more associated with violence. Major stories that became media showcases have revolved around a black athlete, the most notorious was the O.J. Simpson case in which Simpson was found not guilty of murdering his wife Nicole Brown Simpson. The case occurred in 1994 yet in 2016, a miniseries, *The People vs. OJ Simpson: American Crime Story*, was released and easily accessible for Netflix subscribers— two decades later this notorious story still provided dramatized media for American consumption. The drama of this case surrounded a black football player and the murder of his white wife. The next major violent black athlete after Simpson was Michael Vick in 2007 related to his dog fighting ring, in which he pleaded guilty and received a 23-month sentence that he fulfilled.

Michael Vick was an NFL quarterback, which in and of itself was a major accomplishment within the NFL. There has been an increase in black quarterbacks after Vick. There is an elevated type of drama attached to the stories of black athletes that break the rules which were instituted by the white gaze. These two preceding examples showed how the plight of a black athlete gets much more attention from the American public, particularly when there is a condition of violence attributed to it. This notion of elevated attention on violence, leads to a direct example in 1997 with NBA player, Latrell Sprewell of the Golden State Warriors. Sprewell choked and later punched his coach P.J. Carlesimo during a team practice. His punishment with a one-year suspension (Cunningham 41). This incident received a lot of media attention, yet the week earlier a white player, Tom Chambers of the Phoenix Suns, punched his conditioning coach and very little attention was placed upon his unsportsmanlike behavior. Rather Chambers was moved to the Philadelphia 76ers with no penalties (Lane 94).

The choking incident between Latrell Sprewell and his coach Carlesimo began with a verbal battle over the fact that Carlesimo told Sprewell that his ball passing was off. Sprewell choked the coach in response to their continued verbal battling and was ejected from practice. Golden State Warriors' official representation reported to the press that he returned from the locker room and proceeded to punch the coach as well (Dowd). Sprewell's initial punishment was a 10-day suspension, but the white defined gaze would influence the extension of this punishment. In line with elevated public drama for black athletes "the story and the outrage grew, the punishments ballooned. Two days after the incident, the Warriors voided [Sprewell's] three-year, 23.7-million-dollar contract and the NBA announced they were suspending him for one year" (Dowd). Yet, Tom Chambers from a week earlier, was simply traded to a different team. This over extended punishment was rescinded after some legal battles, and Sprewell's contract was reinstated (Dowd). But the white gaze that promoted harsher punishment on Sprewell relates back to the white gaze placed upon Jack Johnson's win against the "Great White Hope," which incited a riot led by whites. The key here is that the white gaze has continued, but simply has evolved.

The type of riot that created an overreach in Sprewell's punishment was not a direct physical one as it was for Jack Johnson, rather it came in verbal, and indirect racial connections to Sprewell, a black man, and violence. Jeffrey Lane shared a clear analysis of this riot type of culture after the Sprewell's incident:

> The mainstream media's handling of the Sprewell episode also suggests why race was relevant. Most in the media insisted that race played no part in the attack and that the Black men supporting Sprewell were disingenuously making a nonracial issue into a racial issue for personal ends. However, while muting the issue of race, they

drew conclusions about the incident and about Sprewell based squarely on racial assumptions. After the attack, Sprewell's status as villain was all too apparent; his name, in many articles, was replaced by negative pseudonyms—"the choker," "the strangler," "the choke artist." One writer dubbed him "a hard shadowy figure." Sprewell was called a "street thug" who had "gone full gangster." Sprewell's identity had been supplanted by aliases generally given to bad guys in comic books, whose actions are guided by smoldering inner evil [Lane 95].

Sprewell became synonymous with being violent, and with the act of violence. And as Lane connects, it is because of Sprewell being black, along with his supportive teammates, that violence was easily associated with them without any moral hesitation. Such violent ideas were placed within the dominant white gaze from images of black gangs throughout media platforms. Don Imus, a well-known radio host, expressed this association when describing the black men standing behind Sprewell at a press conference as "look[ing] like the Bloods and the Crips," two different dominant black gangs in the Los Angeles area. Yet even Imus' combining of the two distinct gangs into one, showcases his gaze on black men as being a group and not individuals. The Bloods and the Crips are historically rival gangs, but they are also historically associated with violence, a type of violence that has no correlation to black men standing behind another black man in support of his fight. However, this was not Imus' only commentary in which he associated black athletes in such a derogatory manner. In 2007, he was fired from his CBS radio show after commenting about the NCAA Rutgers women's basketball team, stating they were some "nappy headed hoes," after first acknowledging they were some "rough girls" that had tattoos. Imus connected the ideas of being rough, and having tattoos with black women, utilizing hair texture and promiscuity commentary as synonymous with black women. Even when there was no violence, Imus, and the white gaze created a narrative of violence. For black athletes there is always potential to be given the narrative of being violent.

Yet is this type of violence on the basketball court, as Sprewell and Carlesimo experienced, truly out of character in professional sports? In an extensive magazine feature by Eric Konigsberg in 1999, his interviews with several NBA sources expressed the occurrence of physical contact between players within practice, and that "what Sprewell did to Carlesimo wasn't out of the ordinary, or that if it was, that's only because it involved a player and a coach instead of two players" (Konigsberg). Several of Sprewell's teammates came to his defense, sharing that Coach Carlesimo was the type to be "verbally abusive" and that he has had confrontations with other players as well. They questioned what would be or was being done about Carlesimo. Not many players speak out about any ill treatment from coaches, as Rasheed Wallace, a player for the Portland Blazers, in 2003 was paraphrased, "the players will take the money because they'd be fools not to, but it confirms that point: part of that cash is hush money" (Lane 101). Players recognize that with such a payment, also comes a lack of power, control, or complaint.

Wrapping up the consistent presence of violent association with black athletes, Sprewell's incident was not the only one, and simply allows for a better understanding of various dynamics at play in regard to violent behavior in sports, and also violent association beyond sports that permeates the narratives of black athletes. Based on the definition of racism, a black male athlete choking a coach was more enticing to criticize and punish than in response to a white player choking a coach because the ideologies towards black men insisted he was extremely violent and a threat to society. However, a white man deserves another chance with no consequences. This is institutional racism, disadvantaging one while the other is privileged. This is not the only case of a double standard in the NBA or NFL. In 1998, Kevin Greene of the Carolina Panthers, a white linebacker, grabbed and threatened his coach, Kevin Steele, on national television. The commentary coming from the team coaches and even the NFL was of less worry and concern, Kevin Steele stated to the *Washington Post*: "Football is an emotional, aggressive game.... Those guys are out there fighting. Kevin is a good person. We've talked about it and worked it out. That's all I have to say about it" (Droschak). Greene was given a one-game suspension the following day, which would cost him under $118,000 of his $2 million contract. The coach that was attacked by Greene, on national television, stated he understood Greene's emotion, and the NFL stated that they were not involved in the decision, yet Sprewell was suspended by the NBA for a year. Sprewell also was not on national television during his altercation with his coach. Of course, the NFL and NBA are two different monsters but the numbers and ownership, and the rules written by a white gaze are parallel.

Personal Dress

In the 1990s, hip-hop permeated American culture. Most noticeably, it became an undertone in clothing, and other wearable attire. Hip-hop also seeped into athletics and introduced mainly by younger black players who were active in such style of dress and play in their everyday lives. These younger players would be a part of the hip-hop generation that Bakari Kitwana establishes in his text. Kitwana's text goes beyond the fundamental elements of hip-hop culture, "music, break dancing, graffiti, dj-ing, style, and attitude," into a more essential break down of the black youth that created and resided in the most progressive years of hip-hop and analyzes their life situation via their interaction with hip-hop (Kitwana xii). As he closes out one of his chapters on the hip-hop generation's exposure and emulation of black culture being unapologetic, he references a major style captain in individuality and hip-hop influence, Allen Iverson. He states that there is a hope-fulness for black youth seeing "b-ballers like Allen Iverson so messiah-like … hip-hop generationers identify with not only their success but where they came from, who they continue to be, *and* the success" (Kitwana 140). Allen Iverson is a prime example of how the white gaze began to police black style and black bodies in professional sports. Also, the five black freshmen basketball starters (Fab Five) at the University of Michigan in the early 1990s would also be a collegiate look at the way that hip-hop would be policed. Both Iverson and the Fab Five, experienced the utilization of their style for institutional profit while they were prohibited from freely expressing their own style. Yet in the 2010s, players in the NFL, like Cam Newton of the Carolina Panthers, often experience the wrath of the institutionalization of rules that police personal dress. These types of experiences demonstrate the evolution of racism in the leagues. In 2016, Newton was benched for the first play of a league game against the Seattle Seahawks (Around the NFL). His benching was not racially charged, but the continual infatuation with his style, or flare in his style, on and off the field relates to the escalation of rule violations by black players. The fact is, many dress code rules hit black players most, aligning with the white gaze definition of appropriate dress.

Connecting Don Imus' statement about the Rutgers players' tattoos and associating them with being rough and violent, the idea of tattoos in sports was a major image issue for Allen Iverson—an image issue within the white gaze. The official publication for the NBA, *Hoop*, edited Iverson's image in 1999; his "diamond earring and some of his tattoos were digitally removed from the cover photo. Other tattoos were obscured by the strategic layering of text over them" (Lane 51). A potential reason for editing the tattoos on his arm, could be what the tattoos represent—"paying tribute to … his deceased friends and old neighborhood" (Lane 42). Yet Iverson, like many young black players, desired to "keep it real" based on Jeffrey Lane's contextualization of their desired connection to their communities. This includes the embracing of the following aspects, which also aligns with the fashion of hip-hop culture at the time: "(tattoos, cornrows, baggy clothes, certain designer labels, big jewelry), speech, and general demeanor that prevail in the Black urban neighborhoods" (Lane 43). Iverson was not the only player to present himself this way, or to be policed in order to obtain an accepted image for the white gaze. Michael Jordan even had a clothing style similar to Iverson, and Jordan too was policed; in fact, his first, and predominately black Air Jordans, were banned in 1985 from the league (Lane 60).

The Fab Five at the University of Michigan were a unique showcase of hip-hop style emerging on the basketball court in the early 1990s (Hehir). They wore longer shorts and black socks. Michael Jordan wore longer shorts in the NBA as well and this hip-hop influence created a new accepted uniform style. Yet in 2005, the NBA "began reinforcing the 0.1 inch above the knee rule, which resulted in several players, including Iverson and some of his Philadelphia 76ers teammates, being fined US $10,000" (Cunningham 45). Cunningham states that during the years leading up to this rejuvenated focus, players were not as policed on the length of shorts issue. It was in 2005 that the NBA also created a player dress code, with the overall general policy for attire off the court to be defined as business casual (National Basketball Association). Iverson was hit with critiques of his off-court attire dating back to before the official rules were created. He spoke out about the league policing him: "Damn, these people want me to wear Italian suits all the time like Michael [Jordan] … want me to act like I'm 25, 26 or 27 years old. Well, I'm not that old yet…. Don't rush me" (Lane 50). Iverson speaks to a very important component of professional sports in the 21st century, the fact that players are younger and still finding themselves. For these young players at best what they can continue to do is "keep it real." Jalen Rose of the Fab Five stated in the ESPN documentary *30 for 30: The Fab Five*, that one of the reasons he and his teammates were so hated by the University of Michigan fandom and alumni was because they had balled heads and tattoos, listened to rap music, and wore earrings. The team received a great deal of hate mail due to their hip-hop style that was often associated with being thugs or a part of a gang, a regular association for black athletes in the contemporary white gaze narrative.

As non-professional athletes, the Fab Five straddled the line of competing in a professional capacity but as amateurs in the NCAA. Despite their lack of payment, they realized that they were profitable, but profits were not going to themselves but to the University of Michigan. The documentary showed the major monetary gain in the first two years of the Fab Five's presence on the court and the years prior. Yet no money or support was going to these five black youth from urban areas, several from Detroit. They protested. They protested in a silent way. They removed University of Michigan emblems from anything they wore during pregame warm ups. They did so because they saw that their title as the Fab Five was advertisement that promoted the sale of the University of Michigan attire. They are a prime example of how sports benefited from hip-hop culture to gain economic prosperity, yet those that provided the style received criticism, and punishment. Lane wrote: "*Sports Illustrated* writer Phil Taylor remarked in 1997 that 'one of the NBA's greatest accomplishments—essential to the way the league has flourished financially over the past two decades—is the way it has not only handled the race issue but also tamed it and used it to turn a profit.' Encapsulated in Taylor's observation is the essence of how Blackness and hip-hop are sold to white America—as an embraced but contained culture—as well as a validation of the NBA's efforts to effectively mediate the hip-hop explosion" (45).

The white gaze on professional, and profitable sports, did not completely police black players and their identities, more so it saw the financial potential and understood how to package their style just right to be desirable to the white consumer.

The NBA and the NFL both have similar trajectories in the treatment of their black players and the culture they bring with them. The NFL Rules and Regulations of 2017 polices their players' appearance under Section 4. "General Appearance. Consistent with the equipment and uniform rules, players must otherwise present a professional and appropriate appearance while before the public on game-day" (Goodell). This is the league protocol, while teams also may implement rules for dress code. The most disappointing about such broad sweeping terms in a diverse cultural nation, is that the white gaze is what defined the "appropriate appearance" qualifier. Herbert D. Simons expresses the lack of cultural understanding by team leadership and ownership, which is predominately white in both the NBA and NFL, in regard to their predominately black players. The ways in which black players present themselves is "a reflection of urban Black male cultural norms, which conflict with white male mainstream norms. The penalties [instituted by professional leagues] are an example of institutionalized racism and white mainstream males' assertion of their right to interpret and control Black behavior" (6). Many fashion aspects that are considered outside of the rules are those that black athletes introduced to sports. In 2005, the NBA stated that "jerseys, all headgear (i.e., baseball caps, do-rags, bandanas, and headbands), sunglasses indoors, sneakers, construction or casual boots, and chains and pendants—bling," were not to be worn (Lane 79). All of these styles can be attributed to hip-hop culture. The NFL also focused on aspects that are related mostly to black players, such as bandanas and stocking caps (Cunningham 45). Players would be monetarily fined for any infraction of the on-field dress code as well. Particularly in the NFL another aspect of style became an issue for policing, especially for the black players, and that was styles of play with particular emphasis on touchdown celebrations. The NBA also would crack down on styles of play most attributed to black players.

Style of Play

Each and every time black players showcase their style of play, they "are resisting white male hegemony and asserting their manhood and cultural identity" (Simons 6). From the way black athletes dress to the way they perform during play and between plays, they bring a part of their own culture to an industry created by a group that has no requirement to understand nor be respectful of their culture. Both the NBA and the NFL have styles of play that were introduced by black players. Both leagues police their styles.

Simmons contests the prescribed concept that censoring these styles of play is meant to make the sport better. Rather he sees censorship and penalizing as disadvantaging at times to the team that the penalties are placed upon.

Sports are theoretically set up in an egalitarian manner, "participants compete under the same conditions and rules. The winner is determined by strength and skill alone and not by extraneous factors such as class, race, politics, wealth, etc. ... [p]enalties are designed to compensate for the unfair competitive advantage and restore the level playing field" (Simons 7). On the field, or on the court, no matter your racial identity, each player is supposed to be judged on their abilities not their personal or community identifiers. The problem has been, with reference to the preceding section on some historical black American athletes rupturing the white norms of play, that this egalitarian ideal is not always applied to black players. It is subtler in the 21st century as the penalties are aligned with aspects of black cultural sports play. Aspects that are not necessarily breaking the egalitarian rules of sport play, because they occur outside of the live play time. Simons explains,

> In football, celebrating, taking off one's helmet, taunting, and inciting the crowd take place after the play is over. In basketball some of the behaviors such as inciting the crowd, trash talking and taunting, using vulgar or obscene language, baiting, or ridiculing an opponent, hanging on the rim, and disrespectfully addressing an official most often do not take place during play.... Although, the overall effect of these 'offenses' on the outcome of the competition is minor compared to the other competitive advantage offenses, they are more harshly punished. The penalties in fact contradict the level playing field justification for penalizing rule violations [and] actually produce a non-level playing field [7].

Not directly breaking the rules of fair play, these styles are being policed in relation to their representation of black culture which disturbs the white gaze.

A major aspect of all forms of black art is that is it not simply created to be consumed but to be interactive. "African orature is orally composed and transmitted and is often created to be communally performed as an integral part of dance and music," it can be fluid, it can be changed based on environment, which is all in the style of play of black athletes (Stewart and Anderson 357). This style of play is contradictory to the concreteness of western desire of presentation. "For Black athletes, sport is a form of entertainment, and the athlete is the entertainer. Thus, all of the theatricalities that Black athletes bring to sport—the highlight reel dunks, the choreographed dance moves after scoring, the trash talk—are endemic of a Black sportsmanship aesthetic that emphasizes individuality and performance" (Cunningham 49). Yet these are the components that are written as against the rules of play and are penalized often financially.

Chad Johnson was one of the NFL's most penalized players in 2003 for touchdown celebrations and not following the dress code. But aligned with the idea of breaking the white gaze, as Simons attested, Johnson stated: "The fine was ridiculous … [touchdown celebrations are] fun…. It's part of the game. They can't take that away from us. I've got to continue to do what I do. That's just Chad" (Associated Press). He was fined 10,000 dollars for the particular touchdown "celebration" in which he brought out a sign he had stashed in the end zone, stating, "Dear NFL, please don't fine me again!!!" (Associated Press). Why not simply follow the rules? The rules that were written by an ownership and a white gaze that does not understand the black style of play or have to respect it. But the ownership will monetarily package the style. It is more than contradictory, but it is unfair, and simply racist to use black styles to benefit the controlling body of the sporting industry, but not allow the players that created the culture to showcase it. Instead they are seen as breaking the rules. In the words of Dr. Martin Luther King, Jr., in his "Letter from Birmingham Jail," it is okay to break some rules because "there are two types of laws: there are just laws, and there are unjust laws … an unjust law is no law at all … any law that degrades human personality is unjust … [a]n unjust law is a code inflicted upon a minority which that minority had no part in enacting or creating because it did not have the unhampered right to vote" (King). Professional black athletes do not vote in the rules and regulations of the sports industry. Even if blacks hold positions to make decisions, they hold a minor portion. Black athletes have a controlled position in the industry. Johnson chose to continue to break the rules, along with other black athletes, in attempt to maintain their identities, whether through personal style outside of play, or their style of play. This, they could control.

In November 2016 at a press conference, Cam Newton was asked about his feelings on the league penalizing players for touchdown celebrations, he himself is a more conservative celebrator but one who is still at times critiqued. He stated: "'Football is hard, man,' Newton said, via ESPN.com. 'I can't stress it enough. The way my body feels right now is not going to be the same way it feels come Thursday. Now I'm sore, but still knowing that Thursday I gotta give everything. And if scoring a touchdown, getting a sack, getting a win … let alone all of that bottled up and staying here until 10 at night and here at 6 in the morning, all of that energy that you put, spending time away from your family, all of that bottled up and being able to do exactly what you planned and foresaw yourself doing, you are owed something'" (Alper). Newton brings attention to the high demand of physical and mental energy in the game, and the desire and in a way the need to truly celebrate. You are owed a touchdown celebration. In 2016, based on the compilation of every touch down celebration that was fined by the NFL, *Newsweek* provides a list that is comprised of all black players—only black players were fined for touchdown celebrations. This is not to say that the rules would not have been equally implemented across racial identity, but it aligns with the fact that this celebratory action is more associated with black cultural style. It was in 2005 that the NFL owners voted 29–3 to penalize excessive celebrations with a 15-yard penalty (Cunningham). Conservative critic Jason Whitlock stated in 2007, in similar fashion as Don Imus, that the "football bojanglers" like Chad Johnson were "caught up in the rebellion and buffoonery of hip hop culture [and gave] NFL owners and coaches a justifiable reason to whiten their roster" (Cunningham 43). Despite the creation of unjust rules, and the continual white gaze type of criticism, black players have attempted to bring their style of play, the play that provided them the opportunity to be drafted, with them and to share it. The reality appears to demonstrate that black players are being penalized for their identities. Not only that, but their style that promotes the sport is packaged for a white audience to ensure the continued monetary success of the industry. This is what occurs contemporarily, which was established and is perpetuated under the definition and ownership of a white gaze.

Contemporary Policing in the Age of Kaepernick

Landing into the sports controversies and debates, a quick discussion of Colin Kaepernick brings to light all the ways in which race still matters and how it is definitively present in the American sports industry. With the preceding understandings and analyses there is no debate that Kaepernick's controversy revolves around race and is influenced by the white gaze. Colin Kaepernick; what violence, what style, what dress did he violate? He violated the tradition of standing, hand on heart, and in silence to the flag. He discussed violence perpetuated on black men, women and children by white individuals and white controlled systems. He began to wear an afro along with his already extensive tattoos. He created another aspect of the game, the pre-game play, one in which the audience watches who stands, who kneels, who sits, who locks arms and who abides by the rules of standing for the National Anthem with hand on heart. He disrupted the unspoken rule for players and fans to salute the flag, a patriotic action defined and created by whites. On May 23, 2018, the rule was no longer unspoken for the NFL. Two years after Kaepernick's first action of protest the NFL owners, comprised of 97.1 percent whites and no African Americans, voted to fine NFL teams if any of their players do not stand for the National Anthem. The rule stipulated that players may remain in the locker rooms during the Anthem if they do not wish to abide by the new rule. Once again those that make the rules, do not resemble those that must abide by them.

The initiation of the National Anthem into sports is a history once again often missing in everyday discussion about why and who stands for the anthem. The story goes that during World War I, before the 1918 World Series of Baseball, the sport was losing its enthusiastic following. The turmoil of the United States being active in the war for 17 months and the continual military draft of professional baseball players depleted the industry and weakened the fandom. The Series was on the verge of being cancelled, until American soldiers abroad expressed that the Series gave them something to look forward to (Waxman). The now National Anthem had been played sparingly at sporting events prior, but the tradition began in the first game of the 1918 series in the seventh inning when the military band played the Star Spangled Banner. A player on leave from the military saluted the war song when it played, and the crowd followed him. The low enthusiasm for the World Series ended there. Over the next decade the song became a staple in the World Series and holiday games until it became the preface to all sporting events as seen today (Cyphers and Trex). The Star Spangled Banner became the national anthem in 1931 when Congress adopted it. However, it "was already a baseball tradition steeped in wartime patriotism. Thanks to a brass band, some fickle fans and a player who snapped to attention on a somber day in September, the old battle ballad was the national pastime's anthem more than a decade before it was the nation's" (Cyphers and Trex). This is a very American tradition as the national anthems of other nations do not accompany all professional games (Gregory). The United States is unique in this connection of patriotism with professional sports.

The American national anthem and the United States flag navigated the same American history as the historical black athletes that had to break down barriers to create the equal access to professional sports for those to follow, and thus its history cannot be deleted, even if it is often forgotten. Colin Kaepernick was well versed and clear about his stance, and his protest pointed at the hypocrisy of the flag not representing all Americans. This aligns with the way the white gaze on sports perpetuates the inequitable way in which the sports industry does not represent, support, understand, or promote black athletes, but rather rejects, and contests them personally. Kaepernick refused to "show pride in a flag for a country that oppresses Black people and people of color," and his protest was a form of patriotic freedom that the World War I veterans had fought for, including black veterans that fought at the time, for a country that was segregated (Flaherty). And as the World Series needed more excitement in the fans, those fans were white, those players were white, and the celebration of the Star Spangled Banner was one with only one lens, one gaze, the gaze of white America, and if to be American is associated with baseball and apple pie, then for sure the white gaze resides over it. And American sports, a favorite pastime, remains for whites only.

WORKS CITED

Alper, Josh. "Surprise! Cam Newton Not in Favor of Celebration Penalties." *NBC Sports*. NBC Universal, 15 November 2016. Web. 8 April 2018.

Around the NFL. "Cam Newton Briefly Benched for 'Dress Code Violation.'" NFL.com. NFL Enterprise, 5 December 2016. Web. 8 April 2018.

Associated Press. "WR Doesn't Agree with NFL Decisions." *ESPN*. 17 December 2003. Web. 8 April 2018.

Belson, Ken. "Kaepernick vs. the N.F.L.: A Primer on His Collusion Case." *New York Times*. New York Times. 8 December 2017. Web. 20 March 2018.

Cunningham, Phillip Lamarr. "'Please Don't Fine Me Again!!!!.'" *Journal of Sport & Social Issues* (2009): 39–58. Print.

Cyphers, Luke, and Ethan Trex. "The Song Remains the Same: The History of the National Anthem in Sports." *ESPN*. 19 September 2011. Web. 8 April 2018.

Dowd, Katie. "It's Been 20 Years Since Latrell Sprewell Choked Warriors Coach P.J. Carlesimo: Where Are They Now?" *SF Gate*. Hearst Communications, 1 December 2017. Web.31 March 2018.

Droschak, David. "Greene Attacks Assistant Coach." *Washington Post*. Washington Post, 14 December 1998. Web. 5 May 2018.

DuBois, W.E.B. *The Souls of Black Folk*. Mineola: Dover Publications, Inc, 1994. Print.

Dyreson, Mark. "Jesse Owens: Leading Man in Modern American Tales of Racial Progress and Limits." Ed. Wiggins, David K. *Out of the Shadows: A Biographical History of African American Athletes*. Fayetteville: University of Arkansas Press, 2006. 111–129. Print.

Flaherty, Bryan. "From Kaepernick Sitting to Trump's Fiery Comments: NFL's Anthem Protests Have Spurred Discussion." *Washington Post*. Washington Post, 24 September 2017. Web. 6 April 2018.

Goodell, Roger. *2017 Official Playing Rules of the National Football League*. 2017. PDF file.

Gregory, Sean. "How Sports Can Move Beyond Lip-service Patriotism." *Time*. (2016): 17–18. Print.

Hill, Justice B. "A True Pioneer: Fleet Walker Is First African-American to Play in Major Leagues." *Major League Baseball*. MLB Advanced Media, Web. 22 April 2018.

Hughes, Langston. "I, Too." Ed. Rampersad, Arnold, and David Roesell. *The Collected Poems of Langston Hughes*. New York: Alfred A. Knopf, Inc., 2004. Print.

King, Martin Luther, Jr. "Letter from Birmingham Jail." Letter. Birmingham, 16 April 1963.

Kitwana, Bakara. *The Hip Hop Generation: Young Blacks and the Crisis in African-American Culture*. New York: BasicCivitas Books, 2002. Print.

Konigsberg, Eric. "The Real Spree." *New York Magazine*. New York Media, 9 April 1999. Web. 31 March 2018.

Lane, Jeffrey. *Under the Boards: The Cultural Revolution in Basketball*. Lincoln: University of Nebraska Press, 2007. Print.

Lapchick, Richard, and Bharath Balasundaram. *The 2017 Racial and Gender Report Card: National Basketball Association*. 2017. PRF file.

Lapchick, Richard, and Saahil Marfatia. *The 2017 Racial and Gender Report Card: National Football League*. 2017. PDF file.

National Basketball Association. "National Basketball Association." *NBA Player Dress Code*. NBA Media Ventures, 20 October 2005. Web. 7 April 2018.

Rhoden, William C. *Forty Million Dollar Slaves: The Rise, Fall, and Redemption of the Black Athlete*. New York: Three Rivers Press, 2006. Print.

Robinson, Jackie, and Alfred Duckett. *I Never Had It Made: An Autobiography of Jackie Robinson*. New York: HarperCollins, 2003. Print.

Sensoy, Ozlem, and Robin DiAngelo. *Is Everyone Really Equal? An Introduction to Key Concepts in Social Justice Education*. New York: Teachers College Press, 2017. Print.

Simons, Herbert D. "Race and Penalized Sports Behaviors." *International Review for the Sociology of Sport* 38.1 (2003): 5–22. Print.

Stewart, James, and Talmadge Anderson. *Introduction to African American Studies: Transdisciplinary Approaches and Implications*. Baltimore: Black Classics Press, 2015. Print.

30 for 30: The Fab Five. Dir. Jason Hehir. 2009. Documentary.

Tomlinson, Alan. "Owens, Jesse (James Cleveland)." *A Dictionary of Sports Studies*. Oxford: Oxford University Press, 2010.

Washington, Robert E., and David Karen. "Sport and Society." *Annual Review of Sociology* 27 (2001): 187–212.

Waxman, Olivia B. "Here's How Standing for the National Anthem Became Part of U.S. Sports Tradition." *TIME*. TIME. 25 September 2017. Web. 8 April 2018.

"Eleven wretched women"

Gender and the Summer Olympics

Benjamin James Dettmar

> The most important thing in the Olympic Games is not to win but to take part, just as the most important thing in life is not the triumph, but the struggle. The essential thing in life is not to have conquered, but to have fought well.[1]
> —Baron Pierre de Coubertin, 1908

Founder of the modern Olympics, Baron Pierre de Coubertin famously supplied the world with the mantra, and oft used sporting cliché: "it is not the winning that matters, but the taking part," when he gave the world his sporting philosophy in 1908 (see above). Unfortunately, women did not seem to fit the remit of Coubertin's admirable attitude. Women were not allowed to compete in the ancient Olympics, or indeed at the first incarnation of the modern Olympics in 1896. When the *New York Evening Post* focused not on the achievement of German athlete Lina Radke winning a gold medal but instead wrote about "eleven wretched women" competing in the 800-meter race at the 1928 Olympics in Amsterdam, they epitomized how women were treated at the Olympics in the long 20th century. This study tells the story of Radke and other female Olympians against the backdrop of conflict, opposition, and struggle that was, and perhaps is, the narrative of women in the Olympics.

"Eleven wretched women"

The quote that forms the title of this piece comes from esteemed sport journalist John Tunis who was at the time writing for the *New York Evening*

Post. He wrote, "Below us on the cinder path were 11 wretched women, 5 of whom dropped out before the finish, while 5 collapsed after reaching the tape" (qtd. in Sailors, 1). Tunis, an esteemed sports writer of his era whom the *New York Times* described as "one of the country's most successful free-lance writers," was not the only journalist to makes such a judgment (Illson). Writing for the *Pittsburgh Press,* infamous Notre Dame Football coach Knute Rockne stated that only six of the nine women finished the race and that five of the women collapsed over the line: "It was not a very edifying spectacle to see a group of fine girls running themselves into a state of exhaustion." The *Chicago Tribune's* William Shirer wrote that five women collapsed at the end of the race and that Florence MacDonald, who came fifth, needed to be "worked over" after "falling onto the grass unconscious" at the end of the race. Shirer also focused on silver medalist Kinue Hitomi of Japan stating that the Japanese athlete required a 15-minute revival period after suffering from complete exhaustion after trying to beat Radke to the gold medal (English).

Ignore, for the moment, the pervasive though alliterative use of the adjective "wretched" in Tunis' report. Nonetheless it should be noted that the information in this quote (and many of the subsequent reports) is both incorrect and misleading. The year 1928 was the first year that women had competed in Athletics events at the Olympics. It would also be the last time that women ran a distance over 200 meters until 1960. The race itself was a close one, with Radke winning the gold medal in a then world record time of two minutes 16.80 seconds. Hitomi of Japan and Inga Gentzel of Sweden were less than a second behind her. Official Olympic reports show that three athletes (not five) dropped out before the finish. Despite the claim by Tunis and others that the athletes "collapsed after reaching the tape" the perceived reality is that the women simply fell to the track in disappointment at not winning gold, or medaling at all. However, even if they had run into "a state of exhaustion" would this be so unusual for elite athletes at an Olympic Games? Just 20 years earlier at the London games of 1908 Italian marathoner Dorando Pietri was famously disqualified after receiving assistance when he collapsed just yards from the finish line; Pietri would go on to become a revered athlete and is one of the most recognizable names in Olympic marathon running. More recently it has become commonplace for Olympic champions to fall to the track in a combination of elation, exhaustion, and disbelief after winning an Olympic medal. There is little doubt that the journalists covering the 1928 Games were not worried about the welfare of the athletes but were worried about female athletes competing in the first place; Tunis' use of the word "wretched" was not accidental. Sadly, for the sport of Athletics, and for the Olympic Games, the draconian views of the men observing the Games were shared by the International Olympic Committee (IOC). Women's Athletics was marginalized for the foreseeable future.

The following table shows how late the IOC was in adopting races for female athletes.

Table 1. Women's Track Events and When They Were First Held at the Olympics

Distance	Olympic Games in Which Female Athletes First Competed at That Distance
100 Meters	1928
100 Meters Hurdles	1972
4 × 100 Meters Relay	1928
200 Meters	1948
400 Meters	1964
400 Meters Hurdles	1984
4 × 400 Meters Relay	1972
800 Meters	1928 (it was then omitted until 1960)
1,500 Meters	1972
3,000 Meters (now discontinued)	1984
3,000 Meters Steeplechase	2008
5,000 Meters	1996
10,000 Meters	1988
10,000 Meters Race Walk (now discontinued)	1992
20,000 Meters Race Walk	2000
Marathon	1984

For comparison, men were running the 5,000- and 10,000-meter races by the Stockholm Olympics of 1912, the Steeplechase by the Antwerp Olympics of 1920, and the 20,000-meter Race Walk by Melbourne, 1956. Men were competing in the 50,000-meter Race Walk, an event still not held for female athletes at the Olympics, by the Los Angeles Olympics of 1982.

The reticence of the IOC in allowing female athletes to compete can also be seen when we analyze women's athletic field events.

Table 2. Women's Athletic Field Events and When They Were First Held at the Summer Olympics

Event	Olympic Games in Which Female Athletes First Competed in That Event
High Jump	1928
Long Jump	1948
Triple Jump	1996
Pole Vault	2000
Javelin	1932
Hammer Throw	2000
Shot Put	1948
Discus Throw	1928

Unsurprisingly, men were competing in all these events (and many others that are now discontinued) by the London Games of 1908.

The treatment of female athletes after Radke's triumph in 1928 cannot, however, be put purely on the shoulders of the U.S. journalists covering the event. Coubertin, who by 1928 was the honorary president of the IOC, was not in favor of allowing women to compete in the Olympics in any form; perhaps explaining the omission of any female athletes in 1896. Olympic historian Allen Guttmann claims that Coubertin was not against women competing in sport but that he did not feel it should be a spectacle for people to watch. "Coubertin, sharing fully the prejudices of his age on this matter, continued to oppose the participation of female athletes in the Olympic Games. He had no objections to women's sports per se, but he felt strongly that such competitions should occur without spectators (whose motives he distrusted)" (Guttmann 46).

"Figures don't lie, but liars figure"[2]

A simple, yet effective, way to look at how women have been treated at the Olympic Games is to look at the raw data regarding the number of female athletes who competed and the number of events in which they were eligible to compete.

Table 3. Total Number and Percentage of Female Athletes at the Summer Olympics, 1896–2016[3]

Olympic Year	Olympic Host City	Number of Male Athletes	Number of Female Athletes	Percentage of Athletes Who Are Female
1896	Athens	241	0	0
1900	Paris	975	22	2
1904	St Louis	645	6	1
1908	London	1,971	37	1
1912	Stockholm	2,359	48	2
1920	Antwerp	2,561	65	2
1924	Paris	2,954	135	4
1928	Amsterdam	2,606	277	10
1932	Los Angeles	1,206	126	9
1936	Berlin	3,632	331	8
1948	London	3,714	390	10
1952	Helsinki	4,436	519	10
1956	Melbourne	2,938	376	11
1960	Rome	4,727	611	11
1964	Tokyo	4,473	678	13

Olympic Year	Olympic Host City	Number of Male Athletes	Number of Female Athletes	Percentage of Athletes Who Are Female
1968	Mexico City	4,735	781	14
1972	Munich	6,075	1,059	14
1976	Montreal	4,824	1,260	21
1980	Moscow	4,064	1,115	22
1984	Los Angeles	5,263	1,566	23
1988	Seoul	6,197	2,194	26
1992	Barcelona	6,652	2,704	29
1996	Atlanta	6,806	3,512	34
2000	Sydney	6,582	4,069	38
2004	Athens	6,296	4,329	41
2008	Beijing	6,305	4,637	42
2012	London	5,892	4,676	44
2016	Rio de Janeiro	~6,538	~4,700	42

Table 4. Total Number of Events Competed in at the Summer Olympics by Male Athletes and by Female Athletes[4]

Olympic Year	Olympic Host City	Total Number of Sports in Which Female Athletes Competed	Total Number of Events in Which Female Athletes Competed (Includes Mixed Events)	Total Events in the Olympics	Percentage of Events in Which Female Athletes Can Compete
1896	Athens	0	0	43	0
1900	Paris	2	2	95	2
1904	St Louis	1	3	95	3
1908	London	2	4	110	4
1912	Stockholm	2	5	102	5
1920	Antwerp	2	8	156	5
1924	Paris	3	10	126	8
1928	Amsterdam	4	14	109	13
1932	Los Angeles	3	14	117	12
1936	Berlin	4	15	129	12
1948	London	5	19	136	14
1952	Helsinki	6	25	149	17
1956	Melbourne	6	26	151	17
1960	Rome	6	29	150	19
1964	Tokyo	7	33	163	20
1968	Mexico City	7	39	172	23
1972	Munich	8	43	195	22
1976	Montreal	11	49	198	25
1980	Moscow	12	50	203	25

Olympic Year	Olympic Host City	Total Number of Sports in Which Female Athletes Competed	Total Number of Events in Which Female Athletes Competed (Includes Mixed Events)	Total Events in the Olympics	Percentage of Events in Which Female Athletes Can Compete
1984	Los Angeles	14	62	221	28
1988	Seoul	17	72	237	30
1992	Barcelona	19	86	257	33
1996	Atlanta	21	97	271	36
2000	Sydney	25	120	300	40
2004	Athens	26	125	301	42
2008	Beijing	26	127	302	42
2012	London	26	140	302	46
2016	Rio de Janeiro	28	145	306	47

The numbers are telling, women have historically been second-class citizens when it comes to Olympic participation. IOC president Thomas Bach, speaking on International Women's Day in March 2018 recognized this and lauded the attempts by the IOC to address the issue. "We are certain that, through the implementation of the 25 IOC Gender Equality Recommendations, we as the Olympic Movement—athletes, officials, commissions, federations and executives—can take real steps to enact effective change together. It is not just the right thing to do. It is in the interest of us all—the fans, the families, and every girl and woman who has been able to fully realize her dreams through athletic participation" ("International Women's Day"). Bach appears hopeful that with the total number of female athletes increasing, along with the events in which they can compete, we are reaching equality in the Olympic Games. This is not exactly true, and although we are getting closer to a form of equality we must recognize how long it took for the IOC to get there. As the 20th century progressed women's sports were slowly added to the Olympic program; the lethargy of the IOC is as important as the current attempt to reach equality.

Another set of figures that are telling when analyzed are the years in which women could first compete in an Olympic sport. Table 5 shows clearly that women were left behind in most sports in terms of when they could first compete, it shows that there is no sport in which women competed before men, but it also shows that the IOC is, perhaps, rectifying past mistakes.

Table 5. Olympic Sports in Tokyo 2020 and When They Were First Contested by Male Athletes and Female Athletes[5]

Sport	First Contested by Men	First Contested by Women
Aquatics	1896	1912
Archery	1900	1904
Athletics	1896	1928
Badminton	1992[6]	1992
Baseball/Softball	1992[7]	1996
Basketball	1936[8]	1976
Boxing	1904	2008
Canoe	1936[9]	1948
Cycling	1896	1984
Equestrian	1900	1952[10]
Fencing	1896	1924
Football (Soccer)	1900	1996
Golf[11]	1900	1900
Gymnastics	1896	1928
Handball	1936	1976
Field Hockey	1908	1980
Judo	1964	1992[12]
Karate	2020	2020
Modern Pentathlon	1912	2000
Rowing	1896[13]	1972
Rugby	1900[14]	2016
Sailing	1896[15]	1896
Shooting	1896	1968[16]
Skateboarding	2020	2020
Sport Climbing	2020	2020
Surfing	2020	2020
Table Tennis	1988	1988
Taekwondo	2000[17]	2000
Tennis	1896	1900
Triathlon	2000	2000
Volleyball	1964	1964
Weightlifting	1896	2000
Wrestling	1896	2004

There are some obvious outliers here. Men competed in Boxing events for a century before women were given the same opportunity. Women wrestlers were first able to compete in 2004, whereas men had the chance to wrestle in every Olympics (except 1900 when no wrestling events where held). The IOC explains some of this with claims that the women's versions of these sports were not competitive on the world stage. There is an argument to be made here, however as the world's single largest sporting event the Olympics could and should have been the catalyst for change, promotion, and acceptance of women's sport. The raw data also show that, especially in the earlier

Olympics, women competed in far fewer events within the sports compared to men. An analysis of sports which have similar events for men and women also shows some alarming disparities. Artistic Gymnastics, for example, sees the men compete in six different events (Floor, Horizontal Bar, Parallel Bars, Pommel Horse, Rings, and the Vault), whereas women only compete in four events (Balance Beam, Floor, Uneven Bars, Vault). This not only gives women fewer opportunities to win a medal in the sport of gymnastics, but also plays on the idea that men are stronger more durable athletes. Further, there are significant differences in how the individual events are judged with women completing their floor routines to music and being assessed on their dance moves and artistry far more than the men.

The IOC, at its organizational level, has also been a place that has seen relatively few women in positions of power. There have been nine presidents of the IOC, all have been men. As of 2018 there are 15 members of the IOC executive board, 11 men and four women; only seven of the 26 IOC commissions are chaired by women ("Statistics"). The first women were elected to the IOC in 1980 and the first female IOC Executive board member, Flor Isava Fonseca, was elected in 1990. Despite the male dominance of the IOC the numbers here have improved over recent decades; in 2007 the IOC charter was updated to include language on gender equality with the following section added: "The mission of the IOC is to promote Olympism throughout the world and to lead the Olympic Movement. The IOC's role is … to encourage and support the promotion of women in sport at all levels and in all structures, with a view to implementing the principle of equality of men and women" (International Olympic Committee, *Olympic Charter* 18). The IOC is trying to rectify its checkered past regarding women's involvement in the Olympics. This is especially true in the admittance of new sports and events to the Games. Since 1991, for a sport to be considered for inclusion in the Olympics, there must be an equality in men's and women's events, or for sports such as Baseball/Softball a close enough equivalent. Tokyo 2020 is seeing far more mixed events than have been held in previous Olympics with disciplines such as Swimming, Athletics, and Table Tennis all incorporating mixed events. The IOC has been accused of pandering to a younger audience and to TV executives with new events such as Sport Climbing, Freestyle BMX, and 3-on-3 Basketball; this might be true (and might not necessarily be a terrible thing) but again to its credit these new events all have equal participation (or very close to) of male and female athletes. IOC President Bach stated that he wants future Olympics to be "more youthful, more urban and include more women," the program for 2020 looks to be setting the tone for this (qtd. in Tokyo 2020). Similarly, IOC sports director Kit McConnell lauds the work of the IOC "[with recent developments] we have taken a really important step forward in terms of gender equality" (qtd. in Tokyo 2020). It has taken over 100 years, but gender equality does now appear to be a viable and achievable aim of the IOC.

Putting Faith in Science: The Troubled History of Sex and Gender Testing in the Olympics

Recent Olympics have seen the sport of Athletics make headlines because of questions over the sex or gender of some of the competing athletes. The IOC has, to its credit, responded and changed its guidelines numerous times over the years. Historically, however, gender testing at the Olympics has been an issue that has left the IOC open to severe criticism.

When Helen Stephens won the 100-meter race at the 1936 Berlin Olympics in a time of 11.5 seconds she was rightly celebrated in her hometown of Fulton, Missouri. Yet the world's press, some in the United States, and the IOC questioned the sex of the "Fulton Flash." The idea that a woman could run that fast seemed impossible to many observers and it was insinuated that some of Fulton's competitors could have won gold if Fulton had run in the men's race—where many observers felt she belonged. So widespread were the rumors about Stephens that German officials conducted a physical exam before clearing her to compete at the games (Pieper 11). Historians generally agree that this was the first official sex test to be conducted at the summer Olympics. This invasive and embarrassing form of testing became the norm for the IOC for the next two decades. IOC officials would use a physical examination, during which they would view the genitalia of an athlete, to determine a competitor's sex. This was done to ensure that men were not competing in female only events; the mass hysteria that had made a folk devil out of Stephens had a lasting effect on female athletes. This practice was also commonplace in Track and Field events with the International Association of Athletics Federations (IAAF) following the lead of the IOC. Of course, an external examination of someone's genitalia is not enough to determine their sex and as our understanding of scientific biology increased so did the IOC's testing; although it remained problematic.

In 1968 the IOC switched to chromosome testing and subsequently banned all female athletes from competing who did not possess XX chromosomes. Olympic historian Lindsay Pieper shows how despite this seeming like a scientific advancement for the IOC, it was equally problematic:

Various chromosomal constitutions regularly undermined the [IOC's Chromosome] test. For example, individuals with androgen insensitivity syndrome (AIS), chromosomal mosaicism, Klinefelter's syndrome, and Turner syndrome all challenged the notion that men and women could be separated neatly into XY and XX. Perhaps most notably in sports, AIS occurs when a person who is considered chromosomally male (46,XY) is resistant to male hormones and therefore demonstrates the physical characteristics of a female. Chromosomal mosaicism exists when an individual possesses cell populations with different chromosomal makeups. For example, a person with 46,XX/XY mosaicism has both XX and XY chromosomes. Klinefelter's syndrome occurs when men inherit extra X chromosomes (46,XXY or 46,XXXY) and, as a result, produce less than average amounts of testosterone.... Turner syndrome is present when women inherit only one X chromosome (46,X0) and consequently do not develop ovaries [Pieper 4–5].

The science behind chromosomal testing is not widely understood by the lay person, however it is indicative of the way the female athletes were treated that the IOC ignored scientific calls to change their testing methods. In the 1990s the IOC advanced from chromosomal testing to DNA testing, using polymerase chain reaction (PCR) to discern the presence of the sex-determining region Y (SRY). In layman's terms the IOC's test looked for SRY in an athlete; SRY initiates production of testosterone and the test was used to determine if the athlete was male (Pieper 5). As with previous methods of testing, however, the test was not 100 percent accurate and there were various conditions that could lead to abnormal test results which could affect the classification of an athlete. The science behind the testing began to interest not just the IOC but also medical doctors, geneticists, and sports scientists. World-renowned geneticist Louis J. Elsas first-authored a 2000 study which roundly criticized the science behind the IOC's historical and contemporary testing methodologies.

> Ultimately, the IOC decided in 1991 to replace chromatin testing with analysis for Y-specific loci using polymerase chain reaction (PCR) amplification of DNA extracted from nucleated buccal cells. This method enabled rapid screening of ever increasing numbers of female competitors.... [This was problematic as] the DYZ-1 region of genomic DNA was not male-specific and produced false-positive results.... [At the 1996 Atlanta games] the presence of the SRY gene was used as a marker of male genetic sex, and an autosomal gene (galactose-1-phosphate uridyltransferase) was used as control to confirm DNA amplification in all samples. Eight of 3,387 female athletes (1 in 423) tested positive. Seven of the eight had the androgen insensitivity syndrome; four had the incomplete and three the complete syndrome. Two of eight had not had gonadectomy. All had full physical examinations and recommendations for follow-up care, including estrogen replacement and appropriate surgical intervention. Letters were written to team physicians explaining the results and, where necessary, recommending further medical evaluation after the Games. One of the eight athletes was found to have 5-a-steroid-reductase deficiency. She had had gonadectomy previously, and so there was no question about her eligibility. All eight who tested positive for SRY were given gender verification certificates in the same batch as their teammates to maintain anonymity [Elsas et al. 251–252].

The science here can be bamboozling, but what is not in doubt is that on-site lab-testing of athletes was not a 100 percent accurate method for the IOC to utilize. Lab-testing to discern the sex of athletes was not conducted at the

2000 Sydney Olympics. Elsas et al. applauded this development, stating that it protected the rights and privacy of all female athletes whilst also recognizing that on-site lab-based screenings of an athlete's DNA was medically and functionally unsound and perhaps even unethical (Elsas et al. 254).

Recently, much focus has fallen on the South African athlete Caster Semenya. Semenya won the gold medal at the 2016 Rio de Janeiro games and came second at the 2012 London Olympics; Semenya's silver medal in 2012 was upgraded to gold when it was discovered race winner Mariya Savinova-Farnosova had been using performance enhancing drugs. The focus on Semenya has been as much on the gender testing she has had to endure as it has been her Olympic titles. After winning World Championship gold in 2009 Semenya was sidelined for 11 months and unable to compete as the governing body of her sport, the IAAF, subjected her to testing to determine her biological sex. The IAAF was severely criticized for the length of time this testing took and for the secrecy that surrounded its methodology compared to the very public scrutiny that Semenya had to endure. Even after the IAAF's process was complete all the public got was a curious statement from then IAAF General Secretary Pierre Weiss who stated: "She is a woman but maybe not 100%" (qtd. in Kessel). To its credit the IOC reacted quickly to the controversy surrounding the treatment of Semenya and sponsored a series of workshops to ensure a much fairer and less invasive process was put in place. In January 2010, The IOC used the second World Conference on the Hormonal and Genetic Basis of Sexual Differentiation Disorders as a platform to discuss its subsequent strategies. Fifteen scientists, medical experts, and sport physicians—many with previous gender verification experience—were invited to help draw up guiding principles for dealing with "ambiguous" gender cases. The group's conclusions became the blueprint for the IOC's final 2011 policy, the "IOC's Regulations on Female Hyperandrogenism" (Pieper 181–182).

A piece of landmark legislation for the IOC, its regulations on female hyperandrogenism ensured that many of the criticisms and discussions of inaccurate or unfair science were consigned to history. The IOC's new guidelines focus only on the levels of androgen production and make no pronouncement of the sex or gender of any athlete.

> Competitions at the 2012 London Olympic Games ... are conducted separately for men and women (with the exception of certain events). Human biology, however, allows for forms of intermediate levels between the conventional categories of male and female, sometimes referred to as intersex. Usually, intersex athletes can be placed in the male or female group on the basis of their legal sex. However, as explained below, intersex female athletes with elevated androgen production give rise to a particular concern in the context of competitive sports, which is referred to as "female hyperandrogenism." In general, the performances of male and female athletes may

differ mainly due to the fact that men produce significantly more androgenic hormones than women and, therefore, are under stronger influence of such hormones. Androgenic hormones have performance enhancing effects, particularly on strength, power and speed, which may provide a competitive advantage in sports [International Olympic Committee, *IOC Regulations* 1].

The focus of the IOC's testing is on levels of androgenic hormones, particularly when they are at levels akin to that of athletes who are using performance enhancing drugs. Importantly, the IOC also states that the administration of these tests shall be conducted by the National Olympic Committees (NOCs) rather than having the tests conducted at the site of the Olympic Games. The IOC also stipulated that the chairman of the IOC Medical Commission would oversee any suspected cases of female hyperandrogenism, and that the chairman would be assisted by an "expert panel" consisting of at least one gynecologist, one genetic expert, and one endocrinologist (International Olympics Committee, *IOC Regulations* 2). The IOC went on to state that only the athlete themselves, a chief NOC Medical Officer, an IOC Medical Commission member, a Medical Officer of the Olympic Games Organizing Committee (OCOG), or the Chairman of the IOC Medical Commission could request a test; thus, ensuring that smear campaigns and snide remarks by other athletes and the press would not lead to female athletes being tested for unscientific reasons. The new regulations also laid out clearly the protocol for testing, how decisions regarding whether an athlete had female hyperandrogenism would be made, who would hear the cases, and the rights of the athletes and the NOCs to appeal any decisions. The regulations repeatedly remarked that all testing, all hearings, and all appeals would be confidential.

Of course, with such secrecy comes accusations of cover-ups and closed-door deals. It is also possible that subsequent scientific breakthroughs could see the IOC's testing for female hyperandrogenism be deemed as inadequate and even draconian. There is a particular worry that this will happen in Track and Field events if the IOC follows recent IAAF protocols. In 2018 the IAAF approved new policies on hyperandrogenism that apply to women who compete in Track events from 400 meters to 1500 meters. "We choose to have two classifications for our competition—men's events and women's events. This means we need to be clear about the competition criteria for these two categories. We have always believed that testosterone, either naturally produced or artificially inserted into the body, provides significant performance advantages" (IAAF). The new regulations focus only on specific events (400 meters to 1500 meters) where the IAAF deems high testosterone levels give female athletes a significant competitive advantage. Curiously, these events include those in which Caster Semenya excels. The new policy ignores events such as the Pole Vault and Hammer Throw in which high testosterone levels also give athletes a specific advantage (Schultz). As the IAAF governs

162 Playing on an Uneven Field

international Track and Field events it is highly likely that the IOC will follow the IAAF's lead on the issue of hyperandrogenism; this will undoubtedly have an adverse effect on many competitors and will hamper the ability of female athletes to compete on the world stage.

To their credit, the IOC's methods of discerning the sex of athletes who compete at the Olympics has markedly improved over the course of the 20th and into the 21st century. However, recent developments and the suspicion that new regulations are being driven by politics as much as science, show that there is still much work to be done in ensuring fairness for all athletes who compete in international competition.

"We could be heroes"

When the British Olympic team came out to rapturous applause, and David Bowie's "Heroes," at the opening ceremony of the 2012 London Olympics the cameras focused on potential medalists Jessica Ennis-Hill, Rebecca Adlington, Jade Jones, and countless other female stars as much as they did the male athletes who were representing Team GB. This is not unusual, despite the slow rise in the number of female athletes at the Games, the Olympics has never had a problem finding female stars.

The first women to win an individual Olympic gold medal, Charlotte Cooper in the women's singles tennis event in Paris, 1900, was already a grand slam champion and would go on to win a further two Wimbledon singles championships before her retirement. Over the course of the next 100 years many more women would become Olympic medalists and either dominate in their sport or prove that their athleticism and achievements were equal to male competitors. Babe Didrikson was, arguably, the first great all-around female U.S. sport star. She won gold medals in the 80-meters Hurdles and the Javelin at the 1932 Los Angeles Olympics, as well as a silver medal in the High Jump. She went on to claim 10 major titles and 41 total titles on the Ladies Professional Golf Association (LPGA) tour. Dutch athlete Fanny Blankers-Koen was the most successful competitor at the 1948 London Olympics. She won gold medals in the 100 meters, 200 meters, 80-meter Hurdles, and the 4x100-meter Relay. She made even more headlines as she did this as a mother of two children, after giving birth in 1941 and 1946. Female athletes who are also mothers still make headlines today; it was almost unheard of in 1948. Blankers-Koen's achievements would lead to her being named female athlete of the 20th century by the IAAF.

Olympic events are split into men's events, women's events, mixed events, and open events. Mixed events, such as doubles badminton or doubles table tennis, have strict rules stating that one man and one women must compete on the same team. Open events are much rarer but have seen success for female athletes competing against male athletes. In 1900 Hélène de Pourtalès won a gold medal and a silver medal as member of the Swiss team in the 1 to 2-ton Mixed Sailing event. Equestrian events at the Olympics have seen success over the years for women competing in the same open events as men. In 1972 Liselott Linsenhoff won gold in the individual Dressage event at her home Munich Olympics. She also won a silver medal in the team Dressage event, adding to the gold she had won in the team event four years earlier in Mexico City.

There is a danger in highlighting the achievements of some of the great female Olympic athletes of the 20th century that we celebrate the victors and forgot the challenges many other women faced in simply trying to compete at the Olympics. By emphasizing the successes of athletes such as Cooper, Pourtalès, Didrikson, Blankers-Koen, and Linsenhoff I do not mean to do this; rather I want to show that there have been heroines. There have been champions who have grabbed headlines and transcended from the sporting world into the realms of popular culture and international stardom. The problem has not been a lack of women wanting to compete, it has not been a lack of women competing at a high level, or even a lack of female superstar athletes, the problem has been a systemic failure of sporting organizations, such as the IOC, to recognize, promote, and push for equality in women's events. This can be seen in the numbers of women competing, the number of events and disciplines in which women can compete, and in the way the IOC has historically treated female athletes. Even as gender equality becomes a more realistic and achievable aim of the IOC the historical ramifications are real. Female athletes often struggle to find sponsorship, earn less in prize money, and have fewer opportunities to compete than men. The IOC and the Olympics, as the world's biggest sporting event, should be the catalyst for change; all too often it has failed in this role. The situation is slowly changing. IOC President Thomas Bach ended his 2018 International Women's Day speech with the following maxim. "As the leader of the Olympic Movement, the IOC has an important responsibility to take action when it comes to gender equality—a basic human right of profound importance and a fundamental principle of the Olympic Charter" (International Women's Day).Whether the next century will see Bach's promise for the IOC come to fruition remains to be seen. Tokyo 2020 is poised to have more female athletes than any previous Olympics, more events in which female athletes can compete, as well as the promise of improved treatment and greater respect for the events in which women are competing. We have come a long way since there were no female competitors at the 1896 Athens Olympics; we still have a long way to go.

NOTES

1. This quote is often attributed to the founder of the modern Olympics, the French-man Baron Pierre de Coubertin, and is referred to as the Olympic Creed or Olympic motto. The modern day International Olympic Committee (IOC) does not refer to this quote as having any sort of official meaning. Professor Amos Oduyale suggests that this quote, which would become de Coubertin's mantra, was first heard in a sermon before the 1908 Games in London and was subsequently used by de Coubertin to signify the role he saw the Olympics playing in the framework of a 20th-century world.

2. This quote is often attributed to Mark Twain. As with many quotes associated to Twain the actual origins of the saying cannot be fully determined.

3. All the information regarding the total number of male and female athletes at the summer Olympics comes from the IOC's official website, www.olympic.org/. Much of the information comes from the IOC's official report on the specific Olympics—for example, the information for Tokyo, 1964 comes from https://www.olympic.org/tokyo-1964. However, if the information given by the IOC was ambiguous, or missing, I consulted "Factsheet Women in the Olympic Movement," this document is housed on the IOC's website. Information for Rio de Janeiro, 2016 is currently unofficial. Many journalistic articles (see Crockett and Warner) that predate the 2016 Olympics claim that the Rio de Janeiro Olympics will have a record number of female competitors and will see the total percentage of female athletes pass 45 percent. However, the (as yet unverified) IOC figures suggest that this was not the case.

4. There are disagreements amongst Olympic historians, and even within the IOC, about what sports and events should be included in official Olympic records. I have attempted here to only use sports that had official Olympic recognition (so not demonstration sports) and sports that have kept that distinction with the retroactive reclassification that has happened within the IOC. Where possible I have used official IOC records.

5. There are, of course, various events within these disciplines as well as many sports and events that have been discontinued; for the sake of brevity I have only included data at the sport level for sports that will be in the 2020 Tokyo Olympics. The title of the sport is taken from official IOC guidelines.

6. Badminton was an exhibition event in the 1972, Munich Games.

7. Baseball was an exhibition event at the 1904, 1912, 1936, 1952, 1956, 1964, 1984, and 1988 Summer Olympics.

8. Basketball was an exhibition event at the 1904, St. Louis Olympics.

9. Canoe was an exhibition event in the 1924, Paris Olympics.

10. Equestrian is now one of the few sports in which men and women compete against each other on an equal footing, not in mixed events.

11. The 1900 Olympics in Paris saw individual Golf events held for men and women, but this changed at the 1904, St. Louis Olympics where only men's events were held. Golf was not in the Olympics again until the 2016, Rio de Janeiro games when men's and women's individual events were added to the schedule. In the build-up to the 2020, Tokyo Olympics there has been much discussion of the Kasumigaseki Country Club's policy of not allowing women to be full members. The IOC is pressuring Kasumigaseki to change its rules and will likely insist that the Tokyo organizing committee move the event to a different course if Kasumigaseki's gender restrictions remain.

12. Women's Judo was an exhibition event at the 1988, Seoul Olympics.

13. Rowing was scheduled to be held at the 1896, Athens Olympics but events were not held due to inclement weather, medals (for men) were first given in 1900 in Paris (International Olympic Committee, *Rowing*).

14. Men's Rugby Union was an event at the 1900, 1908, 1920, and 1924 summer Olympics. Rugby Union Sevens was first played in the 2016, Rio de Janeiro Olympics.

15. Sailing, like Rowing, is a tricky sport to classify. Events were due to be held in Athens, 1896 but were canceled due to inclement weather. It is unclear (although highly unlikely) if any women were due to compete in the 1896 Games. Both men and women competed in 1900 in Paris and sailing (referred to as Yachting by the IOC until 2000) was one of

the few sports (along with Equestrian) were women competed with men in open events (not in mixed events). The first women's only race was held at the 1988, Seoul Olympics.

16. In Shooting, women competed against men in open events from 1968 to 1980. Women only events were introduced at the 1984, Los Angeles Olympics. (International Olympic Committee, *Shooting*)

17. Taekwondo was an exhibition event, for men and women, in 1988 and 1992.

Works Cited

Crockett, Zachary. "More Women Will Compete in Rio 2016 Than in Any Other Olympics." *Vox.* Vox Media, 5 Aug. 2016. Web. 22 March 2018.

Elsas, Louis J., et al. "Gender Verification of female Athletes." *Genetics in Medicine* 2.4 (July/August 2000): 249–254. Print.

Emery, Lynne. "An Examination of the 1928 Olympic 800 Meter Race for Women." *North American Society for Sport History: Proceedings and Newsletter.* 1985. 30. Print.

English, Coleen. ""Not a Very Edifying Spectacle": The Controversial Women's 800-Meter Race in the 1928 Olympics." *Sport in American History.* 8 October 2015. Web. 7 May 2018.

Guttmann, Allen. *The Olympics: A History of the Modern Games.* University of Illinois Press, 2002. Print.

IAAF. *Council Takes Steps to Further Strengthen Athletics. IAAF.* IAAF, 6 March 2018. Web. 7 May. 2018.

Illson, Murray. "John R. Tunis, 85. Author, is Dead." *New York Times* 5 February 1975, 35. Print.

International Olympic Committee. *Factsheet Women in The Olympic Movement.* February 2018. PDF file.

_____. *IOC Gender Equality Review Project.* February 2018. PDF file.

_____. *IOC Regulations on Female Hyperandrogenism: Games of the XXX Olympiad in London, 2012.* June 2012. PDF file.

_____. *Olympic Charter.* August 2015. PDF file.

_____. *Rowing: History of Rowing at the Olympic Games.* March 2015. PDF file.

_____. *Shooting: History of Shooting at the Olympic Games.* October 2017. PDF file.

"International Women's Day: IOC Setting the Stage for Lasting Change in Sport." *IOC.* IOC, 8 March 2018. Web. 7 May 2018.

Kessel, Anna. "Caster Semenya May Return to Track This Month After IAAF Clearance." *Guardian.* Guardian, 6 July 2010. Web. 7 May 2018.

Oduyale, Amos T. "The Importance of Taking Part, Not Winning: The Philosophical Implications." *Olympic Review* 163 (May 1981): 300–301. Print.

Pieper, Lindsay Parks. *Sex Testing: Gender Policing in Women's Sports.* University of Illinois Press, 2016. Print.

Schultz, Jaime. "A Sexist Policy May End the Career of One of the Commonwealth's Greatest Female Runners." *The Conversation.* The Conversation. Web. 8 April 2018.

Sailors, Pam R. "'Organically Sound' Olympians: Gender and Women's Distance Running." *Problems, Possibilities, Promising Practices: Critical Dialogues on the Olympic and Paralympic Games.* (2012): 1–5. *Digital Library Collections.* Web. 7 May 2018.

"Statistics: Women at the Olympic Games." *IOC.* IOC, Web. 7 May 2018.

"Tokyo 2020: Mixed-gender events added to the Olympic Games." *BBC.* BBC, 9 June 2017. Web. 7 May 2018.

Warner, Claire. "How Many Female Athletes Are Competing in the 2016 Olympics? The Rio Games Are Worth Watching." *Bustle.* 24 July 2016. Web. 7 May 2018.

"They still call us Indians"

Colombian Racers and the Barriers of Race, Class and Nation in the Tour de France, 1983–1985

COREY SHOUSE

In 1983, organizers of the Tour de France invited the world's best amateur teams to compete in their event for the first time in the Tour's 80-year history. They did so hoping to capitalize on the dynamics of the Cold War and attract the powerhouse "amateur" squads from the Soviet Union and other Eastern Bloc countries that had been so successful in the amateur-only Tour de l'Avenir during the late 1970s and early 1980s. Ultimately, the only non-professional team to join the field came not from behind the iron curtain, but rather the far away Colombian Andes. On June 29, 1983, when the 10-man Varta-Colombia team lined up for the prologue stage, they became the first amateur and Latin American team to race in the world's premiere cycling event. The unheralded Colombians came to France with modest support from the Colombian Cycling Federation and the unpretentious sponsorship of a battery company (Varta) and dairy (Leche Gran Vía).

In cycling crazed Colombia, the long-anticipated arrival of the Colombian racers to the Tour de France generated a true media frenzy.[1] In 1983, alone three national radio networks sent crews to report on every conceivable aspect of the event for an insatiable national audience. By most accounts the Colombian press corps at the 1983 Tour de France included 50 to 60 full-time television, radio, and print journalists, a contingent so large they occupied the entire second floor of the official press headquarters. The competition to provide the best reporting was so great that it became a news story of its own, and on more than one occasion the directors from competing radio

166

broadcast teams had physical altercations over media turf (Clopatofsky Londoño, "Dos estilos" 3B).

Leading national dailies *El Espectador* and *El Tiempo* sent teams of reporters led sports section chiefs and supported by a cohort of well-respected investigative journalists and commentators. During the glory years of the 1980s, the contingent from *El Tiempo* included sports section chief José Clopatofsky Londoño, special investigative reporter Daniel Samper Pizano, Rafael García as head of their sports magazine *Cronómetro* and racing experts Raúl Meza and Julio "the Bible of cycling" Arrastía Bricca. The team from *El Espectador* similarly included sports section chief Mike Forero Nogués, special correspondent Alexandra Pineda, investigative reporter Cyriad Meck and renowned political commentator María Jimena Duzán. Daily coverage of the Tour de France dominated sports sections and included detailed stage summaries, profiles of upcoming stages and terrain, expert commentary on strategy, health and human-interest stories, frequent translations of European press coverage of the Tour, as well as catch-all columns that compiled a rich stream of anecdotes and event details.

Beginning in 1984, television broadcasters began transmitting as many as eight hours of live and delayed daily coverage that were followed with the same nail-biting intensity as the conclusion of a choice *telenovela* or World Cup. Accounts for the actual number of viewers vary widely, as at this time the Colombian television industry had no Nielsen-style means to accurately measure audiences. However, *El Espectador* and *El Tiempo* all consistently estimated audiences of many millions of viewers of the Tour ("Colombia se 'mordió las uñas'" 1C), and during their broadcast for the American CBS network, long-time Tour de France commentators Phil Liggett and Paul Sherwen claimed that as many as 20 million Colombians watched Lucho Herrera win stage 17 on the Alpe D'Huez in 1984. It is worth noting that at this time the entire national population of Colombia was only 36 million (Palacios 294).

Not surprisingly, the Colombian press celebrated the arrival of their *escarabajos*[2] to the Tour de France as a classic underdog tale, which to this day is still remembered as simply "The Great Adventure" (Urrego Caballero, *El ciclismo colombiano* 67).[3] Writers from sports tabloids to the most prominent newspapers and magazines celebrated their participation as an achievement without precedent in the annals of Colombian history, and from the very beginning touted this as a collective intercontinental struggle of life-and-death proportions. The day prior to the first stage in the inaugural Tour of 1983, the Sports page director for *El Tiempo* framed the Tour a battle of "10 Colombians vs. 130 Professionals" (Clopatofsky Lodoño, "10 colombianos" 2B) with a "Challenge for the *escarabajos* to give it their all for the Americas!" (Clopatofsky Lodoño, "Reto" 1A). The first Colombian advance in this struggle came only 11 days later, when Patrocinio "Patro" Jiménez crowned the storied Tourmalet pass ahead of Bernard Hinault and the rest of the European favorites, making him the first of many Colombians to wear the coveted King of the Mountains jersey. When asked about this feat, Jiménez simply explained: "The only thing I did was to fill the expectations here and in my homeland. It couldn't be any other way ... believe me when I tell you that we will fight to the death here. In a certain way we've already done something important and whatever may happen from here on out is simply decoration. We've shown what we can do, and now we will prepare the tools to win the Tour" (Clopatofsky Londoño, "Me are matar" 3C).

Those familiar with Colombian cycling know that Jiménez' claims were not made in vain. The 1980s was an undeniably spectacular decade for Colombian cycling marked by numerous weighty firsts: in 1980 Alfonso Flórez became the first Colombian to win a stage race in Europe with his astonishing victory over Bernard Hinault in the prestigious Tour de l'Avenir; in 1984 Luis "Lucho" Herrera took Colombia's first-ever stage victory at the Tour de France, and in 1987 he became the first Colombian to win a Grand Tour title (La Vuelta a España); in 1988 Fabio Parra was the first Colombian to earn a general classification podium in the Tour de France; and during one spectacular 24-hour period between November 8 and 9, 1985, Efraín Domínguez became the first Colombian to establish world records for the flying 200 meters, the flying 500 meters and the kilometer time trial (Domínguez). Once unfamiliar and disrespected, by the mid–1980s racers in the professional peloton feared and revered the racecraft and climbing prowess of the *escarabajos*.

At home in Colombia, cycling was a national obsession and generated cultural capital prized by both private industry and the state. Radio, television and print advertisers linked images of cycling to an endless array of consumer products from banking services to fried chicken. *El Tiempo* contracted cartoonist Álvaro Paez to create Colombianito Corredor—literally Little Colombian Racer—a dark-skinned, indigenous-appearing child wearing nothing more than a loincloth, with a Colombian tri-color bandana around his head and crowned with a single feather. The sole purpose of this campaign was to create an affable and easily recognizable cartoon mascot to promote cycling nationwide (Arce et al. 137–138). Colombianito Corredor was quite popular and enjoyed great recognition nationally, appearing in numerous print and television ads for a number of youth-oriented products, including t-shirts, sneakers, chewing gum, stickers and magazines. In their history of Colombian animation, Arce et al. explain that despite the creator's explicit aim to create a positive image of national identity, Colombianito Corredor—like a number of other popular animated renderings of peasants and indigenous peoples in Colombia during the 1980s—borrowed heavily from the racist iconography of the American western, and contained "some of the elements most commonly used in 'traditional' representations of the indigenous child," including almost total nudity, the carrying of a stone axe in one hand, a bandana around his head and an upright feather in his hair [author's translation] (138).

Following Martín Ramírez's shocking triumph over Bernard Hinault in the 1984 Critérium du Dauphiné Libéré, Colombian president Belisario all-but declared cycling the national sport, decreeing it "a sporting practice of special significance for the country and in its representations of Colombia abroad," and formally committed the state resources for cycling at all levels. During the public signing of this decree, Betancur admitted that he, "like all of Colombia," followed the live radio coverage of the event "second by second" as Ramírez was "crowned with glory and asked to listen to the national anthem" ("Gobierno anuncia estímulos" 1C).

Nowhere else were Colombian cycling triumphs more dramatic or significant than in the Tour de France. In 1984, the Colombians came back to the Tour as "Varta-Café de Colombia," a 100 percent Colombian national team sponsored by the Colombian Coffee Federation. That year Luis Herrera became both the first amateur and the first Colombian to take a Tour stage win, dropping favorites Robert Millar, Bernard Hinault and the eventual 1984 champion Laurent Fignon in stage 17 on the historic slopes of Alpe d'Huez. Herrera's win fueled excitement and expectations back at home, with a national survey finding that more than half of the country thought a Colombian to win the Tour within one or two years ("Ganar" 3B). In 1985, Varta-Café de Colombia returned again as a properly professional team, with captain Luis Herrera claiming two more stage victories along with the coveted King of the Mountains prize. During that same Tour teammate and compatriot Fabio Parra was victorious on stage 12, with Herrera following in second, prompting the sports section headline, "Colombia wore the Tour like a poncho" (Clopatofsky Londoño, "Colombia se puso" 1B). In Bogotá alone, more than half a million people participated in the homecoming parade for the *escarabajos*, with similar celebrations taking place around the country ("Inolvidable recibimiento" 1A).

Fully aware of the visibility the Tour provided Colombia, both *El Tiempo* and *El Espectador* were keen to publish articles from the international press that mentioned Colombia and the *escarabajos*. Both papers regularly posted interviews with high profile members of the international cycling community and reprinted translated articles from European news services like the AFP or from newspapers and magazines such as *Le Monde, Paris Match, Velo, L'Equipe,* and *Le Figaro*. Not unsurprisingly, many of these repeated stereotypes and other unflattering observations about all things Colombian. For example, *El Espectador* published a forceful response to a *Le Figaro* article that labeled the Colombians as "distracted and extravagant" ("Distraídos y extravagantes" 1C), while *El Tiempo* published a similar rebuking to public comments by

Irish champion Stephen Roche who described the *escarabajos* as "opportunistic and irresponsible" racers who didn't work for the peloton and attacked only when it was convenient ("Así ven a los escarabajos" 6C).

With the passage of time and accumulated success, however, the *escarabajos* eventually earned their place in the professional peloton. By the late 1980s, most of the European press and racers who had once been openly critical of the Colombians as one-dimensional, distracted, opportunistic and unsportsmanlike, now praised them, and once wary European team directors scrambled to sign *escarabajos* to their rosters (Campillo 3C). Following the 1984 Tour, a group of world's best cyclists, including Laurent Fignon, Greg Lemond, Sean Kelly and Bernard Hinault committed to come and race in Colombia, and Hinault openly declared his desire to have an *escarabajo* on his team ("Hinault vendrá a Colombia" 1C). Undeniably, much like the Brazilians came to dominate the cultural transplant of soccer, in the 1980s Colombia seemed poised to take over the world cycling scene.

Normally this is the stuff of sports fantasy. Setting aside the hyperbole that often flavors sports journalism, these were dramatic years with superlative athletic accomplishments that thrilled a nation. Colombian journalists were right to mark the 1983 Tour de France as a "before and after in the history of Colombian and world cycling" ("Colombia en el Tour" 1B). It is with good reason that sportswriters boast that "in Colombia cycling is culture and religion," and that during the golden years of the 1980s the live voices of Tour commentators Julio Arrastía and Héctor Urrego "rose to the heavens and traveled daily ten thousand kilometers to bring to the country ... a message of happiness, hope, faith and confidence in its men and in their future" (Urrego Caballero et al. 45–47).

Yet during the 1980s Colombian society found itself immersed in profound crisis. These were the worst years of escalating cartel violence, political scandal, and increased foreign intervention. Much to the chagrin of the ruling class, in 1982, Pablo Escobar was both named Latin America's wealthiest man and was elected as an alternate member of the national Chamber of Representatives as part of the established Liberal party (Bushnell 262–263). Equally scandalous were Colombian president Belisario Betancur's clandestine attempts to negotiate a truce with the Extraditables of the Medellín Cartel, as were his efforts to sign an amnesty with Colombian insurgent groups (Palacios 275). In April 1984, the Medellín Cartel gunned down Justice Minister Rodrigo Lara Bonilla in retaliation for his pursuit of an aggressive extradition agreement with the United States (Palacios 281). On November 6, 1985, members of the M-19 guerrilla group occupied the Palace of Justice in downtown Bogotá. The ensuing liberation by the Colombian army—broadcast live on international television—sent tanks through the building's front door and produced a fire that destroyed the building and left nearly a hundred people dead, including 11 supreme court justices (Carrigan). Only one later a volcanic mudslide buried 23,000 people alive in the town of Armero, Tolima. This was a horrific time for many Colombians, and the images and collective memories this period haunted them at home and stigmatized them abroad.

While from the 1950s through the 1980s the Colombian economy expanded at an annual rate of 6 percent or better (Bushnell 241), this growth failed to generate a diversified "trickle-down" expansion of the primary sector economy, and instead concentrated capital managed by a technocratic oligarchy, and further deepened disparities between rich and poor, urban and rural populations (Corredor 30–35). Paradoxically, economic development paralleled the dramatic escalation of urban and rural violence, which in 1987 prompted Fabio Echeverri Corea, the president of ANDI (National Association of Industries) to comment infamously, "the economy is doing well, but the country is doing poorly" (Palacio Castañeda 147). Colombian cities further swelled as rural populations fled escalating violence in the countryside during the mid-century period of partisan conflict and socio-economic known as *La Violencia*. This process accelerated from the 1960s onward during waves of drug cartel violence and armed conflict between the state, leftist insurgencies right-wing paramilitary forces which during the 1980s generated an average of 3,500 politically motivated deaths (*Human Rights Watch* 13–17).

The precipitous expansion of the narcotics trade further stigmatized Colombia abroad, while at home it spurred turbulent transformations that wreaked havoc on long-established sectors of the national economy and fueled the rise of a narcobourgeoisie that threatened the cultural and political hegemony of the traditional elite. While popular cultural representations of drug cartel opulence often lead us to assume that the narcotics trade generated vast sums of wealth in Colombia, in fact it had an overall negative effect on the economy as it created pronounced problems of inflation and distortions in currency value and in key market sectors such as construction and real estate (Reina 75–94). The most distressing symptom of these changes was the escalation of all forms of violence and criminal activity, which skyrocketed from 1970 onward. By 1993, national homicide rates were more than four times what they had been 30 years earlier, leaving Colombia the most murderous country in the world (Safford and Palacios 360). For Colombia's rural, indigenous and Afro-Colombian populations these conditions were particularly severe, as the state's historically weak presence in these communities facilitated what historian Marco Palacios simply describes as a "Hobbesian order" of economic expansion and conflict resolution (275). If there ever was a time when Colombians needed "a message of happiness, hope, faith and confidence in its men and in their future" it was during the 1980s (Urrego Caballero et al. 45–47).

As fate would have it, the two most important periods in Colombian cycling bookend these processes of violence, demographic transformation and economic expansion: the *Violencia* years of the 1950s were the heyday of massively popular national cycling events like the Vuelta a Colombia and the Clásico RCN; while the darkest years of narcotrafficking and insurgency violence of the 1980s coincided with the triumphant entrance of Colombians onto the world stage of international professional cycling. The common wisdom about the cultural importance of cycling during these times was that it functioned simply as a social palliative to comfort and agglutinate a country in crisis. To wit Héctor Urrego Caballero, the most important living Colombian cycling commentator, promoter and journalist, explained, "Say what you may, cycling is still the most important sport in the country ... if we look at results—titles, medals, accomplishments. Colombian soccer hasn't and continues to fail to win anything ... cycling showed the country that we could compete and defeat the world's best on their own terrain ... it brought our people together and fascinated the media and our society precisely because it was a movement capable of making us look good abroad—it was a showcase for the country itself."

At face value, this is a plausible and attractive assertion, but is it accurate? Can the wildly popular images of cycling triumphs combat lived material conditions that suggest something completely different? Is cycling the crux of a robust group of experiences and cultural expressions that generate socially productive practices, or is this simply a populist fantasy? Dozens of interviews with past and present Colombian racers, fans, promoters, bicycle constructors and journalists, newspaper articles on the Tours de France (1983–1985) in the two most important national dailies of the time, *El Espectador* and *El Tiempo*, various accounts of the "glory days" of Colombian cycling in the 1980s characterize Colombian cycling as a rich and dynamic cultural field (Bourdieu) that belies the assertion that cycling is best understood as a simple palliative. Instead, its inner workings reveal a series of competing interests and processes in tension that illustrate the complex dynamics of race, class and national identity for Colombians, both at home and as part of the international community. Specifically,

1. newspaper accounts of the Tour in *El Espectador* and *El Tiempo* reveal an attempt to articulate a centered, coherent and positive image of Colombia and Colombian identity at home and abroad, in which the *escarabajos* function as a conceit for all things Colombian as cast against an uncontrollable tidal wave of negative images, stereotypes and racist fantasies about the Colombians circulating worldwide.

2. the press coverage of these Tours de France often greatly simplifies the complex realities of class and race in Colombia, presenting the

nation as a mestizo racial paradise, and in so doing reiterates what many contemporary historians have critiqued as one of the foundational myths of Colombian identity [Múnera 21].

Given the rhetorical components of this press coverage, a materialist analysis might suggest that those who found meaning, comfort or identity in Colombian cycling do so as the result of top-down discursive manipulations and as an expression of false consciousness. Instead, I understand Colombian cycling as a field wrought with numerous social tensions— between the written and the lived, between official and popular culture, between different ethnic groups and social classes, etc. This model for understanding Colombian cycling ultimately produces a more robust model of Colombian culture; it reveals deeper patterns of conflict in Colombian society and ultimately produces a more robust understanding of popular identity and experience in Colombia during the 1980s.

Cycling as a Showcase

It should come as no surprise that the press coverage of the Colombians in the Tours de France during the 1980s reads like a flagship narrative of national optimism. Interviewers with racers, testimony of fans and press archives[4] consistently demonstrate that the feats of the *escarabajos* on the world stage of professional cycling held an importance that transcended the limits of sport, much like Americans may remember the 1980 "Miracle on Ice" gold medal in Olympic hockey during the nadir of the Cold War, or Argentines might recall the 1978 World Cup victory amid dictatorship and dirty war. It is equally true, however, that the newspaper accounts of the Tour in *El Espectador* and *El Tiempo* also obey a particular set of rhetorical norms that construct a specific image of Colombia, its people and its values as cast against the elaboration of a hostile international context. To begin with, stories written in the plural first person "we" subject pronoun abound, with partisan journalists blissfully subjective in their support of *their* racers in the Tour. Indeed, while the proper sir names of the racers were of course used to celebrate individual accomplishments, just as often authors celebrate *los escarabajos* collectively, and employ them as a metonym for the country as a whole: they are labeled "humble men" in the tour (Mendoza, "Los escarabajos" 1C), "the peddlers for Colombia" or simply "our cycling" (Arrastía Bricca 6B). Noteworthy moments in the Tour were likewise remembered as "a cumbia in the Alps" (Samper Pizano, "Cumbia" 4D), "a nation's hopes and dreams" (Clopatofsky Londoño "Colombia hace historia" 6), "the conquest of the impossible" (Hacia la cima" 4C), a moment of "bitter heroism of the Colombians" (Forero 1A), a stage where "Colombia brought the pepper"

(Clopatofsky Londoño "Colombia se puso pimienta" 3B), or a stinging defeat that Colombia as a whole "pays for with blood" ("Seguimos poniendo" 2C). One editorial went so far as to propose Lucho Herrera as a synecdoche for the country, stating simply, "Herrera is Colombia … we have to point out the enormous showcase that Herrera and his companions had in this live television broadcast to almost all the countries in Europe. This is the good image of Colombia that we all want and that cyclists are carrying around the world" ("Herrera es Colombia" 1C).

The coverage of Herrera's dramatic stage win on July 13, 1985, offers a telling example of how this conceit is employed to narrate one of the greatest moments in Colombian sports history. Recovering from a fall and with blood pouring down the side of his face, Herrera crosses the finish line ahead of eventual 1985 Tour winner and five-time champion Bernard Hinault. This moment generates a series of iconic images highly suggestive of a fallen Christ, a coincidence not lost on the Colombian public, photographers or newspaper editors. *El Tiempo* celebrated Herrera's victory with the headline "Blood, Sweat and Glory" (Clopatofsky Londoño "Sangre, sudor y gloria" 1B) while *El Espectador* proclaimed, "Herrera falls and rises a giant" (Mendoza "Herrera se cae" 1C). In that same edition political commentator María Jimena Duzán penned "A Letter to 'Lucho' Herrera" written in the informal second person *tú* and with an intimate tone of veneration usually reserved for a dear loved one or prayer: "My dear Lucho, after having seen you arrive victorious, despite the streams of blood that ran down your face … you can't imagine, my beloved *escarabajo*, the fright we had when they didn't even let us approach you…. Is Lucho OK? Nothing happened to you? You had taken a real wallop when you fell only a few kilometers from the finish, but immediately you got up, crossing the finish with your arms raised like a Christ in Saint Etienne" ("Carta a 'Lucho'" 2C).

Again, the construction of this metonymic conceit of Colombia-as-*escarabajo* is layered against the elaboration of a contextual backdrop of stereotypes and racist fantasies of Colombians, where the limits between cycling and non-cycling worlds are blurry at best. During the Tours in question *El Espectador* and *El Tiempo* ran frequent articles, editorials and political cartoons explicitly treating cycling as "a showcase" for the country. Unambiguous in this rhetorical construction is the language of exchange. This at times is quite literal. For example, the Minister of Foreign Relations sought to use cycling to promote "a positive image of the country" and proposed a Colombian folk culture float for the massive Tour de France caravan as a means to stimulate tourism and generate a positive image of national culture abroad ("El Tour, una excelente vitrina" 7C). Other times it is more figurative. Gestalt analysis of period front pages with cycling content reveal numerous iterations of this rhetoric of exchange and symbolic compensation. On July 7,

1984, for example, *El Espectador* ran headlines covering controversial dialogues with the Medellín Cartel over their war against extradition, with a headline exclaiming, "Colombia will continue to be a moral power" alongside a photo headline touting the successful fumigation of marijuana fields, while immediately below the fold a headline celebrated an unexpected show of cycling aggression as "Herrera's Rebellion"

In all instances, the currency in this exchange is the imagery of cycling, which is put forward to offset deficits created by the image of drug trafficking, political violence and the *backwardness* associated with Colombia and the developing world in general. In one noteworthy example, *El Tiempo* correspondent Daniel Samper Pizano reflects on casual conversation he had which, for the author at least, lays bare the essence of being a Colombian abroad. He writes,

> The woman was kind. She didn't mention cocaine. Cocaine and coffee are the principal objects of identification of *la Colombie* in France…. Colombia, cocaine and coffee. In that order certainly. Nevertheless, as of two days ago there is a third C. *La Colombie* is also a team of cyclists that awakens the sympathies of people along the roads and the rhetorical admiration of journalists … *les petits colombiens, los colombianitos*. An international cycling power with "a special national identity." And here I have the problem: "national identity, international image." This isn't about only winning a few stages of the Tour de France, nor is it about beating more than 150 competitors. The true rival is the image of Colombia ["Mejora la imagen de Colombia" 6D].

The stigma of this special national identity was particularly pronounced for the darker-skinned, working class *escarabajo* pioneers in the Tour de France. In an interview, Rafael Acevedo—who finished 12th overall in 1984—described those first years as, "a unique experience—at the start the Europeans imagined that Colombians raced in loincloths and with a bow and arrow on our backs. They treated us like underdeveloped Third Worlders—as if we were Indians still!" (Acevedo). Acevedo also recalled that when the Colombian national team was en route to the 1986 Union Cycliste Internationale (UCI) World Championships they were subjected to a six-hour detention that included cavity searches, the destruction of shoes, clothing and even bicycle components by overzealous customs agents "who were certain they'd find coke on the Colombians" (Acevedo). Teammate Patrocinio Jiménez similarly recollected racist insults and having bananas thrown at him by fans as if he were a monkey during the Tour de France in 1985. Martín "Cochise" Rodríguez, the most accomplished all-round cyclist in Colombian history, lamented being treated as "the scum of the earth" and "frequently insulted as a drug addict" by French champion Laurent Fignon and most of the European peloton, both on and off the course (Rodríguez).

El Tiempo and *El Espectador* coverage of the Tour during the mid–1980s is peppered with similar stories of racist encounters that pit the *escarabajos* in an "us vs. them" conflict with the international community vis à vis the professional peloton. In one such story penned for *El Espectador*, special correspondent Alexandra Pineda recalls that Bernard Hinault, "called them midgets, he admitted they made him laugh, that he called them 'cocainers,' and that he insulted them with every imaginable term," only later to find himself begrudgingly needing their help in his ultimately futile quest for the 1984 general classification title ("Los 'coquetos' de Hinault" 5C).

As the previously cited dismissals of the Colombian racers as distracted, extravagant, opportunistic and irresponsible illustrate, the Colombian press paid close attention to how the *escarabajos* were depicted abroad. In general, these depictions assaulted the physical appearance of the *escarabajos* and offered unflattering perceptions of their work ethic and racecraft. The perception that Colombians were dangerous and caused crashes was rampant in 1983 and 1984. While the European press was quick to blame Colombians as a group based on notions of race or culture, they often ignored crashes caused by European racers or those generated by others in the rear of the peloton on the long flat stages where the Colombians—like many other lighter climbers—suffered ("Un tropezón" 1C). Aspects of racial perception and cultural difference were also used to justify the unattractiveness of Colombian racers to European teams. In one telling example from 1985, *El Tiempo* published a summary of French media stories on the Colombian contingent in the Tour, in which the Colombian editor celebrates the fact that Colombians are gaining acceptance as "just another group of cyclists, part of the Tour's folklore, although intelligent." However, the summary also quotes the French paper *Liberation* and its blatantly racist assessment of Luis Herrera's stoic behavior on the podium following his stage 11 victory (July 9, Pontarlier–Morzine Avoriaz): "without a shadow of emotion, with his childlike face, tanned by the sun and impenetrable. That night there were no glasses of champagne nor parties nor laughter. Perhaps this comes from his Indian culture" ("Todavía nos dicen indios" 3B).

The Colombian media was also quick to relate how the European press and professional peloton explained the accomplishments of the Colombians not as the result of hard work, dedication and a drive to escape poverty, but rather as the simple function of their slight stature and the advantageous blood chemistry that comes from living in the high-altitude conditions of the Andes. Even these innate and unearned gifts were often questioned: in one telling article exploring the "myth or reality" of the benefits of life at high altitude, the author summarizes that "Europeans are absolutely convinced that Colombian cyclists compete—and successfully—in the mountain stages not due to their physical or anthropomorphic characteristics. All to the contrary. Their inferior size, the precarious diet, their athletic preparation without scientific guidance, cannot be the elements that produce men who at times seem super-gifted, bionic" (Clopatofsky Londoño "La altura" 6B). Unfortunately, such slurs and racist episodes were common and well-documented experiences for the *escarabajos* in the 1980s. What is worth pointing out here, however, is the rhetorical strategy of exchange and compensatory modernity that the Colombian media uses, deploying the imagery of cycling to counter the cultural and economic deficits created by drug trafficking, political violence and underdevelopment. As Daniel Samper Pizano and the Colombian Consul in Paris Carlos Delgado Pereira explained to readers, *the true rival is the image of Colombia*: "the good image that the cyclists give us through their sweat and pedal strokes is ruined by the Colombians caught with drugs. *Les petits colombiens* constitute a note of vindication for the Colombians in France, for the image of Colombia in France. Like the time that *monsieur* Márquez won the Nobel Prize ("Mejora la imagen" 6A).

This language of exchange is constant in both *El Tiempo* and *El Espectador*'s narrative of Colombian cycling and their *conquest of Europe*. These were indeed groundbreaking years and the Colombians did in fact have much to learn about living and racing in Europe. The Colombian press was correct to remind readers that the *escarabajos* struggled to adjust to race with European tactics and compete on European terrain; that the Colombians arrived to Europe unprepared for the brutal pace of the long, flat stages; that they struggled with the pavé and were initially quite poor time trialists. The Colombian press was also diligent in signaling how the European "experts" and racers attributed the successes of the Colombians to simple physiology and how they lambasted Colombia as a country underdeveloped in terms of cycling culture ("Un ciclismo distinto" 4C). Many also hopefully celebrated the comparative advantages of Colombian altitude training and *escarabajo* racing style to produce "a geographic revolution of world cycling" (Clopatofsky Londoño "La altura" 6B).

Most interesting here is to note how quickly the authors in question took the realm of sport as a foil for discussing Colombia's role in the world. Jorge Child, a socio-political analyst for *El Espectador*, used a famous exchange between 1984 Dauphiné Libéré champion Martín Ramírez and Bernard Hinault as a metaphor to discuss issues of economic development in Colombia. Child writes,

> The dethroned champion Bernard Hinault, when in the last turn of the course realized he was losing began screaming "cocaine! cocaine!" at the new world kind of pedals, Martín Ramírez, and Ramírez answered back, "and marijuana too!" An intense exchange of feelings but certainly in line with the global consumption of hallucinogenics. All of this is part of the contemporary psychedelic market where until recently Colombia was world leader. Fortunately, Martín Ramírez and Francisco Rodríguez have compensated this loss with a new kind of world leadership [author's translation] [Duque Naranjo 13].

Child ends with the quip that while European sponsors literally cover the bikes, bodies and uniforms of European racers with ads for highly desirable global consumer products, "the poor Colombian bikers are only sponsored by two domestic products that are not for export and that nobody knows where to buy: Varta batteries and Gran Vía milk" [author's translation] (13). Again, for authors like Child, the key issue confronting Colombia and Colombians is one of image, market share and development strategies.

Mestizo Paradise?

The Colombian journalists' recurrent use of the international spectacle of cycling as means to promote a compensatory image of Colombian modernity—and to combat the more familiar nefarious spectacles of violence, drug trafficking, underdevelopment—is evocative of Guy Debord's theses on the society of the spectacle. For Debord spectacle is quite simply the ultimate mediator of meaning in late capitalist societies. It is not a simple mass-media ruse but rather the materialization of a worldview that *displaces* meaning generated by lived experience (8). As he argues, the spectacle becomes a separate "pseudo-world" that "presents itself simultaneously as society itself, as a part of society, and as a *means of unification*. As a part of society, it is the focal point of all vision and all consciousness.... But due to the very fact that this sector is *separate*, it is in reality the domain of delusion and false consciousness: the unification it achieves is nothing but an official language of universal separation.... The spectacle is not a collection of images; it is a social relation between people that is mediated by images" (7–8). One could certainly understand the mediated representation of Colombian cycling as such a spectacle. Explicit is the desire to use the images of cycling as a constitutive element of reality—it is the creation of a vision of the world that seeks to articulate a model of national identity and to aggressively negotiate social relations between Colombians and the rest of the world. In terms of the press coverage of the Tour de France in the 1980s, the most obvious consequence of this mediation is that through their shapings of the *escarabajos* an image of national cohesion and unity in time of deep conflict and fragmentation, the press problematically conflates complex categories of race and class in Colombia.

While authors in *El Tiempo* and *El Espectador* are conscious of the racism Colombians experienced abroad, references to experiences of race and class at home are either coded or avoided. In a telling example, in their front-page celebration of the start of that first Tour in 1983, *El Tiempo* exclaimed, "the odyssey of humble men, dedicated to finding economic stability in the rough world of bicycles, has reached its peak and now the Colombian tricolor flag waves proudly over the territory of 'the superstars' of professional cycling" ("Colombia en el Tour"1B). Writing for *El Espectador*, Alexandra Pineda similarly frames the battles between the Colombians and the Europeans as one of "Humility versus Arrogance," and repeats the cliché that the *escarabajos* "are a new style cycling that comes from the New World to the Old Continent," and warns, "be careful with these Colombians, be wary of the threat of these boys of simple appearance that come from the other side of the world, here to snatch the crown from the European kings, to teach them to climb hills and to give them lessons in humility" ("Humildad contra prepotencia" 3C). Numerous similar articles propose images of the *escarabajos* as the incarnation of Colombian order, dignity and decorum, repeating verbatim the positivist concepts of "order and progress" championed by the Enlightenment-inspired elite in 19th-century Latin America (Burns 18).

In all fairness to these authors, Colombian cyclists with very few exceptions are of popular extraction and come from humble backgrounds, and many do not finish high school in order to pursue a career in professional cycling.[5] Along with soccer and boxing, cycling is an aspirational form of athletic endeavor in Colombia. Not surprisingly, Colombian cyclists are also browner, poorer and less-worldly than the elite political class that runs the government and prints newspapers. That said, they are not simple men, nor do they come from simple contexts, but rather represent groups of people who disproportionately suffered the consequences of partisan conflict, urbanization and drug trafficking.

This is particularly true for the *escarabajos* from the 1980s. The richness and complexities of the popular experience of cycling, however, was largely ignored by the Colombian press of the time, who treated these racers as humble yet noble mestizos, happy to represent the country in a manner that did not challenge the conditions of violence and disparity that so profoundly marked this period. The reaction to Luis Herrera's second-place finish in the 11th stage of the 1984 Tour is informative: while the press duly celebrated the first display of Herrera's climbing powers at the Tour, they also did so reminding readers that afterwards this was one of the few moments when "Lucho" spoke without his usual monosyllable vocabulary (Clopatofsky Londoño "En una etapa" 3C). Similarly, in July of 1984, *El Espectador* writer Jorge Enrique Manrique produced a series of multi-installment chronicles of the lives and origins of the *escarabajos*. The most revealing are two series entitled "Lucho's world" and "Rafico's world" that consistently praise the peasant nobility of Luis Herrera and Rafael Acevedo. Herrera is remembered as a simple small-town boy who his mother describes as "honestico, decentico and calladito,"[6] who never swears, loves gardening, honors family above all things and who started cycling using a second-hand bike as a means to get to school ("Espíritu combativo" 2C). Manrique likewise describes Rafael "Rafico" Acevedo as a simple introverted peasant from Sogamoso, Boyacá, who began cycling as a delivery boy and is devoted to the Virgin of Chinquinquirá ("Un campesino" 3C). As such, press renderings of the *escarabajos* bear problematic similarities to the cartoon Colombianito Corredor and fail miserably to develop them as multifaceted protagonists living through one of the most complex periods in Colombian history.

This treatment of the mestizo peasant as a simplified and idealized national subject is consistent with the historiography of race and class in Colombia. Ideas of race in Colombia revolve around the long-standing national ideology that the country is "an egalitarian society, marked by substantial race-mixing and harmonious race relations" without the racism found in segregationist societies like the United States (Urrea Giraldo et al. 88). Historian Alfonso Múnera describes this as the "mestizo racial paradise" model, and critiques it as "one of the foundational myths of Colombian identity [author's translation]" (21), and sociologist Elisabeth Cunin signals this as "a national problematic that ignores differences in the name of republican egalitarianism [author's translation]" (11). Historian Marco Palacios further documents how in the 19th century the governing elite manipulated the myth of Colombian racial democracy in order to consolidate clientele networks and markets generating a socio-racial hierarchy that persists today (17–18). Not surprisingly, contemporary fieldwork on race and class in Colombia reveals that social classes are "colored" and structured in a "pigmentocratic" order, and that racial identity—both in terms of self-perception and perception by others—dictates access to social, cultural, educational and economic capital (Urrea Giraldo et al. 122).

The fact that structures of classism and racism are fused in Colombia should not come as a surprise to anyone familiar with the country. What is important to note here are the ideological consequences of the selective colorblindness with which the Colombian press recorded the national and international experiences of their racers in that first Tours de France, and what this indicates about discourse and civil society in Colombia during this time. Writers from both *El Tiempo* and *El Espectador* create an image of the *escarabajo* and the spectacle of cycling that ultimately reflect social and racial hierarchy in Colombia, these are images that successfully challenge an international context hostile to Colombia (they call us *narcos* and *Indians*) without further provoking tensions at home (they are *humble peasants*).

Further, both newspapers either dismissed the popular experience of the spectacle of cycling as folklore, or treated it with humor and suspicion. José Clopatofsky Londoño offered a relativist chuckle in noting that the civilized Parisians steal bikes just like the ruffians back in Bogotá ("En París" 3B); while an editorial in *El Espectador* questioned the misguided obsession of the "immense majority of Colombians" with cycling as an expression of "chauvinism" and easy nationalism that distorts the country's sense of self and distracts from more pressing needs ("Exceso de patrioterismo" 1C). Novelist and essayist Antonio Montaña came the closest to labeling Colombia's fascination with cycling an expression of false consciousness in an essay published in the literary supplement of *El Tiempo* in 1985. Montaña accused Colombians of having lost the capacity to have a rich interior life, of being incapable of self-reflection, dependent instead on external justifications—the image of cycling triumphs in particular—as the basis for national identity and self-esteem. He laments, "For Colombian identity, the passion of the cyclist, or of his group, becomes an ordeal. And the early bird who tunes into the radio broadcast becomes the spectator of a black judgment of God. But times have changed—this is not the God of the Bible or that of the Gospels. This new, dangerous God is the concept that others have of me—God is the other's opinion. God is 'the image'" (8). He later asks glibly, "Could the party responsible for this stupidification be anything other than the national soul?" (9). Montaña's analysis of the spectacle of cycling is consistent with the ultimate consequences of Debord's thesis on the society of the spectacle: for both it is the ultimate mediator of meaning in late capitalist societies and "the domain of delusion and false consciousness" (7). Daniel Samper Pizano similarly concluded that "[t]he true rival is the image of Colombia" ("Mejora la imagen" 6D).

The spectacle of the *escarabajos* in the Tour certainly does provide a compelling image of late capitalist life in Colombia. It publicly illustrates Colombian access to advanced levels of modern infrastructure and communications technologies. It allows millions of Colombian consumers to see themselves positively in real time on a global stage, demonstrates to the planet that Colombia has the economic, social and physiological means to produce talented racers, and the resources to purchase or produce expensive racing bicycles, tools, equipment and support vehicles. Lastly, the international arrival of the *escarabajos* also demonstrates to the world the existence of legitimate, deep-pocketed corporate sponsors willing to pay for the teams and purchase the ad-driven coverage that makes this an economically viable sporting spectacle.

But cycling also requires bodies: with very few exceptions Colombian cyclists are mestizo and come from humble origins, who like Rafael Acevedo first used the bicycle first to basic employment or transportation and then as a means to escape poverty (Acevedo). Without exception, the cyclists who rose to the world scene of the Tour de France in 1983 were part of a group for whom Patrocinio's declaration that he "would kill himself" to keep the country's first-ever King of the Mountains jersey is more than athletic hyperbole (Clopatofsky Londoño "Me haré matar" 3C). British author Matt Rendell pays painful homage to Gonzalo Martín, Alfonso Flórez, Armando Aristizábal, Juan Carlos Carillo and Rafael Tolosa, all members of this generation of *escarabajos* who were swept-up and lost their lives through contact with drug trafficking and armed conflict in contemporary Colombia (118–119). In another telling example, on June 23, 1984, *El Tiempo* published an obituary for promising young cyclist Edison Arias Fuentes who, like so many Colombians during this time, was killed for reasons unknown ("Se fue 'el Gatico'" 5). For these cyclists and Colombians like them, seeing a Colombian triumph in the Tour de France is not "like the time that *monsieur* Márquez won the Nobel prize" (Samper Pizano "Mejora la imagen" 6A). Instead, the image of the suffering body of the cyclist, of a humble mestizo like themselves literally strapped into the physical, economic and geopolitical machinery of Colombian modernity, has a resonance that goes beyond the limits of *compensatory modernity* and speaks to the depths of the experiences of race and class as a Colombian at home and abroad. While the image of the spectacle of cycling is of tremendous importance to Colombians, this deeper truth of cycling— both as an athletic pursuit and as a cultural field of popular expression—exists in tension to the official imagery. It lays bare the rules and contradictions of race and class in Colombia during this most important and convulsive time in national history.

NOTES

1. One of the most heart-warming parts of this project involved listening to Colombians remember these first Tours de France: stories abound of life coming to a standstill during the Tour, memories of transistor radios stuck to the ears of taxi drivers and stashed under the desks of school kids, and TV broadcasts blaring on every screen in every bar, supermarket and beauty parlor. It is my hope that this essay pays honor to this experience.

2. *Los escarabajos* or "beetles" is the affectionate nickname for Colombian cyclists. Generations of journalists, authors and fans have shaped the *escarabajo* as an idealized archetype of Colombian cycling, both in terms of physique and practice. They are celebrated as physically small and best known as climbers but are also acclaimed for their values as hard working, humble and patriotic Colombians. There is some debate concerning who to credit for creating this moniker: Héctor Urrego Caballero and others tend to credit radio commentator Carlos Arturo Rueda, while Nobel laureate Gabriel García Márquez gives the nod to *El Tiempo* columnist Jorge Enrique Buitrago in his biography Ramón Hoyos ("Nota del redactor" 630). Authorship aside, all historians agree that the term was first used to describe the relentless climbing style of the great Ramón Hoyos, who between 1953 and 1958 won the grueling *Vuelta a Colombia* a record five times.

3. All of the quotations from personal interviews and newspaper stories in this essay are from primary source material originally in Spanish. In the name of reader friendliness, I have translated all quotes to English with bibliographic citations to the Spanish-language originals.

4. While the minute details present in the voluminous coverage of the Tour de France may be of little transcendence more than thirty years later, the sheer volume is impressive in its own right and is indicative of importance of this event for Colombians. During the three weeks of the Tour newspapers regularly dedicated half or more of their sports sections to cycling, with detailed summaries of completed stages, profiles of upcoming stages, discussion of team strategy, as well as notes on course terrain, the history of sites visited by the Tour, injury updates as well as any number of human interest stories.

5. The 1980s great Fabio Parra is often recognized for finishing a university degree

while racing professionally, and the blonde haired, blue eyed Santiago Botero (2002 UCI World Champion in the time trial) comes from an affluent family in Medellín. Almost all of the other world-class cyclists come from working class urban or rural families and populations that disproportionately suffered the traumas of the 1980s in Colombia.

6. Herrera's mother literally describes her son as "honest, decent and quiet," but uses the diminuitive –ico that is impossible to translate and highly suggestive of someone from rural Cundinamarca.

WORKS CITED

Acevedo, Rafael. Personal interview. 4 July 2015.
Angosto-Ferrández, Luis Fernando, and Sabine Kradolfer. *Everlasting Countdowns: Race, Ethnicity and National Censuses in Latin American States.* Newcastle upon Tyne: Cambridge Scholars Publishing, 2012. Print.
Arce, Ricardo, et al. *La Animación en Colombia Hasta Finales de los 80.* Bogotá: Universidad Jorge Tadeo Lozano, 2013. Print.
Arrastía Bricca, Julio. "No Debemos Asustarnos." *El Tiempo* 4 July 1983: 6B. Print.
"Así Ven a los Escarabajos." *El Tiempo* 29 June 1984: 6C. Print.
Bourdieu, Pierre. *Distinction: A Social Critique of the Judgment of Taste.* Trans. Richard Nice. Cambridge: Harvard University Press, 1984. Print.
Burns, E. Bradford. *The Poverty of Progress: Latin America in the Nineteenth Century.* Berkeley: University of California Press, 1983. Print.
Bushnell, David. *The Making of Modern Colombia: A Nation in Spite of Itself.* Berkeley: University of California Press, 1993. Print.
Campillo, Rodolfo. "Ofertas para Cuatro Colombianos." *El Espectador* 19 July 1985: 3C. Print.
Carrigan, Ann. *The Palace of Justice: A Colombian Tragedy.* New York: Four Walls Eight Windows, 1993. Print.
Clopatofsky Lodoño, José. "¡10 Colombianos vs. 130 Profesionales!" *El Tiempo* 1 July 1983: 2B. Print.
_____. "Breves del Tour" 1 July 1983: 4B. Print.
_____. "Colombia Hace Historia en el Tour de Francia." *Cronómetro* 23 June 1984: 6–7. Print.
_____. "Colombia se Puso de Ruana el Tour." *El Tiempo* 11 July 1985: 1B. Print.
_____. "Dos Estilos de Trabajo en la Radio" *El Tiempo* 5 July 1983: 3B. Print.
_____. "En París También Roban Bicicletas" *El Tiempo* 2 July 1983: 3B. Print.
_____. "'En Una Etapa no se Puede Decontar Todo lo Perdido': Herrera." *El Tiempo* 10 July 1984: 3C. Print.
_____. "La Altura: ¿Mito o Realidad?" *El Tiempo* 30 June 1984: 6B. Print.
_____. "Colombia le puso pimienta." *El Tiempo* 13 July 1985: 3B. Print.
_____. "Los Colombianos: 'Ni Muy Buenos, Ni Trabajadores." *El Tiempo* 16 July 1984: 5C. Print.
_____. "Me Haré Matar por Mantener la Camiseta." *El Tiempo* 12 July 1983: 3C. Print.
_____. "Reto para 'Escarabajos'; América 'a Darla Toda.'" *El Tiempo* 1 July 1983: 1A.
_____. "Sangre, Sudor y Gloria." *El Tiempo* 14 July 1985: 1B. Print.
"Colombia en el Tour de Francia." *El Tiempo* 1 July 1983: 1B. Print.
"Colombia se 'Mordió las Uñas.'" *El Tiempo* 16 July 1984: 1C. Print.
Corredor Martínez, Consuelo. *Modernismo sin Modernidad: Modelos de Desarrollo en Colombia.* Santafé de Bogotá: Editorial Cinep, 1991. Print.
Cunin, Elisabeth. *Identidades a Flor de piel: lo 'Negro' Entre Apariencias y Pertenencias: Categorías Raciales y Mestizaje en Cartagena.* Bogotá: ARFO Editores e Impresores Ltda, 2003. Print.
Debord, Guy. *Society of the Spectacle.* Trans. Ken Knabb. London: Rebel Press, 1983. Print.
"Distraídos y Extravagantes." *El Espectador* 14 July 1984:1C. Print.
Domínguez, Efraín. Personal interview. 27 June 2016.
Duque Naranjo. Rafael. *Los Escarabajos de la Vuelta a Colombia.* Bogotá: Editorial Oveja Negra, 1984. Print.
Duzán, María Jimena. "Carta a 'Lucho' Herrera." *El Espectador* 15 July 1985: 2C. Print.

"El Tour, Una Excelente Vitrina para Colombia" *El Espectador* 8 July 1984 7C. Print.
"Exceso de Patrioterismo." *El Espectador* 6 July 1984: 1C. Print.
Forero Nougués, Mike. "Heroísmo Amargo de los Colombianos." 2 July 1984: 1A. Print.
"Ganar: No; Cumplir: Sí." *El Tiempo* 30 June 1984: 3B. Print.
García Márquez, Gabriel. "Nota del Redactor." *Obra periodística. 4* (1982) Bogotá: Oveja Negra, 1982. Print.
"Gobierno Anuncia Estímulos para el Ciclismo Nacional." *El Tiempo* 12 June 1984: 1C. Print.
"Hacia la Cima." *El Espectador* 4 July 1984: 4C. Print.
"Herrera es Colombia." *El Espectador* 10 July 1984: 1C. Print.
"Hinault Vendrá a Colombia." *El Espectador* 22 July 1984: 1C. Print.
Human Rights Watch. *War Without Quarter: Colombia and International Humanitarian Law.* New York: Human Rights Watch, 1998. Print.
"Inolvidable Recibimiento a los Escarabajos" *El Espectador* 26 July 1985: 1A. Print.
Jiménez, Patrocinio. Personal interview. 1 July 2015.
Ligget, Phil, and Paul Shermen. "Luis Herrera 1984 Tour De France," *YouTube.* 17 February 2010. Web. 14 May 2018.
Manrique, Jorge Enrique. "Espíritú Combativo que Floreció en un Jardín." *El Espectador* 15 July 1984: 2C.
_____. "Un campesino entrometido." *El Espectador* 21 July 1984: 3C. Print.
Mendoza, Rafael. "Herrera se Cae se Agiganta." *El Espectador* 14 July 1985: 1C. Print.
_____. "Los 'Escarabajos' Ya No Son Caja de Sorpresas." *El Espectador* 13 July 1985: 1C. Print.
Montaña, Antonio. ¿Por Qué de Pronto Un País…?" *El Tiempo* 8 July 1985: *Lecturas Dominicales* 9–12. Print.
Múnera, Alfonso. *Fronteras Imaginadas: La Construcción de las Razas y de la Geografía en el Siglo XIX Colombiano.* Bogotá: Planeta, 2005. Print.
Palacio Castañeda, Germán. *Globalizaciones, Sstado y Narcotráfico.* Bogotá: Universidad Nacional de Colombia, 1998. Print.
Palacios, Marco. *Entre la Legitimidad y la Violencia: Colombia 1875–1994.* Editorial Norma, 1995. Print.
Pineda, Alexandra. "Los 'Coquetos' de Hinault" *El Espectador* 5 July 1984: 5C. Print.
_____. "Humildad Contra Prepotencia." *El Espectador* 3 July 1984: 3C. Print.
Reina, Mauricio. "Drug Trafficking and the National Economy." *Violence in Colombia 1990–2000: Waging War and Negotiating Peace* Ed. Charles Bergquist, Ricardo Peñaranda, and Gonzalo Sánchez G. Wilmington: Scholarly Resources Inc., 2001. Print.
Rendell, Matt. *Kings of the Mountains.* London: Aurum Press, 2002. Print.
Rodríguez, Martín Emilio "Cochise." Personal interview. 4 July 2015.
Safford, Frank, and Marco Palacios. *Colombia: Fragmented Land, Divided Society.* New York: Oxford University Press, 2002. Print.
Sánchez Gómez, Gonzalo and Donny Meertens. *Bandits, Peasants and Politics.* Trans. Alan Hynds. Austin: University of Texas Press, 2001. Print.
Samper Pizano, Daniel. "Cumbia en los Alpes." *El Tiempo* 17 July 1984: 4D. Print.
_____. "Mejora Imagen de Colombia." *El Tiempo* 11 Uuly 1984: 1A. Print.
"Se Fue 'el Gatico.'" *Cronómetro* 23 June 1984: 5. Print.
"Seguimos Poniendo Cuota alta de Sangre.' *El Espectador* 5 July 1984: 2C. Print.
"Todavía nos Dicen Indios." *El Tiempo* 12 July 1985: 3B. Print.
"Un Ciclismo Distinto" *El Espectador* 24 July 1984: 4C. Print.
"Un Tropezón lo da Cualquiera." *El Espectador* 5 July 1984: 1C. Print.
Urrea Giraldo, Fernando et al. "From Whitened Miscegenation to Tri-Ethnic Multiculturalism." *Pigmentocracies: Ethnicity, Race and Color in Latin America.* Ed. Edward Telles. Chapel Hill: University of North Carolina Press, 2014. Print
Urrego Caballero, Héctor. Personal interview. 27 June 2015.
Urrego Caballero, Héctor, et al. *El Ciclismo Colombiano en el Mundo.* Bogotá: Zeta Comunicadores S.A., 2014. Print.
Vives, Carlos. "Soy de los Que Piensa que el Ciclismo es el Deporte Nacional." *Revista Cromos,* 7 June 2016. Web. 14 May 2018.

Being Good Neighbors

Aston Villa Football Club,
Community Engagement
and Corporate Social Relations

DANIELLE SARVER COOMBS *and* JAKE KUCEK

Sports teams can have a tremendous impact on their communities, both in terms of the people and the physical space. Young fans tack posters to their walls with players' images and team logos. Those with tickets bring home bobble-head dolls and other game-day detritus to line shelves as identity statements. Generations of families make their way into the stadium for home games, celebrating traditions that span decades. These same stadia become the backdrop for countless photographs and memories of hometowns and tourist destinations, enshrined as the cradle for beloved teams that season after season lift you up or, all too often, break your heart. The impact of these clubs and stadia extend far beyond symbolic power or situational prominence as the space where games are played, however. The teams that make their homes within these places can—and often do—play a significant role in the economic fortunes and lived experiences of their neighbors and broader communities.

The grounds of Aston Villa Football Club (AVFC), a founding member of England's football association, are located in the ward of Aston in central Birmingham. This ward has seen significant demographic changes over the past decades and currently is home to a substantial population of Southeast Asian immigrants. For many in this community, the club and its fans are little more than weekly nuisances. The start times of home matches can change at the last minute, disrupting traffic patterns, clogging streets, and taking up all available parking. Because not all residents consider themselves aficionados of the beautiful game or—more frequently—supporters of this venerable club, these frequent life interruptions are a massive nuisance. In this context, AVFC is nothing more than a bad neighbor. Recognizing this, the club has spent the last decade launching initiatives to better engage their local community, offering programs and developing practices that they hope will build positive relationships with these neighbors. More broadly, Aston Villa and its owners have embarked on numerous projects—both large- and small-scale—to deepen its influence and increase its positive impact on greater Birmingham, the second-largest metropolitan area in the United Kingdom. This essay will explore the club's efforts in these areas to better understand how a major football club can be an asset to their community rather than a perceived detriment.

This essay begins with an overview of relevant literature, including brief overviews of corporate social responsibility (CSR), social and community connections, healthy lifestyles and physical education, appeal for reach and recruitment, and current successful community outreach programs run by major sporting organizations in the United States and Europe. We then give a brief history of Aston Villa and the community surrounding its home ground. Next, we review Villa's community initiatives at three key points: 2008–09, one of American owner Randy Lerner's earliest seasons with the club and when optimism was high; 2013–14, when the club's fortunes were beginning to change under Lerner; and finally, the "Supporting Our Own" initiative that launched during the 2017–18 season. Each overview includes brief descriptions of projects that were representative of the club's efforts and direction at that point in time. This case study provides a useful examination of how an influential and geographically dominant sports team can provide community support and leadership designed and intended to promote positive social good in their immediate environs; in other words, to be good neighbors.

Literature Review

Corporate Social Responsibility

Until recent years, corporate social responsibility (CSR) did not play a huge role in professional sports organizations. This has changed. Currently, most professional sporting organizations in the United States have a community affair or community outreach department, with many creating foundations to support social causes in their communities. Babiak and Wolfe state that strong relations with the local community are essential for a sport organization's success, since this is believed to affect an organization's ability to attract fans, secure corporate sponsors, and to have effective dealings with local and state governments (215). As such, sports organizations' outreach programs are growing exponentially across multiple levels, including programs developed or sponsored by leagues, teams, and individual players. For example, professional sport leagues in the United States (including the National Football League, National Basketball Association, Major League Baseball, National Hockey League, and Major League Soccer) have initiated league-wide programs, such as the NBA's "Need to Read." Franchises have also started their own programs to address social concerns, like the Atlanta Braves "Read to Achieve" program. Individual athletes engage in social concerns through their own foundations. Examples include the JJ Watt Foundation, which raised money for Hurricane Harvey relief, as well as the LeBron James Family Foundation's focus on educational success for schoolchildren in Akron, Ohio. These types of programs extend well beyond the United States, however. Barclay's Premier League, which includes teams from England and Wales, is a prominent supporter of the "Kick It Out" campaign designed to reduce racism in soccer. The Fédération Internationale de Football Association (FIFA), soccer's massive international governing body, advocates for a wide range of initiatives addressing everything from environmental sustainability to improving the lives of young children around the world. Finally, major international sporting events such as the Olympics have developed their own social responsibly projects, such as the "Peace Through Sport" program.

Focusing on the relationship between CSR and sports, Smith and Westerbeek came up with the following seven unique features claiming how sports can be used for CSR:

1. The popularity and global reach of sport can ensure that sport CSR has mass media distribution and communication power.
2. Sport CSR has youth appeal. Children are more likely to engage in a CSR program if it is attached to a sport organization or a sports personality.
3. Sport CSR can be used to deliver positive health impacts through program and initiatives designed around physical exercise.
4. Sport CSR will invariably involve group participation and therefore aid social interaction.
5. Sport CSR can lead to improved cultural understanding and integration.
6. Particular sport activities may lead to enhanced environmental and sustainability awareness.
7. Participating in sport CSR activities can provide immediate gratification benefits [8–9].

These seven features show that CSR can and should be tied to sports organizations, as professional sports are a powerful tool to use with community outreach programs. The partnership reaches a large audience as well as leading to an enhanced perception of the reputation and brand of the program.

Sports organizations no longer can consider CSR as an option; instead, CSR is a "must do" due to the substantial benefits that come with these programs, including favorable publicity, positive reputation-building, and building an emotional bond with customers in the community. It does not matter what their motives are, whether its altruistic principles or pragmatic concerns related to the bottom line. It has been argued that sport occupies a unique role in society, and consequently that sport CSR can have a greater impact on issues such as education, health, the environment, and social and cultural enrichment than the development of CSR initiatives by commercial organizations and other industry sectors (Babiak and Wolfe 221).

Social and Community Connection

Sport CSR offers a way to encourage social interaction within the community. Smith and Westerbeek found that a community sports trust can do this in a number of ways by encouraging children to participate in sport activities and offer the means to get them working together and interacting (10). Walters analyzed two UK-based trusts associated with professional football clubs—Charlton Athletic Community Trust and Brentford Football Club Community Sports Trust—and found they offer the opportunity for children to interact in different contexts. The football clubs encourage teams to work together and engage in social interaction through the delivery of social inclusion programs aimed at disengaged children (90). Both the Charlton Athletic Community Trust and Brentford Football Club Community Sports Trust deliver a range of programs throughout several London boroughs aimed at social inclusion. The programs use football coaching and sporting activity to make young people more aware of the dangers of drug abuse, while also looking to improve levels of self-confidence, self-esteem and social responsibility. These initiatives aim to improve community integration and reduce crime, antisocial behavior and truancy (Walters 90).

Community networks are important part in building a positive society and football clubs can be used as an effective vehicle. Thorpe et al. showed that a main benefit identified by participants was the community network that they were a part of through the football club. In general, they found that social and community connection was an important instrument for maintaining cultural values and traditions for Aboriginal people in Australia. The social and community aspects of participating for an Aboriginal football team were just as important to the participants as the individual health benefits gained from participation, indicating that maintaining positive cultural networks is just as important as maintaining physical health when participating in sport (361).

Similarly, researchers have found that sports have a healing potential and are useful in serving the indigenous youth of Canada. McHugh conducted interviews with Edmonton-based indigenous youth and adults to examine the meaning of community within the context of sport. There were five key themes emerged from the interviews. Community was described as: belonging, supportive interactions, family and friends, sport, and where you live and come from. Belonging emulated the feelings of home, and was described as giving the opportunity to engage or communicate with others in a meaningful way. The social interactions component of communities is comprised of people that support one another and the interactions they have with each other are respectful and positive. Family and friends represented familiar faces and people they feel comfortable being around. A feeling of being safe, secure and at ease with people you know (2). Sport itself was described as a community; as described by one youth, "Sport *is* community. On a team, you have to communicate with each other and be like a family. You have to balance everyone out just for them to be happy and successful" (3).

English football clubs can serve an important purpose for their local communities. Kiernan and Porter found that FC United in Manchester is an engaged community partner that creates high levels of trust within and across communities. This is particularly important at times when the responsibilities and pressures on communities are much more significant (860). As government coffers dry up and less money is available for social services, these responsibilities can fall to local businesses and organizations—a void football teams are poised to fill. There was also a significant increase in the employment opportunities created by the club through the Future Job Funds program (858). The economic and employment investment the club made could be an important driver of local regeneration as improved local economic prospects also contribute to community cohesion and the ability to develop community assets (860). FC United helps bind the community together and it is a very successful example of using CSR to link together a community.

Healthy Lifestyle and Physical Education

The association between participating in sport connected to positive health benefits is well established. Walters describes three key ways in which community sports trusts can have a positive health impact. First, most of activities are sports based, and requires that those involved are active. Second, the community's trust can be used to raise awareness of healthy campaigns. Third, they can get involved in several local schools (89).

In their 2016 study, Parnell and his research team explored the relationship between the community and professional football clubs to deliver physical education and school sport (PESS). In 2014, the England's Barclay's Premier League announced the launch of substantial investment in a three-year program of support and delivery of PESS in primary school. The results of their study offered insight into the delivery and partnership potential between professional football clubs and schools. Effective partnership requires quality coaches (236). The coaches were perceived positively by the schools because of their expertise and ability to support the objects set by the PESS (235).

In an earlier study, Parnell et al. aimed to analyze the role and effectiveness of the Premier League's "Football in the Community" initiative. Specifically, researchers investigated the efficacy of this program in terms of promoting positive healthful behavior change in children. The British Government identified football as a key vehicle for addressing wider social issues including health, social inclusion, social regeneration, and increased participation in and access to physical activity (35). The results showed that the Premier Leagues football club "Football in the Community" intervention provided excitement, enjoyment and fun for the majority of the children and teachers it involved (46). The intervention provided an opportunity for the majority of children to engage in further physical activity opportunities.

Appeal for Reach and Recruitment

Sports within the community appeals strongly to children and older adults because of the association with a football club. Walters reported this association could help maintain a strong link between the club and the community, benefit the reputation of the club in the local area and, importantly, ensure that the work of the community sports trust has the potential to have a significant impact (89). Children are more likely to engage in community initiatives run by a community sports trust and respect the coaches because of the association with the football club than activities run solely by a local council (85).

Older adults are at a high risk of chronic conditions and it has been suggested that physical activity can potentially reduce the severity and likelihood of these conditions. As such, professional sports clubs have been recommended as an option for health improvement programs. Lifestyle programs for fans and locals put on by professional football clubs are an important contribution to the social and public health of individuals and the teams' community. Pringle et al. used the Burton Albion FC to conduct tests on 54 older adults to support the Golden Goal pilot program of physical activity led health improvements for adults 55 years or older. The findings support the potential of professional football clubs for recruiting both male and female older adults into health-improvement plans, suggesting programs in professional sports settings can be acceptable to both men and women (909). A previously identified issue of older men being reluctant to join a health program was negated by their acceptance of the program being delivered in a professional football setting (910).

This shows that football remains a popular activity to both men and women in health improvement programs. In order to reach wider audience engagement, the activities were packaged with language that focused on sport and fitness rather than merely on health. It was also shown that participating in football could provide girls with the opportunity to resist traditional gender norms and perform alternate scripts of femininity (Rutherford et al. 961).

Curran et al. found that the brand of the football club acted as the major catalyst for attracting our participants to physical activity and health interventions. Football was able to draw in members of the community that were the most at risk because its appeal to the masses by being one of the largest sports globally and most popular in the United Kingdom. The kids enjoyed going to the stadiums and were "wowed" by being around a professional football club (940). The professional sports clubs can lure in older adults as they differed from a traditional gym.

Current Successful Community Outreach Programs

As stated previously, currently most professional sports organizations have a community affair or community outreach department, with many creating foundations to support social causes in their communities. According to a Gallup poll conducted at the end of 2017, the main three sports leagues in the United States are the National Football League, Major League Baseball, and the National Basketball Association (Norman). Each league is doing their part to contribute to the community. The National Football League considers themselves the twin pillars of the community, which represents all 32 teams in the NFL, along with current and former players. Since 2007, the league has committed more than $325 million to grants, health and fitness programming for youth, and media time for public service announcements. The NFL and its clubs have supported programs in more than 73,000 schools nationwide, giving more than 38 million children the chance to boost their activity levels (National Football League Foundation). Major League Baseball has formed core partnerships with Boys & Girls Clubs of America, Stand Up to Cancer and the Jackie Robinson Foundation. They focus on youth baseball and softball participation, consistently emphasizing the need for young people to become constructive members of their communities (Major League Baseball). Lastly, the NBA Cares is the league's global social responsibility program that builds on the NBA's mission of addressing important social issues. Participants have provided more than four million hours of hands-on service and created more than 1,115 places where kids and families can live, learn or play in communities around the world. The NBA also engages more than 18 million youth annually, inspiring play and teaching the values of the game (National Basketball Association).

In comparison, European football clubs are also finding success with community outreach. The Manchester United Foundation has 16,195 total participants engaged in their program, consisting of males, females, children and disabled. Manchester United Foundation uses football to engage and inspire young people to build a better life for themselves and unite the communities in which they live. Dedicated staff delivers football coaching, educational programs and personal development, providing young people with opportunities to change their lives for the better (Manchester United Foundation). The Norwich Community Sports Foundation helps over 38,000 people every year. The main programs they run include Kicks, which consists of weekly sports activities and educational workshops for young people, PL Enterprise, which gives youngsters the opportunity to develop key business skills, the National Citizen Service program, which gives 16- and 17-year-olds the chance to give something back to their local community, and the CSF College Football program which provides scholars the chance to combine an intensive football training and fixture program with a Level-3 BTEC Extended Diploma in Sport (Community Sports Foundation). In a final example, Everton in the Community aims to use the power of sport to motivate, educate and inspire people in their local communities to improve their life chances. Through its 120 dedicated full-time staff, 72 casual staff, and 144 volunteers, the charity offers 60 programs covering a range of social issues including health, employability, anti-social behavior, crime, education, dementia, poverty, youth engagement, youth justice and disability (Everton).

Birmingham and Aston: Understanding the Community

Birmingham is a highly diverse city. Slightly more than half (53.1 percent) of Birmingham residents identify as white British, significantly lower than the average across England (Birmingham City Council, "Population"). Birmingham's population is younger than most of the other "core cities," including Bristol, Leeds, Liverpool, Manchester, Newcastle upon Tyne, Nottingham, and Sheffield (Birmingham City Council, "Demographic"). Census projections expect Birmingham's population to grow substantially over the next 20 years. This marks a change from fairly recent history and, often, perceptions of Birmingham as a place people leave—a perception grounded in reality during the latter part of the 20th century. Since 2011, however, the population has steadily increased ("Birmingham Demographic Brief "). This increase has been attributed to international migration, with residents "arriving from many different parts of the world, including Eastern Europe, Africa, and the Middle East" (Birmingham City Council, "Population").

The Aston ward, located north of the Birmingham city center, amplifies many of the demographic trends seen in greater Birmingham. The most recent data comes from the 2011 census as reported in the Aston Ward Economic Key Facts sheet (Birmingham City Council Economic Research & Policy). According to these data, residents of the ward tend to be younger than average, while ethnic minority residents are overrepresented compared to the city average. The ward struggles with poverty, meaning "worklessness and unemployment rates are well above the city average" (Birmingham City Council Economic Research & Policy). Only 37 percent of Aston residents ages 16 to 64 are employed full time, which is far below both the Birmingham (57 percent) and England (68 percent) averages; the "economically inactive" total (including those who are retired, students, looking after homes/families, long term sick/disabled, and "other") is at 44 percent, compared to the Birmingham average of 31 percent and 23 percent across England. There is a slightly higher representation of full-time students (9 percent in Aston, compared to 5 percent in Birmingham and 4 percent in England), possibly due to the presence of Aston University. Despite this, the educational qualifications of Aston residents fall far behind the rest of the city and the country. Twenty-eight percent of Astonians have no qualifications at all, compared to 21 percent in Birmingham and 15 percent in England. Furthermore, the large population of immigrants introduces some language proficiency challenges. Among residents ages 16 to 64, 37 percent of Aston residents speak a main language other than English (compared to 17 percent for Birmingham and 10 percent for England), and 13 percent indicate they cannot speak English at all or not well, compared to 5 percent for Birmingham and 2 percent for England. These conditions are part and parcel of the poverty with which Aston residents live.

As these data clearly demonstrate, Aston and, more broadly, Birmingham represent an amplification of some of the most striking economic and demographic trends that have defined recent British population shifts. A large influx of immigrants moved into a poor area with low employment rates. Education levels are substantially lower what is seen in other parts of the country. With a decrease in social services available from the government to help alleviate the challenges of poverty and deficiencies in access to education and language services, the ward and its residents continue to struggle. It is in this context that we must examine the contributions of the ward's most famous resident, Aston Villa Football Club.

Aston Villa Football Club

With one of the most storied traditions in soccer history, Aston Villa Football Club has played a central role in the development of the structure that still guides footballing in the United Kingdom. The team was first conceived on a wintry night in 1874, when members of the Villa Cross Wesleyan Chapel cricket team—in search of a winter sport to keep them moving during the offseason—went to a meeting to learn more about rugby. During their walk home, they stopped under a lamppost to discuss what they had learned. They agreed that rugby was not the sport for them; instead, they opted to launch a football team ("Timeline"). Within just a few short years, the team found success, winning their first Football Association (FA) Cup in 1887. The next year, Villa chairman William McGregor conceived what would become the Football League, inviting teams from around England to compete within an organized structure. The first matches attracted thousands of fans across the north and midlands of England, and the league was a success. Villa's first match against fellow midlands side Wolverhampton Wanderers ended in a 1–1 draw. Their fortunes improved, however, and in 1987 Villa achieved a "double," winning the League Cup as well as topping the table as Football League champions.

Over the decades, Villa's fortunes have risen and fallen. They moved between leagues, being relegated as low as third division before fighting their way back into the top tier of English football. In 1981, Villa celebrated their first league title in 71 years. Their success on the pitch continued over the next few years, much to the delight of fans who had stuck with the team through their relegation and promotion battles. The apex of Villa's success came in 1982, when the team was crowned champions of Europe after beating German rivals Bayern Munich in Rotterdam. European success continued the next year with victory in the Union of European Football Associations (UEFA) Super Cup. Firmly cementing their role as leaders in English soccer, Villa were among the teams founding the Premier League in 1992, a place they continued to hold until relegation to the Championship after the 2015–2016 season. At the time Villa were relegated, their 105 years in England's top football league was second only to Everton's 113 (Reed).

Since the turn of the century, ownership transitions have been marked by fan unrest and calls for selling. "Deadly" Doug Ellis, a Birmingham-based businessman, owned the team from 1982–2006, his second spell as chairman of the club. His relationship with fans had soured due to what they perceived as lack of investment in ensuring the team improved in quality both on and off the pitch. The Villa faithful publicly called for him to sell the club, organizing protests and displaying banners at matches that forcefully reminded Ellis, "We're not fickle, we just don't like you" (Coombs and Osborne 311).

While Lerner was welcomed with open arms by fans expecting—and receiving—robust investment in the team and an owner demonstration a passion for all things Villa, Lerner's ownership experience eventually soured. After flirting with the bottom three for consecutive seasons, the team finally was relegated to the Championship at the end of the 2015–16 season, its first drop from top-flight football since the creation of the Premier League. Fans demanded Lerner's exit. In May 2016, Lerner agreed to sell Aston Villa to Chinese businessman Dr. Tony Xia for an estimated about $90 million, an astonishingly low sum for a team that had been valued in the hundreds of thousands of pounds in earlier years—and for $5 million less than his purchase price a decade earlier, despite the skyrocketing values of Premier League clubs.

Both Lerner and Xia faced challenges coming in as foreign owners of an English football club with substantial heritage and ties to a local community. While Ellis had the benefit of being a Brummie, the local shorthand reference for those from Birmingham, neither of the two most recent owners had any sort of local ties. As such, local and regional fans could rightfully question how much investment these owners would make in their area immediately surrounding Villa Park. Would they have a commitment to the community, recognizing the importance of being thoughtful stewards of the clubs now under their control? Or would they be "foreign invaders" (Osborne and Coombs 309), asserting their influence to benefit the club over the community around it? The remainder of this essay will explore the community-based approaches adopted by both Lerner and Xia at three specific points in time: Lerner's 2008–09 and 2013–14 and Xia's 2017–18 seasons. Each of these marked a significant change in the team's outreach and engagement. By understanding how club stewardship and community engagement were approached under each of these owners, we can develop a useful understanding of the role a club can play in a local community, even with varied approaches and priorities.

2008–09 Season: "Proud History, Bright Future"

A year into Lerner's tenure as owner of Aston Villa, the team was flying high. Fans were thrilled with their new American owner, someone characterized in the press as a "savvy custodian" (Osborne and Coombs 304)—an owner driven by a long-term commitment, clearly invested in both the club and the community, "characterized as having an authentic appreciation for football and, more important, for the traditions of his club" (Osborne and Coombs 312). The promise of investment and opportunity extended to the broader community and Aston and Birmingham. Lerner embraced this role to much success. In fact, by 2009, Villa were ranked at the top of the Premier League "stewardship table," which was "designed to recognize those who work toward 'handing something on to the next generation in better shape than you inherited it, and not just the next quarter's results'" (Shore).

The previous season, Aston Villa had launched a significant rebranding campaign that established the context and set the tone for how the club would approach their constituencies under the Lerner regime. Grounded in consumer research with fans, community members, and other stakeholders, the team made a splash with its new brand launch. In addition to fairly substantial media coverage of the revised badge, the team adopted what was considered to be an American approach to consumer outreach. Each season ticket holder from the previous year was mailed a branded package that included a variety of Villa-related materials. It opened to a letter from then Chief Executive Officer Richard FitzGerald, heralding their new approach and inviting fans to join the team at Villa Park this season. A fold-out poster boasted of reduced season-ticket prices, clearly reflecting fans' concerns that the skyrocketing cost of going to matches was making the average fan unable to attend. The large, plastic envelope also included a "complimentary brand book and DVD, which introduces the club's new vision, values, personality and message" (FitzGerald). The brand book made Villa's mission for the future clear: "We aim to compete in the Champions League in the coming years. We also want to fill the stadium week-in and week-out and to create the infrastructure to create a top club" (*Aston Villa Football Club Brand Book*). The book itself described the symbolism behind the new crest as well as introducing and explaining the club's new vision, motto, and personality: "With a quiet confidence, based on a pride in our history and our successes; with a passion for the club and its fans; with energy, enthusiasm and a spirit that befits a club with a lion as its mascot; with an engaging personality that welcomes all-comers; and with a professional attitude at all times—on and off the pitch" (*Aston Villa Football Club Brand Book*). The book also included quotes from a range of sources intended to reflect the high profile of this new brand across a range of perspectives, including business (Villa's CEO; the vice-president and general manager of Nike UK), on the pitch (celebrated club manager Martin O'Neill), and among fans (a consumer sales representative and two supporters).

This consumer-focused orientation was a change from Ellis' system, and this was credited to Villa's new American owner. The brand values were cited and credited during discussions about Villas operating principles and standards, even a year later. As one senior executive noted, "We want to make sure that we have made them happy. That is the American model to customer service, right? It is like when I visited Disney World. Everyone works to make you happy. That is what we are trying to do now" (Coombs and Osborne

208). Recognition of this change was not limited to internal constituencies, however. Rather, the club was being given credit for these changes externally as well, particularly in terms of Villa's approach to community engagement and CSR.

Acorns. Within the Premier League, kit sponsorship—paying to have your name and branding fully associated with the team, including emblazoned on the front of players' game-day uniforms as well as every replica kit sold—is a massive deal. Internationally prominent brands like Chevrolet, Emirates, and others seek these opportunities to leverage association with teams to get their names in front of enormous audiences. For Aston Villa in the early days of Lerner's ownership, this was a huge opportunity. Speculation was rife about who would come on as sponsor, particularly with the announcement that the new kit would be produced by Nike—a palpable indicator that Villa's brand was going places. Through the end of the 2007–08 season, kit sponsor was 32RED.com, a gambling website. Lerner made clear that he did not want to continue that relationship, preferring instead to find a kit sponsor more in line with his values and those of the "new" Villa. Ultimately, rather than entering a partnership with a brand they did not feel matched their revised brand values, Villa donated their sponsorship to Acorns, a West Midlands charity that provided support and services for life-limited children who are not likely to reach adulthood. Acorns three hospices offered services free of charge to these families, an expensive proposition. They needed financial support, and Villa were poised to step into that breach.

The launch event to introduce Acorns as the new Villa kit sponsor occurred on June 3, 2008, at Villa Park. The opening video featured stories from local children and their families, foregrounding the incredible impact this support would have on the children and their families. The framing of this as being evidence of Villa's commitment to their community was explicit, and that carried over into media coverage, as represented in these opening paragraphs of the *Guardian's* article describing the deal:

> Aston Villa will carry the name of a children's charity on their shirts next season after announcing a partnership with the West Midlands–based Acorns Children's Hospice. The charity's logo will feature on the club's shirt for free in the 2008–09 season after their lucrative sponsorship deal with internet gambling website 32RED.com came to an end.
>
> The club said the decision to promote the hospices would help Acorns to raise funds and "give something back" to the community. Duncan Riddle, Villa's head of community, added that commercial offers had been turned down in favour of supporting the charity.
>
> Villa's American owner, Randy Lerner, manager Martin O'Neill and the board had been fully behind the decision to opt for a non-commercial partner, said Riddle, before adding: "Yes, the shirts have monetary value, but they also have emotional value to fans and this is something to give back to them" [Gardner].

As Villa executives discussed at the launch event, this deal was intended to provide a platform for Acorns to use to build their donation network as well as other partnerships. Representatives from both sides emphasized that the partnership worked because the two organizations had shared values and a common vision of community needs and how to address them. In a later interview, Acorns chief executive David Strudley said he was "over the moon" with the "amazing and groundbreaking possibilities" (Strudley). He further noted, "As a platform for an organization seeking to raise funds, this is almost more significant than I could imagine."

The Acorns deal set the tone for how the new-look Aston Villa would engage with their broader community. As a club representative noted, "At the end of the day, football clubs are about their fans and community. We want to focus on our local surrounds." This included tapping into existing organizations who had, in the past, experienced difficulty with convincing Villa to partner and support their initiatives.

Partnering with community organizations. During interviews with community organizers and representatives from Aston-based charities, it was clear that Lerner's arrival had sparked a real change in Villa's approach to community engagement. As one noted, "It was a bit like when the Berlin Wall came down—suddenly they decided, 'hello, neighbor!'" (Community Organizer C). Under Ellis, engagement was hit or miss at its best; things soured when the local community pushed back against an expansion of the stands at Villa Park. The perception among community members was once they stopped Villa from building what they wanted to build, relationships shut down almost entirely—it was as if "the club closed ranks" (Community Organizer B). During that time, "there was no attempt on the club's part to engage with the community or other key stakeholders, especially after the community resisted building a new stand" (Community Organizer B).

In these early days of Lerner's ownership, community groups noted much more engagement, characterizing it as "complete openness with the new regime" (Community Organizer C). Because Aston Villa was one of the largest single employers in the area, it made sense to host an employment event there working with local organizations focused on the substantial unemployment numbers in the area. They also hosted a "business think tank" at Villa Park, offering Villa an opportunity to link in to local business. During this time, they were giving out grants quickly and with minimum of fuss, even some of considerable size. For example, AVFC donated 15,000 pounds to support a "Mobile Skills for Life" bus that would go into hot spots of unemployment, without the requester having to go through what in the past had seemed to be an impossible gauntlet.

In addition to these business-focused engagement points, Villa tried to engage with those in their immediate environs. They hosted a Diwali "festival of lights" celebration, characterized as a "convenient way for them to get right into the community—they can easily get involved" (Community Organizer A). They also made space at the grounds available to other community organizations who wanted to partner on relevant issues, including a health-related event that had a wide range of providers, services, and information available to help tackle some of the more pressing health concerns in the area, including nutrition and wellness. Events at Villa Park were intended to say "We are open. We often hear, 'we have never seen you here before.' That needed to change" (Club Official C).

While lauded, these efforts were still perceived to be limited in that they tended to be on Villas terms. The club was criticized because they did not always get involved when they could, limiting how they spent their resources. The perception among community groups and organizers was that Villa either were in charge or they would not really participate. This led to some suspicion about their intentions: Was the purpose to actually make change in the community? Or was Villa engaging to be *perceived* as active? As a local community organizer noted, the question was whether or not Aston Villa's "key is to be seen as active in the community" (Community Organizer A).

Some of these criticisms were softened by recognition that this shift at Aston Villa meant structural and cultural changes within the organization that would take some time. Community organizers noted silos with the club meant not everyone at Villa or their partners always knew what was going on, noting, for example, that it often was unclear who would be the point of contact for various initiatives. This was compounded by the suspicion noted above that Villa's intentions might be grounded in something other than true, authentic interest in the community. Ultimately, however, the Acorns sponsorship helped alleviate some of this concern; because it was "an astonishing thing for anyone to do" (Community Organizer A) it immediately built trust among organizers in the community.

Building relationships with neighbors. Executives and staff within Aston Villa recognized the need to engage in more meaningful ways with the community, particularly in terms of the population groups immediately surrounding Villa Park. One executive noted the stadium meant the Aston neighbors "live next door" and thus it was important for Villa to serve as an advocate for them. The club ramped up their participation in the "Kick It Out" campaign against racism launched by the Premier League, coordinating with their own "Villa in Harmony" initiative. The club took a proactive approach to hearing the concerns of their neighbors, spending time in neighborhoods meeting the Aston citizenry as well as holding meetings and focus groups to better understand their concerns. One direct outcome of these conversations was the creation of the Community Communication tool, used to share information about fixture changes as early as possible with those who would be directly affected due to traffic and parking concerns.

During this period, Villa also increased their specific outreach to minority organizations and communities in their area. For the Chinese New Year, the club designed celebratory flyers that were distributed around areas with significant Chinese populations. Rather than following what a typical design approach would be for Aston Villa communications, the flyer incorporated traditional Chinese iconography—red envelopes, Chinese dragons—and noted that it was the Year of the Rat. The flyers also included information on ticket sales. As a club official noted, while these outreach efforts had a primary objective of building relationships with local communities, they also were focused on "winning Birmingham" (Club Official B). The club recognized that cultural events needed to be a big part of this effort: "Being open to their culture is a good way to show we recognize this is important to you and to say you are welcome in our home too, so to speak" (Club Official C).

This idea that increasing ticket sales and leveraging local populations to expand Villa's fan base—ultimately, working to benefit Villa versus the community—was subtle but present in many of the interviews with club officials. While they all seemed to genuinely believe in the importance of what they were doing, there was recognition that it was at least in part driven by less-than-altruistic objectives in mind. Because of this, investment in resources to support these initiatives was fairly limited. The aforementioned Chinese New Year flyer, for example, was outsourced to a designer because their in-house team were focused on other projects. Much of the work to coordinate and develop these outreach efforts fell to one person, and his plate often was overflowing. While ambitions were high, he noted that he "wanted to do things on a grander scale but no time or budget this year." This club official specifically noted the challenges surrounding staffing at events: "I usually struggle for volunteers—that is a strain on what we can do. If we had more staff, we could have arranged it better." He was proud of their work they were doing, but the frustration of trying to cobble materials and people together to pull off events was causing a strain.

Summary. Clearly, the efforts Lerner and his team were putting into building relationships and supporting causes within the Aston and Birmingham communities were noticed and appreciated. It is important to note, however, that while Villa were getting extraordinary credit for the work they were doing, the bar was really low in the wake of "Deadly Doug" and his team's refusal to work with community organizations. That said, there was evidence that the team genuinely was trying to be a good neighbor and leaders in their community. The Acorns deal generated an extraordinary amount of goodwill and positive publicity for both Lerner and Aston Villa. The club gave out grants that could be sizable, and they were more open to partnering and collaborating with other local organizations than they had been in the past. However, the commitment to this cause did not lead to the commitment of resources. While culture change was evidenced as being in process, the structure did not yet support it. Club officials realized that they should not expect instant results, acknowledging, "This is a long journey. We cannot build relationships in eight or nine months. It will take time and people have to recognize that" (Club Official C).

2013–14: Facing Relegation and "Villa Vitality"

While optimism characterized the mood in and around Villa Park in 2008, the tides had shifted yet again by the 2013 season. No longer aiming toward Europe, the club was now fighting to remain in the Premier League. A 15th-place finish at the end of the 2012–2013 season had left fans disillusioned. Lerner's promise to deliver the club success had not borne out, and fans were turning against him. Despite frustration on the pitch and in the stands, Villa continued to be committed to community engagement during this period.

The club continued reaching out to local communities, including religious groups. Players and staffers visited Sikh temples and Islamic mosques, and Aston Villa had representation at almost all major cultural events in Birmingham. They used these opportunities to both celebrate and build relationships with community members. Through these efforts, Villa was attempting to "instill that Aston Villa is their local club—you know, what football used to be" (Club Official D). This was in part to the release of updated census information. These new data demonstrated that the demographic "rate of change (was) staggering" (Club Official D). The "traditional" fan base for Aston Villa—white, male, and working class—was moving farther away from Villa Park than ever before. The core of the city was made up of immigrants, many of whom had no affinity to football in general or Aston Villa in particular. While the club knew this from their own observations, the census confirmed that these trajectories were accelerating. This crystallized Villa's commitment to developing a positive, productive relationship with these communities. As a club official (F) noted, "We want to be more than a football brand. We are good neighbors. It is important to be a caring institution." Over time, Villa began to see the fruits of these efforts, increasing both positive feedback from community groups and anecdotal observations that there was a notable increase in people from diverse backgrounds coming into the stadium each week.

To help ensure they could have a direct impact, Villa partnered with a range of community and civic organizations on myriad projects. One of the most successful was Villa Vitality. A signature initiative at this time, Villa Vitality program was a "flagship health initiative and one of Birmingham's biggest childhood obesity prevention initiatives" (Aston Villa Foundation, *Impact Report*). In partnership with Birmingham Public Health, Villa Vitality's work was centered on children living in areas of Birmingham with the highest obesity levels. Designed to address the nutrition and exercise needs of these children, Aston Villa and partners developed a plan that would increase physical activity opportunities with the school day, increase healthy eating knowledge, improve food preparation skills, and increase participation in physical activity out of school hours. Its impact was measured by a team led by University of Birmingham researcher Peymane Adab. In their attempt to analyze the effect football clubs have on local schools, Adab and his team of researchers conducted a study to analyze the body mass index score of about 1,000 children aged five to 10 years old split across 50 schools. Villa Vitality proved to be a tremendous success.

Throughout the course of the study, participants attended sessions at the Aston Villa training ground. These two-day sessions included promoting healthy eating and physical activity through participation in various activities, including physical activity games and ball skills, two nutrition education sessions, dance mats, preparing a meal in the team kitchen, a tour of the stadium, and a session in the team radio studio. During the six weeks of the program, children were encouraged to participate in weekly health challenges, and participated in a class project about healthy living. The children also received a 60-minute physical activity session by a Villa coach. Follow-up qualitative research teachers, parents, and children in the study indicated that the Villa Vitality program was often well received (Adab et al. 13):

- "It was fantastic and combining the sport and the nutrition was brilliant" [Teacher].
- "There's no doubt about it they have loved it, yeah … so it's been really good for them and that's what it's all about really isn't it" [Teacher].
- "I teached [sic] my mum how to cook it when we cooked in Aston Villa. And I chop a bit at home because I learned how to chop at Aston Villa" [Child]
- "Because I have done my exercise I can think harder and try" [Child].

Villa's work with this program reinforced its role as a leader in the community, particularly in relation to health issues—a continuation of the efforts from five years earlier touched on in the previous section.

While Villa continued to try to make a difference off the pitch, the team's struggles to survive in the Premier League were taking a toll. By the end of the season, Lerner admitted that the club was for sale. By the spring of 2016, Villa were headed down to the Championship, relegated for the first time since the inception of the Premier League. They also were in the hands of a new owner, Chinese businessman Dr. Tony Jiantong Xia.

2017–2018: "Supporting Our Own"

When Xia took over the club, he was welcomed by fans as a breath of fresh air in the wake of Lerner's increasingly disastrous ownership. Promising to infuse cash into the club and build toward promotion back into the Premier League, Xia quickly made moves designed to help meet those goals. Off the pitch, he worked toward re-inspiring his employees as well. A new face, Guy Rippon, was brought in to head up the Aston Villa Foundation. After assessing Villa's initiatives as they stood, Rippon realized that the club's community engagement efforts needed to be pulled under one umbrella. After pitching his ideas to various stakeholders both within and outside of the club, "Supporting Our Own" became a reality.

The Supporting Our Own initiative brings together the various strands of Foundation support Villa had offered in the past. According to the club, "Supporting Our Own is a community relations and corporate social responsibility strategy led by the Aston Villa Foundation which will enhance and expand the work of the Foundation and Football Club in the local community" (Aston Villa Foundation, *Supporting Our Own*). The program is presented as eight spokes on a wheel: There are four spokes on the "Local Community Based" side: project delivery, community grants, community action, and community MVP. On the "Club Based" side, the four sections include the Former Player Benevolent Fund, charity partners, charitable requests, and grassroots support scheme. These eight spokes represent what the club was already doing, but this revised structure allows for more integration and internal support. The initiative is funded through a range of opportunities, including a share of gate receipts from a pre-season match, company donations, match day 50/50 lotto drawings, fundraising events, donations and sponsorship, and supporters organizing their own fundraising events. Foundation support focuses on four strategic themes: health and well-being, education and learning, inclusive opportunities, and community relations. The launch of Supporting Our Own went remarkably well internally, with quick buy-in from across the organization.

While staffing was a real concern in the past, the structure under Xia's leadership has more stability. A team of 26 people are involved in Foundation projects in some capacity, allowing for a larger pool of resources upon which to draw when organizing and hosting events. Because these contributors are spread across various departments within the club, Supporting Our Own allows for quick response when opportunities arise. For example, on March 3, 2018, Aston Villa's Saturday afternoon match against league rivals Queens Park Rangers was postponed due to inclement weather. The head of catering found himself with hundreds of packed lunches that had been prepared for the fans in attendance. Knowing the food would spoil and recognizing this could meet a need, he went into action. Rippon put a call out on Twitter: "FOOD DONATION: Following the cancellation of today's @AVFCOfficial v @QPRFC game, we have over 700 packed lunches to be donated to homeless charities in Birmingham. Please contact Guy Rippon on [cell number] to find out more details." The response was instant and wildly positive. The initial tweet generated over two million impressions, and universal praise came from all corners. As Rippon noted, "We want fans to be proud of the club," and this was a fantastic opportunity to both do good in the community by helping a vulnerable population during a dangerous time and to generate some much-needed goodwill from the Villa faithful.

During Lerner's tenure at Aston Villa, an undercurrent of their community engagement and CSR efforts focused on selling tickets and building out their fan base. Under Xia, that has faded into the background. Rippon explicitly notes that it is not about selling more tickets or to target areas for fans; instead, the focus for the Foundation is on making an impact in critical areas (health, education, inequality) for their local environs. To ensure that these promises are kept, the Foundation's work is built into the club's five-year strategic framework. This commitment is important. The work done under the umbrella of Aston Villa and Supporting Our Own fills a gap left by budget cuts and cuts to social services across the United Kingdom.

Despite the progress made under Lerner, the difficulties of his last few years as owner brought back some of the distrust between the community and the club. The team has had to work to build or, in some cases, rebuild relationships with local people and organizations, some of whom posit they have "never been able to work with Villa" (Club official G). The goal, according to Rippon, is to have Villa seen as an asset rather than a nuisance on match day.

Conclusion

As these three exemplar seasons indicate, effective community engagement and CSR is something multiple owners and officers at Aston Villa Football Club have prioritized. This echoes Babiak and Wolfe's belief that CSR is now a must-have for professional sporting organizations; regardless of motivation, clubs and teams need to be active in their communities (221). In this case, Aston Villa can directly impact the citizenry in one of the most economically depressed areas of the UK, delivering social services that might otherwise be lost (Kiernan and Porter 860). The areas of focus—health, fitness, education—are ones that often are considered essential for a community's well-being. Through the efforts of local clubs and sporting organizations, the playing field can be leveled—more will have access to a healthy start to life than might otherwise.

While Villa certainly plays an important role in the more typical areas of CSR, they also recognize the importance of being good neighbors to those in the Aston community. Rather than focusing efforts on their traditional fan base, many of whom have moved out of the area, Villa has opted to do specific outreach into their community. This allows them to better hear the concerns of their neighbors and, as possible, address them by providing up-to-date information on game schedules and changes, hosting job fairs, and offering health wellness opportunities at Villa Park. These efforts are intended to ensure that Villa Park will continue to be a positive force in their neighborhood.

Works Cited

Adab, Peymane, et al. "A Cluster-Randomised Controlled Trial to Assess the Effectiveness and Cost-effectiveness of a Childhood Obesity Prevention Programme Delivered Through Schools, Targeting 6–7 Year Old Children: The WAVES Study Protocol." *BMC Public Health*. 15 (2015): 1–10. Print.
Adab, Peymane, et al. "Effectiveness of a Childhood Obesity Prevention Programme Delivered Through Schools, Targeting 6 and 7 Year Olds: Cluster Randomized Controlled Trial." *BMC Public Health* (2018): 1–15. Print.
Aston Villa Football Club Brand Book. 2007. Print.
Aston Villa Foundation. *Aston Villa Foundation Impact Report*. 2015. Print.
Aston Villa Foundation. *Supporting Our Own Introduction*. 2017. Print.
Babiak, Kathy, and Wolfe, Richard. "More Than Just a Game? Corporate Social Responsibility and Super Bowl XL." *Sports Marketing Quarterly* 15 (2006): 214–222. Print.
Birmingham City Council. "Birmingham Demographic Brief." *Birmingham City Council*. Birmingham City Council, Web. 17 February 2018.
Birmingham City Council. "Population in Birmingham: Key Statistics." *Birmingham City Council*. Birmingham City Council, Web. 17 February 2018.
Birmingham City Council Economic Research and Policy. *Aston Ward Economic Key Facts Sheet*. PDF file.
Community Sports Foundation. "Offering Facilities, Activities and Opportunities across Norfolk," *Community Sports Foundation*. Norwich City Community Sports Foundation, Web. 12 March 2018.
Coombs, Danielle Sarver, and Osborne, Anne C. "A Case Study of Aston Villa Football Club." *Journal of Public Relations Research* 5 (2012): 201–221. Print.
Curran, Kathryn, et al. "Ethnographic Engagement from Within a Football in the Community Programme at an English Premier League Football Club." *Soccer & Society* 15.6 (2014): 934–950. Print.
Everton. "Our History." *Everton Football Club*. Everton Football Club, Web. 12 March 2018.
FitzGerald, Richard. Letter to Aston Villa supporters. 2007.
Gardner, Alan. "Aston Villa to Promote Charity in Place of Shirt Sponsor." *Guardian*. Guardian, 3 June 2008. Web. 9 March 2018.
Kiernan, Annabel, and Porter, Chris. "Little United and the Big Society: Negotiating the Gaps

Between Football, Community and the Politics of Inclusion." *Soccer & Society* 15.6 (2014): 847–863. Print.

McHugh, Tara-Leigh F. "Sport Is Community." *Alberta Center for Active Living* 27.12 (2016): 1–5. Print.

Manchester United Foundation. "About Us." *Manchester United Foundation*. 12 March 2018.

Major League Baseball. *MLB in the Community*. 2017. PDF file.

National Basketball Association. "Mission." *National Basket Ball Association*. NBA Media Ventures, Web. 12 March 2018.

National Football League Foundation. "Community." *National Football League Foundation*. National Football League Foundation, Web. 12 March 2018.

Norman, Jim. "Football Still Americans' Favorite Sport to Watch." *Gallup*. Gallup, 4 January 2018. Web. 7 May 2018.

Osborne, Anne, and Danielle Sarver Coombs. "Enthusiasts, Invaders, and Custodians: Media Characterizations of Foreign Owners in Barclays Premier League." *International Journal of Sport Communication* 2 (2009): 297–318. Print.

Parnell, Daniel, et. al. "The Pursuit of Lifelong Participation: The Role of Professional Football Clubs in the Delivery of Physical Education and School Sport in England." *Soccer & Society* 17.2 (2016): 225–241. Print.

Parnell, Daniel, et. al. "Football in the Community Schemes: Exploring the Effectiveness of an Intervention in Promoting Healthful Behaviour Change." *Soccer & Society* 14.1 (2013): 35–51. Print.

Pringle, Andy, et al. "Effect of a Health-improvement Pilot Programme for Older Adults Delivered by a Professional Football Club: The Burton Albion Case Study." *Soccer & Society* 15.6 (2014): 902–918. Print.

Reed, Tom. "Former Browns Owner Randy Lerner Reportedly Hemorrhaging Money and Taking Last-place Soccer Team into Relegation." Cleveland.com. Advance Ohio, 14 March 2016. Web. 7 May 2018.

Rutherford, Zoe, et al. "'Motivate': The Effect of a Football in the Community Delivered Weight Loss Programme on Over 35-year Old Men and Women's Cardiovascular Risk Factors." *Soccer & Society* 15.6 (2014): 951–969. Print.

Shore, Ben. "Football Clubs Must Think Long-term." *BBC*. BBC, 20 August 2009. Web. 9 March 2018.

Smith, Aaron C.T., and Hans M. Westerbeek. " Sport as a Vehicle for Deploying Corporate Social Responsibility." *Journal of Corporate Citizenship* 25 (2007): 43–54. Print.

Strudley, David. Personal Interview. 2008.

Thorpe, Alister, et al. "The Community Network: An Aboriginal Community Football Club Bringing People Together." *Australian Journal of Primary Health* 20.4 (2014): 356–364. Print.

"Timeline." *Aston Villa Football Club*. Aston Villa Football Club, Web.9 March 2018.

Walters, Geoff. "Corporate Social Responsibility Through Sport." *JCC* 35 (2009): 81–91. Print.

About the Contributors

LaToya T. **Brackett** is a visiting assistant professor of African American studies at the Race and Pedagogy Institute at the University of Puget Sound. Her work has been published in books as well as in a special edition of *FairPlay, The Journal of Philosophy*, and *Ethics and Sports Law*. Her research interests have focused on the struggle of the black athlete and the representation of black professional characters on television series.

Danielle Sarver **Coombs**, professor in the School of Journalism and Mass Communication at Kent State University, is an author, media commentator, and consultant on areas related to politics, sports, and the politics of sport. Her work has been published in a range of journals, including *The International Journal of Sport Communication* and *Sport in Society*. She is a coauthor of *Women Fans of the NFL: Taking Their Place in the Stands* (Routledge, 2016).

Benjamin James **Dettmar** is an archivist and historian who teaches classes in history and political science at Salt Lake Community College. His research interests include Olympic history, specifically cities that have bid to host the summer games in the 20th century and how these bids have changed those cities (for better or worse). He has published on the history of baseball, soccer in the United States, game-playing pedagogy, archival history, and popular culture.

Glen **Duerr** is a former semi-professional football/soccer player and an associate professor of international studies at Cedarville University. He is the editor of *Secessionism and Terrorism* (Routledge, 2019) and the author of *Secessionism and the European Union* (Lexington Books, 2015). Other publications have focused on the links between sports and politics.

Meghan E. **Fox** is an assistant professor of athletic training at Grand Valley State University as well as a certified and licensed athletic trainer in the state of Michigan. She has worked with sports programs in the community both as a heath care professional and as a researcher. Her primary research interests involve exploring youth concussions and their age- and gender-specific effects as well as evaluation of youth concussion assessments.

Linda K. **Fuller**, professor of communications at Worcester State University, has produced 250-plus professional reports and authored or (co-)edited more than 30 books—including *Sport, Rhetoric, and Gender* (Palgrave Macmillan, 2006), and the two-volume *Sexual Sports Rhetoric* (Peter Lang, 2009). For more, visit www.LK FullerSport.com

Andrew **Guest** teaches psychology and sociology at the University of Portland in Oregon. His research focuses on youth development in activity contexts, with particular attention to sports and development across cultural and community settings. He has played, coached, watched, and written about soccer in places ranging from Michigan to Malawi, with particular interest in the game's evolution in the United States and its importance across sub–Saharan Africa.

Robin **Hardin** is a professor in the Department of Kinesiology, Recreation, and Sport Studies at the University of Tennessee. He teaches courses focused on collegiate athletics, event management, and research methods. His research interests include examining sport governance and the development of sport management curriculum. He is also interested in program and curriculum evaluation.

Cedrick **Heraux** is an assistant professor in the Department of Sociology and Criminal Justice at Adrian College. His areas of expertise are in police behavior, particularly the use of force, and homeland security. His research interests extend to the connection between sociology and sports, focusing on how social dynamics impact the participation in, and consumption of, sports at all levels.

Yuya **Kiuchi** is the graduate director for Great Plains IDEA's graduate programs in youth development and family community services and is an assistant professor in the Department of Human Development and Family Studies at Michigan State University. He has authored, coauthored, edited and coedited more than 10 books in English and Japanese. He also serves on the editorial advisory board for *The Journal of Popular Culture.*

Jake **Kucek** is a doctoral student at Kent State University in the communication and information program. His research focus is in sports identification, sports fandom, corporate social responsibility in sports organizations, and framing/priming in social media. He was a member of the Youngstown State baseball team and was a second team All-American and second team Academic All-American student-athlete.

Joshua R. **Pate** is an associate professor in the Hart School of Hospitality, Sport and Recreation Management at James Madison University. His research is in sport for people with disabilities with an emphasis on the experiences of individuals and media coverage. He teaches undergraduate courses in sport sociology and graduate courses in facilities and event management.

Corey **Shouse** is an associate professor of Spanish and Latin/o American studies at St. John's University in Minnesota. His areas of academic interest include sport and national identity in the Americas, Colombian literature, postmodern fiction in the Americas, and contemporary Latin American cinema. He is also researching a book on the history and culture of cycling in Colombia.

Francisco A. **Villarruel** is a University Outreach and Engagement senior fellow and a professor in the Department of Human Development and Family Studies at Michigan State University. He is involved in policy reform related to Latino youth in U.S. juvenile justice systems. He has worked with numerous community, state, and federal agencies to address the involvement of Latino youth in juvenile justice systems programs.

Index